Spirituality in Ministerial Formation

Religion, Education and Culture

Series Editors:
William K. Kay (Glyndŵr University, UK)
Leslie J. Francis (University of Warwick, UK)
and Jeff Astley (Durham University, UK)

This series addresses issues raised by religion and education within contemporary culture. It is intended to be of benefit to those involved in professional training as ministers of religion, teachers, counsellors, psychologists, social workers or health professionals while contributing to the theoretical development of the acedemic fields from which this training is drawn.

Spirituality in Ministerial Formation

The Dynamic of Prayer in Learning

ANDREW D. MAYES

UNIVERSITY OF WALES PRESS
CARDIFF
2009

British Library Cataloguing-in-Publication Data
A catalogue record for this book is available from the British Library.

ISBN 978-0-7083-2224-6
e-ISBN 978-0-7083-2270-3

www.uwp.co.uk

Printed in Great Britain by CPI Antony Rowe, Wiltshire

Contents

Part III
Possibilities for the Future

Preface by the Bishop of Chichester

Andrew Mayes makes an important contribution to the under-standing of the formation of those preparing for ordained ministry. He directs attention to the importance of prayer in the curriculum and thus to the fundamental place that should be given to 'life in the Spirit' for ordinands themselves and for seminaries and theological colleges and courses.

It is not always easy to find the right language in which to describe that particular form of growth in discipleship which is involved in this task. 'Education', 'training' and 'formation' suggest different ap-proaches, and may imply different understandings not only of the process of preparation itself but also of the quality, character and task of ordained Christian ministry and those admitted to it.

The pressures on the seminary curriculum have become acute in recent years, but that may itself be an indication of how far spiritual formation has moved from the centre of the preoccupations of many churches. Whereas 'theological education' ought to imply 'growing in the knowledge of God', all too often it is reduced to 'imparting information about religious subjects', and whereas 'training for ministry' suggests 'growing in the patterns of life and practice required for the cure of souls' it is often understood to mean 'how to respond to personal or social problems or how to run an institution'.

Things are not as bleak as this, of course, but, as this timely study reminds us, constant vigilance is required if ministerial formation is to remain both living and life-giving. The most important thing of all is that God's gracious provision of ministers for the Church is to be met by a corresponding concern to ensure that those who are ordained are shaped for a lifelong journey of discipleship in which they are fellow pilgrims alongside, as well as for, those they are called to serve.

+ John Hind

Introduction

One of the most urgent issues facing the Church today and underpinning the central research question of this book is the crucial question of how Christian leaders and priests are created and sustained for the challenges of this new millennium. What processes are required to develop the kind of Christian leaders who are needed for today's Church? This is, first of all, a question about what training is necessary for those to be ordained or commissioned as the Church's ministers, but it is also a question about what is needed to sustain and equip them throughout their ministry. While the focus of this book is the formation of the ordained, it speaks also to the formation of all the Church's ministers, including lay ministers, parish leaders and readers. It is hoped that it will be a stimulus and inspiration for both theological educators and students, and prompt them to consider creatively the dynamic interplay between the journey of learning and formation and the practice of prayer.

The emerging holistic paradigm of ministerial formation, in contrast to former models of training or theological education, has the potential to enrich and deepen approaches to this issue, but there exists in the Anglican tradition in the UK no developed theology of formation and no clear idea about it. This is also the case in the US. Winkelmes writes: 'Most seminaries have yet to reach a definition of formation for their students that all faculty can accept comfortably. This lack of consensus may contribute to some faculty's retreat from actively supporting formation in order to focus more explicitly on course subject matter' (Winkelmes, 2004: 214). This book seeks to advance our understanding of the formation paradigm and especially to explore the role of spirituality within it.

The *Hind Report*, which proposes the biggest shake-up and revision of Anglican training for 150 years, calls out for such research (Archbishops' Council, 2003). It offers only tentative and undeveloped ideas about formation, and displays an ambivalence towards spirituality in theological education: while arguing for a strengthening of the academic and intellectual rigour of theological studies, it concedes equal weighting to 'growing in faith, discipleship, prayer and vocation'. The role of spirituality in formation, however, demands greater clarity of understanding, for it is an issue not of marginal but of central significance in theological education in all major Christian traditions.

Episcopalian Professor van den Blink has written: 'It is no exaggeration to say that theological education in our time is in a state of crisis. The widespread lack of grounding of theological curricula in any authentic spirituality is . . . a major contributing factor to this state of affairs' (van den Blink, 1999: 430). Alan Jones puts it more strongly: 'There is also an idolatry with regard to the material that is supposed to be covered [in theological training] instead of an emphasis on how to pray, to think and behave from a theological perspective grounded in faith' (Jones, 1987: 19). Evangelical educators agree. Miller-McLemore observes:

> Within many institutions of theological education, it is hard to shake the dominant liberal Protestant view of religious formation and spiritual fervour as secondary to cognitive knowledge and intellect . . . [this] has obscured the essential interconnections between faith and knowledge . . . Separating spiritual practices and theoretical reflection is a modern aberration in the history of philosophical and theological thought.
>
> (Miller-McLemore, 2002: 52)

George Lindbeck concurs:

> the difficulties of special spiritual formation within the seminary are increasing. There is a growing gap between it, on the one hand, and the academic and pastoral skill aspects of the curriculum, on the other . . . While ministerial candidates have less spiritual formation than before, the need seems to be greater.
>
> (Lindbeck, 1988: 10–32)

The Episcopalian scholar John Westerhoff, among others, similarly argues that the stress on knowledge and skills at the expense of spiritual development and formation of priestly character is the major weakness of recent theological education (Westerhoff, 1982). James

(2002) observed in the US, 'little research has been conducted with faculty to understand how they relate teaching to spiritual growth.' A rare example of such research in the US is afforded by Foster et al. (2006).

In the UK, too, there is a widespread dissatisfaction with the pragmatic and functionalist approach of the last decade, which has focused on the development of ministry skills and the imparting of basic theological knowledge. As Kenneth Leech wrote, in respect to a basic textbook by the then head of the Church of England's Ministry Division, designed to be read by those enquiring about ministry: 'So much of recent writing on ministry has been functionalist. What about the Christian minister as a person of prayer? "Prayer" does not even appear in the index of Dr Kuhrt's book' (Leech, 2005; Kuhrt, 2000). Even more telling is the total absence of references to spirituality or prayer in a further major textbook from Ministry Division (Kuhrt, 2001; see also Sheridan, 1999).

In the UK, the role of spirituality in formation has been treated with ambivalence, with intellectual caution towards its subjectivity, and academic overload/lack of time and space have combined to squeeze it out of the curriculum. A recent guide for new theological students cautions: 'one of the odd things about a period of preparation for ministry is that, in reality, people find that time for worship and prayer is continually pushed to the edges of their time and energy' (Croft and Walton, 2005: 18). It is noted that this 'student handbook' commends 'quiet times' and prayer-times but fails to integrate prayer into the learning process.

There has opened up within training a gulf between theology as a *habitus* – an existential orientation towards God (knowledge of God) and theology as an academic discipline (knowledge about God). There has also been a dichotomy between knowledge and experience, between theology and spirituality: academic theological reflection often divorced from the lived experience of prayer. This divorce can often be aggravated by what Hughes (2003: 3) calls 'split spirituality' – piety which has become adrift from life. As Catholic William Johnston (2002) put it: 'The split between theology and spirituality is one of the main causes of the crisis in the priesthood. Seminarians and students of theology assert almost unanimously that their theological studies did little for their life of prayer.'

This is paralleled by a divide between emotional/affective development and intellectual development (the 'head and the heart').

Other problems undermining the effectiveness of the ordained ministry – including a loss of vision and passion, ministerial fatigue, shallowness of theological reflection amongst ministers and confusion about the identity and role of the minister – point to an urgent need to understand the significance of spirituality in ongoing formation.

This book identifies ways in which the emerging paradigm of ministerial formation can help to heal some of these rifts and explores the ways in which different types of prayer have the potential to be a significant integrative, cognitive, healing, empowering influence in ministerial formation. Its central research question is 'what should be the role of spirituality in ministerial formation?'

The book derives from the first thesis accepted by the University of Wales Lampeter for the award of Doctorate of Ministry, written under the supervision of Dr Neil Messer and Dr Mark Cartledge. It is hoped that its publication in this form will afford an example of the kind of investigations appropriate for this: thus it includes some details about the process of empirical research. The Doctorate of Ministry, being part of a new generation of professional doctorates, is designed to advance practice in the field of Christian ministry, and thus this book is essentially practical and not theoretical. Thus there are questions for individual or group reflection at the end of each chapter, and photocopiable sheets at the end of the book which can be used either in personal reflection or by groups of teaching staff or students.

Plan of the book

Part I Formation, past and present

The book opens with an historical perspective, surveying six models of clergy training as developed in the last two millennia, antecedents of the formation paradigm, identifying the place of prayer and different approaches to the task of theology. This includes examination of a range of documentary sources and texts. The evolution of the formation model of training is traced in the major traditions, and their key documents related to this are examined. An ecumenical and international perspective is gained from interviews conducted with theological educators in Orthodox, Catholic and Free Church traditions (enabled by five overseas visits by the author to seminaries and theological centres). Part I concludes by identifying the issues and questions which emerge from each historical and contemporary tradition of theological education encountered, and clarifies an understanding of the process of formation within five major themes.

Part II The role of prayer in formation: findings and reflections

This presents the findings from empirical research, informed by a range of theological and psychological perspectives on prayer, among a sample of newly ordained clergy and tutors in the UK. The research uncovers what particular expressions and types of prayer contribute most to the process of formation. It identifies what transformation is achieved in candidates for ordination and the newly ordained through the practice of prayer. We consider both the teacher's perceptions of aims and methods in theological training and also the learner's perspective: the experience of 'being formed' and the role of prayer in this. Each chapter is in two parts: first reporting findings of the research and secondly offering theological reflections. These are explored through the use of a powerful metaphor which conveys the dynamic character of prayer in formation, with special attention given to the role of the Holy Spirit, suggesting elements for a theology of formation.

Part III Possibilities for the future

The concluding chapter reviews the evidence about the usefulness and limits of the formation paradigm, and summarizes the function of prayer in formation. In the light of this, the chapter offers a range of creative ideas, deriving from the research, for a renewed understanding and praxis of the role of prayer in learning and training and elements of a spirituality of ministry are identified. This practical perspective makes proposals to the Church of England and its ecumenical partners about the integration of spirituality into the revised training programmes now being formulated for use in the new Regional Training Partnerships. It also seeks to address the wider ecumenical community of theological educators. Finally, it identifies implications of the research for continuing (lifelong) ministerial education and for the training of lay leadership and calls for a clearer articulation of a spirituality of education as needed by our present culture and context.

Part I

Formation Past and Present

1

Models of theological education in the first millennium

Introduction to chapters 1 and 2

At the heart of this study is the concept of ministerial formation, and chapters 1 and 2 explore its historical antecedents – paradigms of leadership training that have served the Church in the last two millennia. They will identify six major models and describe their chief characteristics, especially as they touch on issues of concern to this study: What concept of theology is in view here and how is this related to spirituality? What forms of prayer does this model require and what are their purposes? What view of leadership/priesthood does this model engender? How does this model challenge contemporary training of priests and leaders?

While a comprehensive historical account is not attempted, successive (and overlapping) models will help to tell the story of how the Church has prepared and equipped its leaders over twenty centuries. The methodology involves returning to key figures and primary texts. In our encounter with these texts we shall be guided by Sheldrake's (1991a: 165) advice about a two-way conversation: 'What is needed is a receptive and at the same time critical dialogue with a spiritual text in order to allow the wisdom in it to challenge us and yet to accord our own horizons their proper place.' Thus the exploration of the past both gives a sense of perspective and of origins, and raises issues about current forms of training, to be taken further into the present research.

Praxis – action/reflection model

In the synoptic gospels, the relationship between Jesus and the disciples is expressed in different ways, including rabbi/master and disciple (*mathetes*), leader and follower. As Kittel (1967: 441) points out, this word 'always implies the existence of a personal attachment which shapes the whole life of the one described as *mathetes*, and which in its particularity leaves no doubt as to who is deploying the formative power'. Such discipleship pictures Jesus as a trainer and the disciples as apprentices who learn 'on the job'. Within this pattern of training, it is possible to identify the significant inclusion of both prayer and reflection on ministry.

In Mark's gospel, the Twelve are chosen (chapter 3) 'to be with him and to be sent out' – for a learning process and an apostolate. Early on Jesus chooses a small team (Peter, James and John) who are given privileged access to his way of working and healing behind closed doors (Mk 1: 29; cf. 5: 37, 9: 2). In the first part of Mark's gospel, the Twelve learn by observation of Christ's healing and teaching techniques, and at an early stage (6: 7) they are sent out in pairs. In Mark 8, in the journey together towards Jerusalem, Jesus invites his disciples to copy him, to take up their cross and follow him (Mk 8: 34). As Best (1981: 39) notes: 'There is thus here the beginnings of an *imitatio Christi* theology.' Processes of interaction between Jesus and the disciples, allowing for reflection, are also identified in Robbins (1984).

This perspective is echoed in Luke's account, and the missions of the Twelve and the Seventy reveal key aspects of the learning process. First there is a period of intense training, which includes listening to Jesus, watching his pastoral approach, comprising ministry both in the marketplace (Lk. 7: 32) and in the home, and sharing meals with outcasts. Then the Twelve are sent out (9: 2) and report back to Jesus (9: 10). Next Jesus withdraws with them to a place apart, a 'lonely place' (9: 12) for a time of shared reflection.

This pattern is repeated in the experience of the Seventy, sent out in pairs (10: 1) for a ministry of preaching the Kingdom and healing, modelled on Christ's. Upon their return there is reflection, debriefing and feedback on the exercise (10: 17–20). Banks (1999: 104) identifies four elements in this process: 1. induction: the disciples hear the basic message; 2. observation and participation: they are drawn into helping with Christ's 'hands-on' ministry; 3. modelling: Jesus exemplifies patterns of ministry; 4. fellowship: the experience of being together a learning community. What also stands out as a highly significant aspect is the time given over to debriefing and reflection, in which the first, tentative experiences of ministry can be reflected on and lessons drawn out (cf. Lk. 10: 19 where the concept of authority is reflected upon).

Both Mark and Luke emphasize the role of prayer and silence in the example Jesus sets before the disciples, following the forty days of prayer, struggle and preparation in the desert. In Mark chapter 1, a hectic twenty-four hours of ministry is followed by prayer before dawn in an *eremos* – lonely place (1: 35): the time of prayer is both the conclusion of an intense period of ministry and the prelude to the next stage. This rhythm of prayer and activity is repeated in the disciples' experience, as they go to a place of retreat enabling rest and reflection after first incursions into ministry and giving an account to Jesus (Mk. 6: 30, 31). As Lane (1974: 81) points out: 'In each instance reference to the wilderness-place is preceded by an account of Jesus' preaching and power; he then withdraws from the multitude which seeks his gifts.' After this retreat, another time of ministry (6: 35–45) is followed by Christ's retirement into the hills for prayer at night (6: 46): the pattern of intense activity and solitude is repeated.

Luke gives a similar picture. Jesus withdraws to the hills and prays through the night after a demanding period in which great crowds gathered for preaching and healing (Lk. 6: 12). After another time of intense ministry, there is further prayer which becomes the context for learning and questions: 'Once when Jesus was praying alone, with only the disciples near him, he asked them, "Who do the crowds say that I am?"' (9: 18).

This passage vividly highlights Jesus modelling solitude to the disciples and the thin line between teaching and prayer. Eight days later, the pattern is repeated as Jesus goes up on the mountain to pray with Peter, James and John. This prayer experience becomes a learning experience in a different sense, in the encounter of the transfiguration (9: 28–36). In the return of the Seventy after their mission, within their debriefing and reflection with Christ, perspectives arising from prayer are shared; as Wright (2004: 125) puts it: 'Jesus in prayer had seen a vision . . . [he] had seen, in mystical sight, the heavenly reality which corresponded to the earthly victories won by the 70.' There is a further example of the integration of prayer and learning, as Christ spontaneously moves into thanksgiving 'at that same hour' (Lk. 10: 21), in which he celebrates *apokalupsis*, disclosure or revelation, taking place in the pastoral experience of the Seventy. As Dunn (2003: 561) puts it, we should note 'the degree to which Jesus provided a model to his disciples as a man of prayer ... To be a disciple of Jesus was to pray as Jesus prayed.'

Christ's practice of modelling a balance between prayer and activity is communicated to the disciples not only by his own personal example but by appeal to other expressions, notably in the passage about Mary and Martha (Lk. 10: 38–42) in which Mary chooses 'the better part'. This prompts the disciples to request particular training in prayer (Lk. 11: 1). Christ speaks of the kind of prayer that involves bringing questions and puzzlement to God: 'Ask, and it will be given to you; search, and you will find; knock and the door will be opened for you' (Lk. 11: 9).

As Jeremias (1974: 78) puts it, with Christ's approach to God as *Abba* 'a new way of praying is born'. Jeremias (1974: 76) points out that, in giving the disciples the Lord's Prayer in Aramaic vernacular, 'he removes prayer from the liturgical sphere of sacred language and places it right in the midst of everyday life'. Also significant is a daring, radical fluidity in respect to the traditionally fixed Jewish *Shema* of Deuteronomy 6: 5, so that Mark (12: 33) commends loving God with heart, understanding and strength, while Luke (10: 27) advocates loving God with heart, soul, strength and mind. While this may point to the replacement of the recital of the *Shema* by the Lord's Prayer, it also points to a holistic approach to prayer encompassing both affective/feeling elements and intellectual/thinking dimensions (Jeremias, 1974: 80). In his study of the prayer-life of Jesus, Thomson (1959) identifies it as a crucial source of inspiration and illumination for his ministry. In a more recent study, Chilton (2002) characterizes Jesus as a 'mystic'; for a more cautious approach to the prayer of Jesus, see Cullmann (1995). Borg (1993) sees Jesus as a 'Spirit person', interpreting the long periods of prayer mentioned by Luke (6: 12) implying Jesus' use of contemplation or meditation.

Paideia – holistic model

Paideia represents a second model of learning that developed throughout the Greek world and forms the background to theological thinking in the first centuries of the Church. Werner Jaeger, in his major study *Paideia: The Ideals of Greek Culture* (1945: 286), understands *paideia* as a holistic approach to learning that enables a person to participate fully in the culture, with the formation of character and virtue as its central aim:

> *Paideia* was now connected with the highest *aretē* possible to man – it was used to denote the sum total of all ideal perfections of mind and body – complete *kalokagathia* [nobleness and goodness], a concept which was now consciously taken to include a genuine intellectual and spiritual culture.

Thus *paideia* represents the process of instruction that made a person complete in body, mind and soul. This shaping of a virtuous person took concrete expression in the earliest schools of the Church, of which the catechetical school of Alexandria is the greatest example. Here Christian leaders were trained alongside pagan seekers after truth. Founded in about 180 by Pantrenus, it has been called 'the first Christian academy' and 'the first catholic university' (Wilkin, 1984: 15). Pre-baptismal catechesis led to an exploration of the Christian tradition and of philosophy understood as 'living the virtuous life'. It was not so much a school as a network of students, enabling one-to-one tuition or learning in small groups with a tutor.

Clement of Alexandria

Clement of Alexandria (*c.*150–*c.*215) gives us insight into the educational process of *paideia* in his treatise *Paedagogus* on 'Christ the Teacher'. For Clement, education is concerned with living the ethical life: what matters are behaviour, attitudes, values. What is the aim of the teacher? 'His aim is thus to improve the soul, not to teach, and to train it up to a virtuous, not to an intellectual life . . . [he] first exhorts to the attainment of right dispositions and character' (Clement, 1997a).

He develops his view of *paideia* through the concept of *gnosis*, in which he presents true Christian knowledge in opposition to the heretical esoteric *gnosis*. As Jaeger (1961: 61) says: 'The true *paideia* is the Christian religion itself, but Christianity in its theological form and conceived in Clement's own system of *gnosis*.' For Wiles (1977: 182), Clement represents 'the first extensive synthesis between Christian faith and Hellenistic philosophy' while, for Danielou (1973: 453), Clement enables 'an interplay and encounter between Greek *paideia* with elements originating from the Judeo-Christian apocalyptic tradition'. In Clement's (1997b) *Stromateis* VII: 10, 'Knowledge *(gnosis)* is added to faith, and love to knowledge, the heavenly inheritance'. There is a progression: "'O taste and see that the Lord is good." Faith will lead you in, experience will teach, the Scripture will instruct . . .' (Clement, 1986: 54).

The content of the *gnosis* is essentially the Christian tradition, but Clement is concerned not only with knowledge about God, but rather knowledge of God. He urges his students to seek the experiential vision of God he calls *theoria*: 'Embracing the divine vision not in mirrors or by means of mirrors, but in the transcendently clear and absolutely pure insatiable vision which is the privilege of intensely loving souls . . . this is the function of the Gnostic . . . to have converse with God' (1997b, II: 7).

'Converse with God' is Clement's favourite phrase for prayer, which is crucially important because 'does not he who always holds uninterrupted converse with God by knowledge, life and thanksgiving, grow at every step superior [to the good man] in all respects – in conduct, in words, in disposition?' (1997b, II: 7). In Clement's *paideia*, prayer becomes thoroughly integrated into the learning process, which itself is a prayerful process of discernment, while also allowing for dedicated time and space for wordless prayer and contemplation:

> While in silence, while engaged in reading or in works according to reason, he in every mood prays. If he but form the thought in the secret chamber of his soul, and call on the Father with unspeakable groanings, he is near . . . Prayer, then, may be uttered without the voice, by concentrating the whole spiritual nature within on expression by the mind, in undistracted turning towards God (1997b, II: 7)

Flew (1934: 25) appreciates Clement's approach: 'The perfection to which believers are called by the *Stromateis* is *theoria*, a full unification of the powers of the soul. There is knowledge in it, but there is also love (*Stromateis* VII: 2), complete harmony of purpose and desire.' Meredith (1986: 115) observes: 'The personal note apart, there is little in Clement's conception of perfect prayer to distinguish it from the private intellectual contemplation outlined by Plato in the *Republic* and Aristotle in the tenth book of the *Nicomachean Ethics.*' Yet Clement has been hailed as 'the founder of Christian mysticism' and 'the creator of mystical theology' (McGinn, 1991: 101). Clement does encourage a contemplative, reflective approach to study and there is a balance: 'Our philosophy is concerned, therefore, with three things: first, contemplation (*theoria*); secondly, the fulfilment of the commandments; thirdly, the formation of the man of virtue' (1997b, II: 10). The teacher has the highest vocation: 'he who has undertaken the first place in the teaching of others . . . mediates contact and fellowship with the Divinity' (1997b, II: 9).

Origen

Origen (*c.*185–*c.*254), who succeeded Clement as the third head at Alexandria after 202, develops this further. Gregory Thaumaturge (*c.*213–*c.*270) tells us in his *Panergyric of Origen*:

> Nothing was forbidden to us, nothing hidden from us, nothing inaccessible to us. We were to learn all manner of doctrine – barbarian or Greek, mystical or political, divine or human . . . [Origen] went on with us . . . directing us, pointing out to us all that was true and useful, putting aside all that was false.
>
> (Murray, 1957: 157)

Prestige (1940: 51) observes: 'Origen wanted the minds of his pupils to retain a fluidity and independence – a very important point in the education of young clergymen . . . so long as the process leads in the end to acquiring powers of judgement and decision.' Kelsey reminds us (1993: 9): 'The goal of *paideia* cannot be taught directly, by simply conveying information about various philosophers' doctrines regarding virtue. Knowledge of the Good only comes through contemplation, the ultimate fruit of which is an intuitive insight, a *gnosis* of the Good.' At the heart of this *paideia* lay a process of discernment leading to the application of wisdom. The relation of Origen to his students can be understood in terms of 'spiritual direction' (Wilkin, 2004: 53). Wilkin (1984: 19) puts it: 'The teachers of Alexandria were not interested solely in conveying knowledge or transmitting intellectual skills. They were interested in moral and spiritual formation.' A process of inner transformation was nurtured within a mentoring kind of relationship, in which the teacher fulfilled a function combining role model, instructor and spiritual companion. What was the role of prayer in this process? One commentator writes:

> Worship went side by side with study in the School. Teachers and their students practised prayer, fasting and diverse ways of asceticism . . . The dean and his students did not isolate the study of religion, philosophy and science from their church life nor from their daily life. They believed in a one integral life in Christ . . . They lived not only as scholars but as true worshippers, ascetics and preachers.
>
> (Coptic Orthodox Church Network, 2008)

Gregory of Nyssa

The Cappadocian tradition offers additional insights. Gregory of Nyssa (330–95), one of the Cappadocian Fathers and brother of Basil, communicated *paideia* through a dynamic vision of the Christian life as continually evolving and progressing, energized by the Holy Spirit. His key text was the resolve of Paul: 'Forgetting what lies behind, and straining forward (*epekteinomenos*) to what lies ahead, I press on toward the goal, for the prize of the heavenly call of God in Christ Jesus' (Phil. 3: 13–14). For Gregory, this concept of *epektasis* infuses *paideia* with an energy and motivation: we should never stand still, but continually stretch ourselves towards the 'upward call'. Gregory (1962: 51, 52) encourages the learner to discover his or her full potential in Christ:

> the finest aspect of our mutability is the possibility of growth in good . . . let us change in such a way that we may constantly evolve towards what is better, being transformed from glory into glory, and thus always improving and ever becoming more perfect by daily growth.

For Gregory, each stage reached in the spiritual journey is but a beginning, not an end. The pilgrim can never say he has arrived. In Gregory's eyes, the greatest sin is that of complacency, of resting on one's laurels. Gregory's educational vision is one of lifelong learning or, rather, eternal progress. He develops this through an allegorical approach to biblical figures. In *The Life of Moses*, each new summit the patriarch conquers is but an invitation to see wider horizons and higher ascents to be made (see Malherbe and Ferguson, 1978: 113).

This unceasing development in *paideia* is a question of a partnership between human effort and divine help. The Holy Spirit enables participation in the divine life itself, which animates, vivifies and completes human life: 'The rich and ungrudging Spirit is always flowing into those accepting grace . . . for those who have taken possession of this gift sincerely, it endures as a co-worker and companion in accordance with the measure of faith' (Callahan, 1967: 129). Gregory pictures the Holy Spirit as a dove who not only broods over human life, but actually gives the person wings to fly, never staying put for long upon the mountain, but ever ascending: 'the soul keeps rising ever higher and higher, stretching with its desire for heavenly things "to those that are before" as the Apostle tells us, and thus it will always continue to soar ever higher' (Musurillo, 1962: 57).

Above all, Gregory brings the ideals of *paideia* into the developing monastic life, as Jaeger (1961: 100) reminds us: 'It was Gregory of Nyssa who transferred the ideas of Greek *paideia* in their Platonic form into the life of the ascetic movement that originated during his time in Asia Minor and the Near East and that soon was to display an undreamed-of power of attraction.'

Ascesis – monastic model

From its beginnings in the fourth century, monasticism has provided a variety of expressions of ministerial training. The end of the persecutions heralded by Constantine's Edict of Milan and the establishment of Christianity as the state religion by Theodosius in 380 revolutionized the status of the Church and its ministers. Now they had a role as public servants, and enjoyed the privileges and responsibilities of civil administrators. Monasticism developed as the 'white martyrdom' in reaction to this, opening up new pathways in the training of clergy. Patsavos (1976) reminds us of the significance of the monastic model: 'From the first half of the fourth century it was becoming customary to select bishops from among monks distinguished for their holiness and learning. Many of the qualifications defined for monks apply equally to candidates for the priesthood . . .' We focus on the writings of four major leaders.

Basil

The guidelines or *Rules* first written by Basil (330–79) for the evolving monastic life continue to guide the Eastern Church today, and the practice of choosing bishops from the monastic community continues. In the West, Basil's ideals were adapted and developed by Benedict so finding their way into western monasticism, acknowledged in *Rule of St Benedict* 73: 5. Basil is also the link between the Desert Fathers and the Church of Nicea, for it was after making a tour of early monasteries in Syria and Egypt soon after the death of Anthony in 356, that Basil developed his monastery at Pontus. Cautious about the extremes of the eremetical solitary life, Basil champions the advantages of cenobitic learning and growing in community: while Anthony was inspired by Matt. 19: 21, Basil's key text is the communitarian Acts 2: 42.

Four closely related concepts underpin Basil's concern to develop a monastic life that would become the seedbed for clergy in the

Church. The principal model Basil advocates, *ascesis*, translated as training or exercise, derives from the Pauline image of the spiritual athlete (cf. 1 Cor. 9: 24–7). He speaks of the community as 'a stadium in which we exercise ourselves as athletes, a training school that pushes us to make progress, a continuing exercise of perfecting the commandments of God' (*Regulae fusius tractatae 7*, quoted in Cola, 1991: 38). In a letter Basil puts it:

> The solitude (*eremia*) offers a very great advantage for our task ... Let there the site of the monastery be most like our place here [Annisi], free from the commerce of men, so that nothing may come from without and break the continuity of the *ascesis*, for a pious *ascesis* nurtures the soul with divine thoughts.
>
> (Basil, 1986: 49)

The *ascesis* which Basil commends seeks to integrate into one lifestyle the study of Scripture, common prayer, silence (*hesychia*) and fasting, and aims to achieve a balance between talking and listening. The key to this is his second key concept of *anachoresis* – withdrawal. Basil radicalizes this concept of detachment in relating it not only to a physical separation and retreat from the world but also to an inner state that can be carried into the active arena of ministry: 'Now this withdrawal (*anachoresis*) does not mean that we should leave the world bodily, but rather break loose from the ties of 'sympathy' of the soul with the body ... making ready to receive in our heart the imprint of divine teaching' (Basil, 1986: 48).

Basil's own life reveals a dialectic or movement between the poles of solitude and active engagement, between the desert (Pontus) and the city (Caesarea). His *Rules* are emphatic about the need for monasteries to be outward looking in compassion to the needs of the community, themselves serving as hospitals and centres of care for the poor (see the *Asceticon* in Holmes, 2000). His question to the monks is: 'whose feet will you wash?' (Holmes, 2000: 139). Basil wants to nurture in those in training an 'interior withdrawal' where mind and heart become focused on God, and where prayer is receptive and listening in character. We shall see later how the idea and practice of *anachoresis* inspired a detached view of theological training in remote seminaries separated from the world.

His key aim (*skopos*) in this is *diathesis* – an undistracted disposition which enables a life pleasing to God (*eusebia*). His concept of *diathesis* seems to influence not only Gregory of Nyssa but also the later Maximos the Confessor, expressing 'the essentially dynamic quality of his spiritual anthropology' (Holmes, 2000: 117). *Diathesis* also refers to the environment, atmosphere or ethos of the community which can foster and nurture the inner disposition. At the heart of the monastic community, for Basil, are an inter dependency and mutuality in which spiritual direction is given by experienced members. As Rousseau (1994: 219) puts it: 'A constant programme of consultation, encouragement, and advice was central to Basil's view of what the ascetic community was for.'

Basil, in helping to lay the foundations of organized monastic life, also reveals his understanding of the relationship between knowledge and the divine Spirit, forged in the context of hot debate with Eunomius. He begins his treatise *On the Holy Spirit* by establishing that knowing God is closely connected to becoming like God: 'What is set before us is, so far as is possible with human nature, to be made like unto God. Now without knowledge there can be no 'making like' – and knowledge is not got without lessons' (Basil, 1997: 1).

Teaching that the Holy Spirit forms human beings in virtue, Basil's major concern in monastic and clerical training is the pursuit of *eusebia* – 'a life pleasing to God', training for godliness characterized by compassion and prayer. As Charry (1997: 115) puts it: 'Unless educated to grasp God's majesty and grace, we should fail to understand God properly and be moved to virtuous living as a consequence.'

In his teaching on the illumination of the Holy Spirit, Basil teaches about 'the gradual progress of our education', combining a progressive, dynamic view of *paideia* with a concept of intellectual illumination. Meredith comments:

> It would, however, be unfair to argue either for Origen or for Basil that their reaction against too great a stress on the emotions led them to adopt an aridly intellectual approach to the life of the spirit. Mind/spirit/*nous* must not be conceived too narrowly in the Platonic tradition. Mind and heart go together and both need the Spirit's help if they are to be properly activated.
>
> (1985: 34)

Augustine

The best-documented early monastic model is that of Augustine (354–430). In the years prior to his conversion, Augustine had himself enjoyed a period of study, theological exploration and reflection with friends in what he called the *Christianae vitae otium* under the hospitality of Ambrose, bishop of Milan. (Ambrose had been impressed by Bishop Eusebius' experiment at Vercelli, where clergy lived together under a rule.) This experience of learning and reflecting in community at Milan was in the background when Augustine, as bishop of Hippo, resolved in *Sermon 355*: 'I wanted to have in this bishop's house a monastery of clerics (*monasterium clericorum*).' This was to train priests and deacons for the Church in north Africa, and *Sermons 355–6*, preached by Augustine in 425–6, give us some clues about this monastic school for clergy: 'We thus live in the house which is called the bishop's house so that, as far as we are able, we may imitate those holy men and women about whom the Acts of the Apostles speaks: "No one called anything their own, but everything was in common for them".'

Taking their inspiration from the apostolic life of Acts 4: 32, the ordinands lived a covenanted common life of worship and learning. *Sermon 356* reveals its make-up: two subdeacons, five deacons, two priests, one bishop. The *Rule* attributed to Augustine, relating to a small lay community in Hippo, which has close verbal similarities with *Sermon 356*, highlights the significance of the community library and the place of biblical study (see Mary and Bonner, 2004). The evidence suggests that

> In both the *monasterium fratrum* and the *monasterium clericorum* there was a regular program of table reading, combined with opportunity for private study, leading to serious guided conversation, rigorous yet fraternal dialogues . . . Together they read, studied, prayed and dialogued, the Scriptures providing the course of study and training. Augustine's early *dialogues* and *questions and answers* are suggestive of how this education could have potentially unfolded.
>
> (Martin, 1999)

Three characteristics of Augustinian monastic pedagogy emerge. First, the lively dialogue and dialectic in the small community were balanced by a call to 'interiority', as Augustine wrote:

> After teachers have used words to explain all the branches of learning that they claim to teach, including those dealing with virtue and wisdom, students ponder interiorly if what is said is true, that is, they contemplate the inner truth according to their capacity.
>
> (The Teacher, 45, quoted in McCloskey, 2004)

Secondly, this is a holistic process, using the three faculties of the mind Augustine identifies as memory (=consciousness), understanding and will. As McCloskey observes:

It involves mind *and* heart. Augustine knew from experience that the heart brings the learning tools of will, motivation, passion and power to bear as the mind navigates among the varied trajectories of knowledge toward wisdom. This movement of the will toward understanding impels one to action.

(2004: 18)

Thirdly, the aim of the educational process thus is a wisdom that leads to virtuous action. Learning issues in *praxis*, which is itself the catalyst for further reflection. Augustine's *monasterium clericorum* has parallels with today's 'reflective practitioners' – encouraging a dynamic cycle of thought that leads through reflection, discussion, consideration of Scripture and tradition, to decisive ministry – notably, in the context of a small community of prayer and learning. Such is another dimension of the monastic *ascesis* in ministerial formation.

Benedict

In England, the greatest monastic influence on clergy training was through the *Rule* written by Benedict (480–550). The Church in England has had a special relation with the *Rule* since its inception because generations of clergy were trained in Benedictine monasteries. Gregory the Great, a contemporary of Benedict who wrote a biography of him, chose to evangelize Britain by sending Augustine with a company of forty monks. Barry (1995: 14) notes: 'It is highly probable that Augustine had St Benedict's *Rule* with him when he landed in Kent.' Wilfrid (634–709) promoted the *Rule* by encouraging new monastic foundations. In 674 Benedict Biscop (628–90) opened the monasteries of Wearmouth and Jarrow, which soon became centres of great learning, where Bede studied and wrote (673–735), while smaller foundations like Malmesbury under Adhelm (d.709) likewise functioned as places of clerical training.

On the continent, a leading theological school was established by Boniface (680–754) at Fulda in 744. In such places there was an integration of the classical disciplines within monastic training. Rabanus Maurus, abbot of Fulda in 822, required that the *trivium* (grammar, rhetoric, logic) and the *quadrivium* (mathematics, geometry, music and astronomy), making up the seven Liberal Arts, be adapted to Christian faith and studied in juxtaposition to the Scriptures (Rooy, 1988: 58). Elsewhere on the continent, the monastic school at Bec in Normandy later became a significant centre of monastic learning producing the scholars Lanfranc (1010–89) and Anselm (1033–1109), both destined for the office of archbishop of Canterbury.

Thus in many places ordinands and novices studied side by side. Throughout England, the minsters or *monasteria*, as in Ireland, brought into juxtaposition the monk and priest as co-learners and co-workers (Hylson-Smith, 1999: 206). The reforms of Charlemagne (742–814) implemented by Alcuin (735–804) insisted that wherever Benedictine schools had been limited to their own members, they were to be opened up for the training of secular priests too (Bullock, 1969: 4).

Clerical training was shaped powerfully through the Benedictine approach to time. Benedict's *Rule* states: 'Idleness is the enemy of the soul. Therefore, the brothers should have specified periods for manual labour as well as for prayerful reading' (48: 1–5). Benedict calls his readers to live within an ordered rhythm of prayer, which celebrates the primacy of God and his resourcing in ministry. He allows proper time for labour, study and creativity. The very layout of a Benedictine monastery reveals a sense of balance: there is the church, the chapter house, dormitory, refectory, kitchen, each reflecting different commitments and tasks, all held together by a common walkway, the cloister walk, and, at the centre of it all a large open space of the cloister-garden, where stands a spring or fountain. This conveys the need for life to be lived not in fragmentedness but in connectedness, in unity and integrity, a place of cleansing, refreshment and stillness at the very centre. The *Rule* powerfully shaped training for ministry in its call to hold together disparate commitments: the call to community, the call to solitude; the desert and the city; the needs of body, mind and spirit; human decision-making and divine grace; standing still in stability and moving out in continuous conversion. But, in many areas, proportionally few clergy were probably able to benefit from a monastic education, and instead benefited from an apprenticeship model which persisted through the centuries.

Gregory the Great

It was *The Pastoral Rule* of Gregory the Great (540–604) that helped to mediate monastic ideals to the parish clergy over several successive centuries, commended, for example, by the Councils of Mainz and Rheims (813). The book was written as a rule for bishops and pastors, modelled on the monastic rule, to guide the development of ministry: indeed, it became the secular clergy's equivalent of the monastic rule. Translating it into Saxon in 871, Alfred the Great wrote of the desperate need for such a manual:

> There were very few on this side Humber who could understand their mass-books in English, or translate a letter from Latin into English; and I ween that there were not many beyond the Humber. So few of them were there that I cannot think so much as a single one south of the Thames when I came to the throne.
>
> (from the 'Preface to the Cura Pastorolis',
quoted in Moorman, 1958: 42)

Underpinning the manual is the Benedictine ideal of *consideratio*, a careful balance between body and soul, between contemplation and action, between individual and corporate responsibilities that maintains a heavenward orientation in the midst of earthly duties (Purves, 2001: 61). As Gregory puts it:

> Let the ruler not relax the care of the inner life by preoccupying himself with external matters, nor should his solicitude for the inner life bring neglect of the external, lest, being engrossed with what is external, he be ruined inwardly, or being preoccupied with what concerns only his inner self, he does not bestow on his neighbours the necessary external care.
>
> ('Regula Pastoralis', II: 7: 68 in Gregory the Great, 1978)

What Gregory aims to do in his *Pastoral Rule* is unite both the monastic and the apostolic: to show that it is possible for active ministers to be energized by an inner life to which monasticism testifies. This document, integrating monastic values into ministerial and episcopal life, was studied widely throughout Europe, became required reading for priests and bishops, and exercised a profound influence on the training of the clergy. It can be viewed as an expression in some kind of continuity with patristic thinking about priesthood – an evolving classical tradition.

Questions for reflection

✦ What does each model say to your present educational practice or to your experience as a learner?

✦ What insights do you think each model offers to understanding the process of ministerial formation?

✦ How does each model question us?

✦ How would we want to question each model?

2

Models of theological education in the second millennium

Scientia – university model

During the eleventh century theological schools attached to the cathedrals became more important than the monastic. Some training had been offered in episcopal households since the Council of Toledo in 531 required the instruction of ordinands 'under the eyes of the bishop'. Now, bishops created the post of chancellor for the express purpose of providing lectures for clergy. They hired teachers to equip the clergy with a basic Christian education: the training centred on the learning of Latin, familiarity with plainchant and some basic mathematics to enable clerks to undertake parish book-keeping (Moorman, 1958: 87).

This shift from the Benedictines to institutional structures of the Church, diocese and bishop was encouraged by Pope Gregory VII (Hildebrand, 1021–85) as part of his reform programme. This also included promoting a strictly celibate model of priest-hood, conceived as a caste increasingly separate and removed from the laity. This was furthered by the Fourth Lateran Council of 1215 in its stress on the priestly powers of absolution (see Hughes, 1961).

The geographical shift from the monasteries of the countryside to the cathedral schools of the new towns represented a profounder change in the teaching of theology, especially with the establishment of the first universities which grew out of the episcopal schools in the twelfth century. Paris became a leading centre for theological study at this time, paving the way for other large cities to develop autonomous universities, organizing their own curriculum and administration outside the structure of the Church. There began to be a distance between the study of theology and the life of the Church. Theology came to be studied as a separate discipline. This was encouraged by the new translations of Aristotle, and the analytical mode of theological enquiry that came to be called scholasticism, eptimomized by Thomas Aquinas (1225–74) with his *Summa Theologica* representing the attempt to defend Christian truth from the standpoint of reason.

Theology as *habitus* and *scientia*

Two different approaches to theology began to compete. Theology was understood as a *habitus*, 'an enduring orientation and dexterity of the soul . . . a cognitive disposition and orientation of the soul, a knowledge of God and what God reveals' (Farley, 1983: 35). Thomas Aquinas and the Schoolmen, adapting an Aristotelian anthropology, saw theology as a human, theoretical *habitus*, enabling systematic study of theology as speculative and theoretical discipline, taking its place alongside law, physics and medicine in the university. Indeed, theology becomes the 'queen of the sciences' and is viewed as a science, a body of knowledge or *scientia*, the Latin word *theologia* taking on the meaning of 'the discipline of sacred learning', with a clear emphasis on the systematic and academic study of the doctrinal aspects of faith.

In contrast, the so-called 'Churchmen', maintaining the Augustinian-monastic tradition – thirteenth-century theologians such as Scotus and Alexander of Hales – were concerned about the implications of neglecting the practical side of theology. They advocated theology as a practical habit of the soul, a wisdom, inseparable from the practice of prayer and the virtues. For them, *habitus* is a divinely given capacity arising from prayer. Bonaventure (1217–74) advocated a mystical theory of knowledge stressing the priority of prayer in knowing God. He wrote:

> Let no one believe that he can be content with reading without inspiration, investigation without devotion, research without wonder, circumspection without exaltation, hard work without piety, knowledge without charity, intelligence without humility, zeal apart from divine grace, vision apart from divinely-inspired wisdom.
>
> (Cousins, 1978: 55)

It is an oversimplification to consider *habitus* as subjective and *scientia* as objective: nevertheless, the former encourages an existential approach in which the learner is in a personal relationship with God, while the latter tends towards an academic scholarly approach. In this way, scholarship became separated from *ascesis*. As Sheldrake puts it:

> The theological enterprise was no longer to be focused in centres that were explicitly dedicated to a religious way of life. The new scholarship in the narrow sense created centres that existed primarily to foster teaching and learning. The new theology gradually gave birth not only to distinctions between disciplines such as biblical theology, doctrinal theology and moral theology. It also produced a belief that the discipline of the mind could be separated from the discipline of an ordered lifestyle or *ascesis*.
>
> (Sheldrake, 1998a: 39)

Towards an academic ideal: the training of clergy in England

In England, Oxford and Cambridge were the centres of such theological education that was available. Students often began their university studies at about fourteen years of age: before the Reformation, many of these would already be in minor orders, and some had already been instituted to livings (Moorman, 1958: 135). The curriculum was governed by the seven Liberal Arts, the whole course taking seven years to complete. Theology was a postgraduate course taken by few clergy.

After the Reformation, the Church of England's new Ordinal in *The Book of Common Prayer 1549* summarized the basic requirements of candidates for the diaconate: 'And the bishop ... after examination and trial finding him learned in the Latin tongue, and sufficiently instructed in Holy Scripture, may admit him.' The Canons of 1604 embody the same broad ideas: a candidate must have taken an Oxford or Cambridge degree or at least be able to yield an account of his faith in Latin, according to the Articles of Religion and to confirm the same by sufficient testimonies out of holy scriptures (Bullock, 1955: 7).

There was some increase in the proportion of clergy attending university as such ideals began to be realized. In Oxford diocese, in 1560 a third of clergy were graduates, rising to two thirds by 1620 and over 90 per cent by 1640 (Jones, 2000: 223) but Oxford was not a typical diocese. For centuries, throughout the Church of England, only a privileged few received education at Oxbridge. However, in the eighteenth and nineteenth centuries the majority of clergy were graduates (Hinton, 1994: 105).

Even after the Reformation, the education given at the two English universities continued to be very general and academic, and no pastoral or professional training was offered. Divinity continued to be taught as a subject alongside the other disciplines (arts, classics, mathematics) and this was required of all students, whether ordinands or not. It was not until the 1870s that Oxford and Cambridge provided for a BA degree in theology. These general studies could be supplemented by attendance at extra divinity lectures, but these were still extra-curricular and optional. Diligent candidates could find guidance for the pastoral ministry in such works as George Herbert's *Priest to the Temple* (1652), Jeremy Taylor's *Rules and Advice to the Clergy* (1661) or Richard Baxter's *The Reformed Pastor* (1656): this was a matter for individual initiative. Rooy (1988: 60) makes a negative evaluation of Oxbridge: 'There was a lack of the basic elements of theological education and absolutely no spiritual formation.'

In fact, the ethos of the Oxbridge colleges was profoundly Christian, with all dons required to be clergy and the chapel lying at the heart of each college community. With its full round of daily offices and other services, it provided a liturgical framework for study. After university, it was common practice for candidates to live with a priest for a few months before their ordination, reading the subjects required by the deacon's examination and gaining some pastoral experience. It is to be recalled that Nonconformists, excluded from the universities of Oxford and Cambridge, founded Dissenting Academies from the eighteenth century, where generations of Free Church ministers were trained. These were characterized by a broad curriculum, including science, philosophy and history, and a practical application of knowledge.

Seminarium – the seminary/theological college model

The key concept of the *seminarium* was a place of training that could be a seed-ground or nursery, where seeds of faith and understanding could be nurtured and fed and come to maturity.

Seminary in the Roman Catholic Church[1]

In the Roman Catholic Church, the Council of Trent decreed in 1563 that seminaries be set up for the proper training of the priesthood, modelled on the paradigm pioneered in England by Cardinal Pole in 1556. Clerical laxity had widely been identified in the reformation debates, and the need for proper training of clergy had become an urgent priority. Seminary training came to consist of seven years' study devoted to philosophy, scripture, church history, apologetics, dogmatic and moral and ascetical theology, supplemented with liturgical studies and canon law.

Charles Borromeo (1538–89) in Milan and Frances de Sales (1567–1622) in Geneva gave early leadership to the implementation of the ideals of Trent. Most instrumental in advancing its directives were the Jesuits, Ignatius Loyola (1491–1556) himself establishing in Rome the Collegium Romanum (which was to become the Gregorian University). Thus Ignatian and monastic ideals were quickly incorporated into the new model and the seminary functioned as a religious community, with the Office and Mass providing the daily framework for learning. In the Ignatian tradition of seminary life two other features were notable: the discipline of slow, meditative reading of Scripture and the use of the *Examen,* a daily act of recollection and reflection (Mottola, 1964).

It was in France that the seminary ideal was most effectively established in the course of the seventeenth century by Vincent de Paul (1580–1660), Jean-Marie Eudes (1601–80) and Pierre de Bérulle (1575–1629). De Bérulle's spirituality became typical and highly influential, later mediated to Britain in the writings of Abbot Marmion (1952). Key objectives included sanctification and growing identity, characterized by an acute sense of the otherness of the priest, who was not to be like other men:

> Priests and seminarians were to associate themselves with the role of the risen Christ as eternal priest and victim. As priests they were representations of Christ the victim-priest, imparting grace through the ministry of the sacraments. The seminarian's interior identification with Christ was accompanied by an attitude of self-abnegation, or even self-annihilation, so that Christ would live in him.
>
> (White, 1989: 12)

[1] Seminary in Roman Catholic and Anglican traditions are considered here prior to the advent of the formation paradigm.

A manual for use among aspirants to the priesthood entitled *Ecclesiastical Training* expresses the aim of the seminary thus:

> A seminary is not primarily a place of study . . . A seminary is a place the only essential object of which is to train to a truly spiritual and supernatural life those to whom God has made known . . . his invitation to share in the Eternal Priesthood of his Divine Son.
>
> (Bourne, 1926: 3)

After the French Revolution and the reactions against what was identified as 'modernism' and 'rationalism', two features became increasingly marked: standardization and specialization (Duffy, 1992: 170). Using the same Latin textbooks for dogma, moral and canon law and liturgy, uniformity was enforced through the use of a common model of the priesthood expounded by successive pontiffs, typified by Pius IX and the First Vatican Council. Such seminary training is sometimes called 'the priest factory' or even 'a paramilitary approach . . . a highly regimented system designed to produce a uniform product . . . it emphasized obedience to hierarchical authority, formalism in spiritual exercises and devotions, conservatism in doctrine, and self-control in all things' (Hoge and Wenger, 2003). Specialization revealed itself in a separation of the disciplines noted in the Reformed tradition: here, ascetical theology and the practice of prayer were entirely detached from dogmatic theology.

Seminary in the Anglican tradition

In the Church of England, there had been attempts to supplement the academic provisions of the university. At the beginning of the eighteenth century, bishop of Salisbury Gilbert Burnet established a 'nursery' where he could provide instruction in 'matters of learning and piety, and particularly of such things as related to pastoral care' (Bullock, 1955: 10). The experiment was short lived, due to opposition from those in Oxford who took this as an affront to the university.

English theological colleges mainly developed in the nineteenth century. Their origins owed nothing to any central planning or initiative, but grew as a result of private individuals or groups, partly influenced by the evangelical and catholic revivals, both of which advocated the distinctiveness of the clergyman. The 'common life' was understood in varying ways. At Ridley Hall, in the evangelical tradition, the model was the Christian family, with evening prayer at 9.45 pm considered the household devotions (Jacob, 1990). In the catholic tradition H. P. Liddon, first vice-principal of Cuddesdon, saw the college's role as 'the systematic cultivation of piety'. The preliminary Theological Examination, first held in 1874, aimed to establish some norms and standards in training, but colleges persisted in independent approaches to curricula. In 1912 a Central Advisory Council of Training for the Ministry was established, seeking to bring some oversight to training: from 1921 it established as a benchmark the General Ordination Examination (GOE), with its required papers on doctrine, Bible, church history, worship and Christian morals, together with Latin and Greek. Pastoral topics were studied but not examined within GOE, and there was little emphasis on academic standards, though the Durham Report of 1944 proposed the requirement of a theological degree before ordination. This was echoed in the Bunsen Report of 1968 which recommended the closest relationship between college and university.

Since 1960 a range of regional courses has evolved for the training of candidates while still at secular work. Once designated 'non-residential' it is now recognized that these incorporate significant residential elements, both at weekends and longer periods through the year. Since 1979 all the regional courses were validated for the training of both non-stipendiary and stipendiary candidates (Hodge, 1986).

Context and prayer in the seminary model

The first Roman Catholic seminaries established after 1563 were built close to the cathedral in the heart of the city and enabled students to share in the cultural life of the locality. In the nineteenth century, in the wake of the French Revolution and Pius IX's struggles against modernism there was a change. Gualdrini explains:

> The seminary changed from its original open stance to a closed one and distanced itself from society in order to protect candidates for priesthood from the negative influences of the world. Separation from urban life often became geographical as well. In remote surroundings the students came to be formed . . . in a neoscholastic theology which found dialogue with modern culture difficult.
>
> (quoted in Pepe, 1991: 18)

Costello (2002: 268) calls this an 'ethical-pessimistic' anthropological approach: 'This gave rise to a juridical approach . . . which emphasizes the vulnerability of human nature and the need to isolate the candidate from a contaminated world.' At times, what was aimed for was described in semi-monastic terms of safeguarding a protective *anachoresis*. In 1900 Archdeacon Sandford, chairing a committee for the Convocation of Canterbury on ordination training, could point out that theological colleges

> created the spiritual atmosphere which was a necessary part of all true training for the pastoral office. They enabled men to go into retreat for a season before they approached the holy mysteries and the holiest of all duties . . . It was the supernatural side of the priestly office which was brought forward in these colleges.
>
> (quoted by Jacob, 1990: 74)

The colleges were marked by a well-defined *ascesis* with strict disciplines in place for both community prayer and individual meditation.

Wissenschaft – the professional model

The rise of the professional paradigm

In the eighteenth and nineteenth centuries a combination of factors led to the emergence of a professional paradigm for theological training which, on the surface at least, left little room for prayer and spirituality.

The Enlightenment's quest for rational enquiry led in Continental Protestant universities to the emergence of a fourfold theological encyclopaedic approach to theology: Bible, church history, dogmatics and practical theology. This began a process of fragmenting theology into different objective sciences, specialisms or discrete disciplines. At the same time, continental pietism stressed the need for the proper training of the minister for the specific tasks of ministry, equipped with the necessary skills. When in 1811 Frederick Schleiermacher needed to justify the creation of a faculty of theology in the new secular university of Berlin he helped to formalize this double-trend by advocating the study of theology in terms of *Wissenschaft* – orderly, critical research needed to resource and train the leaders of the Church that they might serve society well. In his *Brief Outline of Theological Study* (1811), Schleiermacher conceived the training of pastors in terms of supporting a professional model of ministry: clergy able to uphold an intellectually defensible Christianity, not necessarily connected with the living tradition of the Church. Paralleling trainee doctors' and lawyers' need for being equipped with the relevant knowledge of medicine or law, clergy as an emerging profession needed training in theological knowledge – hence Farley (2003) calls this the clerical paradigm; as Kelsey reminds us (1993) *Wissenschaft* has a bipolar character, between research and professionalism.

Schleiermacher proposed three major areas of study: historical theology, philosophical theology and practical theology – not at this stage understood in terms of ministerial skills but as a body of theory related to ministerial practice. Schleiermacher's approach to theology had its influence beyond the Protestant churches of Germany, and resonated with parallel developments in Victorian society. The rapid development of the professional class in Victorian Britain led to the rise in expectations and status of the clergy, helping to justify the existence of theological colleges in terms of the training of the clerical profession (Russell, 1984).

Limitations of the professional paradigm

The professional paradigm sits uncomfortably with those aspects of ordained ministry which stress the humility and servant character of the priesthood. It could encourage an elitist, exclusivist and separatist view of the priesthood, fostering a dependent laity, in contrast to collaborative models. The stress on expertise needed, in terms of competencies to be acquired, can foster a success ethic in ministry whereby 'effectiveness' and success become the paramount goals (compare the 'capability procedures' in Archbishops' Council, 2005). As Kelsey (1993: 24) observes: 'Neither intuitive experience of God nor capacities for such experience are cultivated, not even indirectly, by engaging in *Wissenschaft*.'

There is a danger that professional techniques could become more important than personal qualities. Competencies can become standardized institutional requirements encouraging the cloning of ministers rather than people's development in Christ according to their unique combination of the gifts of the Spirit. Pastoral skills, in addition, could be more highly valued and be considered as 'more relevant' than biblical or historical skills. The professional model can encourage a secularized view of ministry as a career rather than as a vocation, causing conflict within the curriculum: 'The vocational character [of studies] may exert itself over the professional with an insistence from some students and faculty that courses must first and foremost nourish one's spirituality and personal growth, with knowledge and skills subordinate to this primary aim' (Schner, 1993: 6). If the development of useful professional skills is the highest priority, where does that leave the place of prayer and spirituality, which seem rather less useful and pragmatic?

Questions for reflection

+ What does each model say to your present educational practice or to your experience as a learner?

+ What insights do you think each model offers to understanding the process of ministerial formation?

+ How does each model question us?

+ How would we want to question each model?

3

The advent of the formation paradigm in Roman Catholic and Anglican traditions

Introduction to chapters 3 and 4

The aim of chapters 3 and 4 is to chronicle and document the evolution of the paradigm of formation within the main Christian traditions, in order to discover the difference that this model makes in approaches to training of the ministry. The main methodology employed is the study of primary official documents. This will be supplemented where greater clarity is necessary by interviews with theological educators. Particular attention will be paid to the concept of spiritual formation, as it develops in different churches. These chapters seek to identify further issues to be addressed in the research, from each of the main ecclesial traditions considered here.

Formation in the Roman Catholic Church

No research into the origins of the development of the concept of formation has been published. This section will attempt to trace the advent of the word and its evolving meaning over the last century.[1]

Use of formation language prior to Second Vatican Council
Like the word spirituality, the word formation in its educational use entered the English language from the French, where *formation*

---

[1] Researched in the libraries of St John's Seminary, Wonersh, the Monastic Library of the Benedictine Abbey of Worth, Sussex, and access to documents from the archives of the Community of the Holy Name, Oxford.

means 'training/education' and the verb *former* means to form, shape, fashion, teach. Many Roman Catholic religious orders in England in the nineteenth century have French origins or betray French influence. Widely used was the manual written by Valuy (1871).

Examination of original foundation documents of these orders reveals early use of the language of formation, especially of the verb 'to form'. For example, the 1850 *Constitutions of the Society of the Holy Child Jesus* speak of the novice mistress 'moulding the hearts of the Novices, according to their different capacity and mind, so as to form them all according to the good pleasure of Him to whom they are consecrated' (Connelly, 1850a). The *Customal* of the same order directs that the novice mistress 'must take care to form and mould the Novices as far as possible to strength of mind and reason . . . All ought to form themselves according to their vocation and thence to the spirit of the Society' (Connelly, 1850b). In these examples the word 'form' is used in the sense of shape or mould interior dispositions or attitudes. It evokes a sense of 'conformity' to a religious or monastic ideal and a surrender of individual characteristics to the predominant religious norm.

An early use of the language of formation is to be found in such manuals for seminarians as Cardinal Bourne's *Ecclesiastical Training: being a Short Treatise on the Spiritual Formation of Aspirants to the Priesthood*. This uses the word 'formation' interchangeably with the language of Christian perfection, sanctification and the cultivation of a 'supernatural life': 'From beginning to end it [the training] must aim at giving to every candidate, young and old, a true, real, and solid formation in the spiritual life, making of him a supernatural man' (Bourne, 1926: 9). There are faint hints of a holistic vision, of incarnating spiritual life in the natural, daily round, but these stand in tension with the language of the 'supernatural life' of priests.

Seminary training in England was influenced by French terminology in parallel manner to religious orders. Reference has already been made to the impact of Eudes and de Bérulle, and also to Marmion of Louvain. Fr Garrigou-Lagrange's work *De Sanctificatione Sacerdotalum* (1954) is translated as *The Priesthood and Perfection* and where the language of formation is used it denotes priestly sanctification. His later work, *The Priest in Union with Christ* (1961), anticipates the struggles of the Vatican Council in the question of the unity and integration of theological studies. Writing of the 'priest's intellectual and spiritual formation' he calls for a careful balance between intellectual study and the nurture of the 'interior life' and for the avoidance of the perils of superficiality, where intellectual questions do not impact on the spiritual life: 'Therefore, what is required? A greater unity, depth, and elevation of life, so that the priest may live under the continual impulse of the theological virtues and under the inspiration of the Holy Ghost' (Garrigou-Lagrange, 1961: 93). Here we begin to detect a movement in the use of formation language towards the big issues of fragmentation and integration of priestly training. It is no longer used in the earlier isolated sense of 'moulding' according to a predetermined (Tridentine) template of priestly life.

The first use of the language of formation in papal documents is in Leo XIII's 1890 encyclical *Dall'alto dell'Apostolico Seggio* which contains a brief reference (in official English translations of the Latin document) to 'the formation of the clergy learned and full of the spirit of Jesus Christ'. In his encyclical *On the Education of the Clergy*, Leo XIII struggles with the tension between cultivating a 'fitting culture of soul and mind' (para.13) and the need to respond to the demands of the world:

> Certainly in the formation of the clergy and the sacerdotal ministry, it is reasonable that regard should be had to the varied conditions of the times . . . Now he can never fully correspond if he is not well versed in the science of divine and sacred things, if he is not furnished with that piety which makes a man of God.

But he concludes with the necessity of separate, even elitist training: 'Keep them removed from contact and still more from living together with youths who are not aspiring to the sacred ministry' (Leo XIII, 1902: para. 5, 11).

In his Apostolic Exhortation *Haerent Animo*, Pius X (1908) talks of his duty to urge the bishops 'to devote themselves unceasingly and efficaciously to the formation of Christ in those who, by their calling, have the responsibility of forming Christ in others'. In this, he refers to Paul's usage of formational language in Galatians 4: 19.

Throughout the twentieth century there is an ambiguous usage of formation language. Sometimes it is used to be equivalent to education; at other times it is interchangeable with holiness. For example, Pius XI in his 1935 *Ad Catholici Sacerdotii* used 'formation' as equivalent to 'education', and the encyclical maintains the prevailing scholastic and philosophical approach to theological studies. Pius XII in his 1950 Apostolic Exhortation *Menti Nostrae* 'On the Development of Priestly life' speaks once of 'the formation of the clergy' in connection with personal sanctification; otherwise educational references are to 'intellectual, literary and scientific training', 'philosophical and theological training' and 'spiritual and moral training'.

In 1959 it is possible to note a shift in the use of the language. In his *Princeps Pastorum* John XXIII uses formation, for the first time, in the general sense of the Christian education for all disciples. Its priestly use, however, is confined to the nurture of the virtues: 'Regarding the requirements of a perfect priestly formation and education, it is necessary that seminarians be induced, tactfully but firmly, to espouse those virtues which are the prime qualification of the priestly calling, that is the duty to achieve personal sanctification.' However, it is to be concluded, that the main word for education or training in the Catholic tradition prior to Vatican II was *institutione*. Rarely is the language of formation employed and, where it is, it denotes sanctification or education as noted above.

Use of formation language in the Second Vatican Council

The Second Vatican Council facilitated a major shift in Roman Catholic ecclesiology. *Lumen Gentium* registers a movement away from institutional and juridical models of the Church towards the dynamic paradigm of the pilgrim people of God (Dulles, 1976). Thinking about the priesthood evolved more hesitantly, with a gradual progression from a cultic model towards a paradigm which has been called the 'servant-leader' model (Schwartz, 1989).

The 1965 *Decree on the Ministry and Life of Priests* published as *Presbyterorum Ordinis* attempts to achieve a balance between an ontological understanding of priesthood as 'sign' and the essential priestly functions described in terms of ministers of God's Word, ministers of the Sacraments and rulers of God's people. It reiterates traditional calls to priestly perfection and holiness. There is but one reference (article 7) utilizing the language of formation, in the call for a progressive formation or *continua formatione* (see Tartre, 1966).

The Decree *Optatam Totius* (1965) was the fruit of fierce debate in the three sessions of the council about the training of priests. It embodies two major trends.

The first is a movement from fragmentation in priestly studies towards greater unity. The existing seminary system, built upon its scholastic and Tridentine legacy, characterized by divisions into separate branches of study, was to be renewed through a unifying of studies with the single aim of training pastorally minded priests after the model of Christ, teacher, priest and shepherd: 'all the elements of their training, spiritual, intellectual, disciplinary, should be co-ordinated with this pastoral aim in view.' (*Optatam Totius*, art. 4, in Flannery, 1975). However, such 'coordination' falls short of integration, and there is little exploration of the possible fruits of cross-fertilization between the 'elements'; the questions of how prayer might feed theology, or pastoral encounter might impact on prayer, are not considered.

The second movement in *Optatum Totius* is towards a new focus on developing the personality of the candidate in terms of the model of Christ noted above. There is a fresh seriousness about the humanity of the priest, and a gentle critique of Trent's desire for seminaries to 'protect' candidates from the world in isolated training marked by abstracted and dehumanized approaches. Archbishop Hurley writes of a new concern for the nurturing of human nature:

> One of the drawbacks of the past was our lack of understanding of the ministerial priesthood. We thought of it, as we thought of most other Christian values, too much in juridical terms . . . The *Decree* is deeply concerned about correcting this deviation . . . We are not dealing with supernatural life. We are dealing with human life transformed by the supernatural.
>
> (Hurley and Cunnane, 1967: 181)

These two movements represent tentative steps forward in the development of a theology of ministerial formation, but they hold back from endorsing the language of formation which is used rarely in the Latin text. Indeed, the proposed title for the document *De Sacrorum alumnis formandis* was rejected in favour of the traditional language: *Decretum de Institutione sacerdotali* – the static language of the institution preferred over the dynamic language of formation (Vorgrimler, 1968: 373). Nevertheless, in English translations of the text, the term *institutione spiritualis* is often given as 'spiritual formation', indicating that the language of formation was becoming attractive in English-speaking areas, if not in Rome. The translation in Flannery (1975) thus affords an early example of the terminology of spiritual formation: 'spiritual formation should be closely associated with doctrinal and pastoral formation' (*Optatam Totius*, art.8). There is here the call for 'close association' of prayer with other studies but no exploration of this relationship. Spiritual formation is explicated in terms of a Trinitarian and paschal lifestyle: it

> should be conducted in such a way that the students may learn to live in intimate and unceasing union with God the Father through his Son Jesus Christ, in the Holy Spirit. Those who are to take on the likeness of Christ the priest by sacred ordination should form the habit of drawing close to him as friends in every detail of their lives. They should live his Paschal Mystery in such a way that they will know how to initiate into it the people committed to their charge.
>
> (*Optatam Totius*, art.8)

As Archbishop Hurley comments: 'This is true Christian ontology, with its emphasis on union with the indwelling Trinity and identification with Christ in his person and in his Church. These are the realities that constitute authentic Christian mysticism . . . Such mysticism is of its nature apostolic' (Hurley and Cunnane, 1967: 192).

Thus Vatican II witnesses to the first tentative use of formation language, but the interrelation of spirituality and pastoral and doctrinal studies is left unexplored.

The immediate Post-Vatican II Period

The practical out-working of the resolves of Vatican II about priestly training were detailed in the 1970 document *Ratio Fundamentalis Institutionis Sacerdotalis* produced by the Sacred Congregation for Catholic Education and translated in English as *The Basic Plan for Priestly Formation* (Congregation for Catholic Education, 1970). This provides an outline for a programme of training within four dimensions: human, spiritual, intellectual and pastoral formation. It gives the purpose of spiritual formation as

> the end of spiritual formation is the perfection of charity, and it should lead the student, not just by dint of his ordination, but from the intimate fellowship of his whole life, to become in a special way another Christ, deeply penetrated by his spirit . . .
>
> (*Basic Plan*, para. 44)

The role of the spiritual director is highlighted and seven features of spiritual formation are specified: living in communion with the Trinity; finding Christ in prayer; faith rooted in Scripture; the

Eucharist; devotion to the Blessed Virgin Mary; attention to the Fathers and Saints; self-examination and the use of the sacrament of penance. But such 'churchy' disciplines are to be supplemented by engagement with the world, itself considered in some way part of their 'spiritual preparation' for ministry (*Basic Plan*, para. 58).

The *Ratio Fundamentalis* was used throughout the world as a template for priestly training, with each national episcopal conference charged with producing its own programme. In England and Wales this was developed through the Commission for Priestly Formation, publishing in 1979 the *Cherwell Report*, putting forward proposals arising from a significant piece of research among seminarians in the 1970s. Nearly half of those who took part considered the spiritual direction they received in seminary as less than adequate. In addition, just 16 per cent of the sample registered a sense of growth in prayer during their seminary years, while less than half considered the support they received to help people with prayer to be adequate. Similar sentiments were reported in *Early Thoughts: An Interim Statement of the Working Party of the Commission for Priestly Formation,* in which students 'found a lack of instruction and experience in personal prayer' (quoted in Tolhurst, 1982: 368). More than 10 per cent voluntarily called for greater emphasis on spiritual training. Yet, the *Cherwell Report* gives only a brief and unnuanced account of spiritual formation, betraying an undeveloped sense of the role of spirituality in the formation process.

The degree of struggle with the question of spiritual formation in seminaries throughout the world in this period caused the Congregation for Catholic Education to see the need to issue an impassioned plea for renewed attention to its significance and implementation in its 1980 *Circular Letter concerning Some of the More Urgent Aspects of Spiritual Formation in Seminaries.* Its introduction talks of a deep longing

> to find in our priests real 'teachers of prayer' with a firm knowledge of tradition, priests who experience God in a fervent way, who are capable of being wise and prudent 'directors of souls' following the paths of the great masters, and who are also responsive to the needs of the time ... the future of the Church at the present moment depends most of all on the spiritual formation of future priests.

This letter to all Catholic bishops places high emphasis on the need for 'interior silence': candidates 'must receive an experience of interior silence. They must acquire a genuine sense of it. They must become capable of communicating it to others . . . students must be taught to pray.'

However, the document concedes a very real problem. In calling for a 'spiritual propaedeutic period', its conclusion says:

> Thus something could be achieved at the beginning which might be very difficult or impossible to achieve later on when seminary training is taken up with a great deal of intellectual work. Then students often do not have the leisure and the freedom of mind to accomplish a real spiritual apprenticeship.

Once again the document reveals a divorce or dichotomy between spiritual formation and intellectual study and concludes that it is desirable to attend to the former at the outset of training, because there may be no room for it later on. Any role for prayer in the process of intellectual reflection is not envisaged.

Developments and debate, 1980–92

The 1980s and early 1990s were a very significant period for evolution of Catholic thinking and practice about formation and the role of prayer in it. In the wake of Vatican II thinking about formation, there were significant developments, summed up in three major documents.

The Rite of Christian Initiation of Adults

This document from the Sacred Congregation for Divine Worship, embodying a radically fresh catechetical and liturgical programme for basic Christian formation, began to be used widely in Catholic parishes throughout the world during the 1980s (Thomas, 1982). It represented a major development in thinking about the formation of Christian disciples, moving from the traditional didactic and instructional model to a more participatory one which encourages spiritual growth (with the use of retreats, quiet days and meditative exercises) and participation in the Christian community, complementing training given in groups.

Directives on Formation in Religious Institutes

Published by the Congregation for Institutes of Consecrated Life and Societies of Apostolic Life, for the training of religious sisters and monks, this used formation as the main paradigm, as it took shape during the 1980s. It notes an interplay between the formation of identity and the experience of God: 'The primary end of formation is to permit candidates to the religious life and young professed, first to discover and later to assimilate that in which religious identity consists' (para. 6). Elsewhere, the *Directives* make plain:

> Whatever the insistence placed upon the cultural and intellectual dimensions of formation . . . the spiritual dimension retains its priority. The principal purpose of formation at its various stages, initial and ongoing, is to immerse religious in the experience of the Good and to help them perfect it gradually in their lives.
>
> (para. 35)

The document represents an attempt to reach greater clarity in the use of the formation paradigm. But, as Faber pointed out,

> Integral formation with its spiritual, physical, moral and intellectual needs is recognized, but the psychological and emotional dimensions are not considered, yet such consideration is essential if we are to form the whole person . . . A more surprising lacuna lies in the whole area of prayer . . . it is as though nothing has been learned about 'doing theology' or about the formative experiences of other communities and groups, especially, perhaps, Basic Christian Communities. At least an unhealthy emphasis on piety (spiritual bandages for emotional wounds) has been avoided.
>
> (1991: 62)

The Code of Canon Law

With its new canons issued in 1983, *The Code of Canon Law* laid down particular requirements to sustain spiritual formation. This stated that 'the spiritual and the doctrinal instruction of students in a seminary are to be harmoniously blended'. The new canons require increased use of retreats, appointment of spiritual directors in every seminary and the writing by each national episcopal conference of a charter of priestly formation, to enable detailed programmes to take into account regional and local circumstances and context.

Ecumenical consultations

Roman Catholic educators contributed to important ecumenical consultations which helped stimulate thinking on spiritual formation in this period across the traditions (Lonsdale and Sheldrake, 1986; Amirtham and Pryor, 1989; Pobee, 1997). After a preparatory consultation at Iona in 1981, came a global consultation at Yogyakarta, Indonesia, convened in 1989 by the World Council of Churches'

Programme on Theological Education. Its aim was to clarify understandings of spiritual formation and to ask the question 'What
spiritual resources do Christian leaders need for their ministry?' It
worked with this definition:

> Spiritual formation can be understood as an intentional process by which
> the marks of an authentic Christian spirituality are being formed and
> integrated ever anew . . . this needs some deliberate cultivation in any
> process of theological education; its development cannot be left to hap-
> hazard choice and unplanned growth.
>
> (World Council of Churches, 1987)

Ten characteristics of 'authentic spirituality' were identified: it is to
be reconciling and integrative; incarnational; rooted in scripture and
nourished by prayer; costly and self-giving; life-giving and liberative;
rooted in community and centred around the Eucharist; expressed
in service and witness; waiting for God's surprising initiative; attentive to the unfolding of the loving purposes of God here on earth;
open to the wider *oikoumene* (WCC, 1987).

Responding to this vision of spirituality energizing formation,
Bishop Francesco Marschisano (1989) raised the question of the
relationship of spirituality to the curriculum in seminaries: 'It is
therefore supremely important that teachers should be fully aware
that . . . they share in a unitary teaching scheme which has as its aim
an authentic spiritual formation [and] bear witness to this unity and
awareness.'

Roman Catholic approaches to formation also contributed to
what came to be known as the Theological Education Debate which
was advanced by consultations convened by the Association of
Theological Seminaries in the USA (see, for example, Fiorenza,
1988, in Astley, Francis and Crowder, 1996).

Evolving Catholic thinking crystallized in the publication in 1992
of Pope John Paul II's Apostolic Exhortation *Pastores Dabo Vobis*,
which has become the touchstone and normative guide to Catholic
practice in this area. Costello (1998: 269) concludes that this represents a major shift from the Tridentine juridical and ethical-
pessimistic anthropology to one designated 'rational-optimistic
which gave rise to an empirical approach to priestly formation' taking into account human nature, individual freedom and the search
for spiritual maturity. *Pastores Dabo Vobis* explores more fully than
before the four dimensions of ministerial formation:

Human formation: this is explored in terms of the development of human maturity. Emotional stability and coming to terms with one's sexuality are recognized as key factors influencing the formation process: for Roman Catholic priests, of course, this entails the commitment to celibacy.

Spiritual formation is understood in terms of maintaining communion with Christ the Good Shepherd: 'for every priest his spiritual formation is the core which unifies and gives life to his *being* a priest and his *acting as* a priest' (John Paul II, 1992: 122). The necessity of time in prayer is stressed: 'the priest will only be able to train others in this school of prayer, if he himself has been trained in it and continues to receive its formation' (John Paul II, 1992: 130).

Is prayer understood mainly in terms of 'devotional life', and how is the relation of prayer to theological reflection or demanding ministry in the world explored? There is a dialectic between interior spiritual life and exterior ministry:

> The spiritual life is, indeed, an interior life, a life of intimacy with God, a life of prayer and contemplation. But this very meeting with God, and with his fatherly love for everyone, brings us face to face with the need to meet our neighbour, to give ourselves to others, to serve in a humble and disinterested fashion, following the example Jesus has proposed . . .
>
> (John Paul II, 1992: 134)

Intellectual formation incorporates study of the Fathers and tradition and also serious theological and philosophical reflection, which does not take place in a prayerless vacuum: 'To be pastorally effective, intellectual formation is to be integrated with a spirituality marked by a personal experience of God' (John Paul II, 1992: 141).

Pastoral formation is understood in terms of communion with the charity of Jesus Christ the Good Shepherd. This underlies the Christological model of ministry which predominates in the text, but the relationship between pastoral formation and prayer is not considered.

It is in this document that the paradigm of formation becomes the central model in Catholic approaches to priestly training. But what is the relation between these four dimensions? Reference is again made to 'the co-ordination of the different aspects of human, spiritual, and intellectual formation directed to a pastoral end' (John Paul II, 1992: 154). The four dimensions are set out side by side; some lines of contact are drawn between them, but there is still a sense in which the potential of complex interpenetration and cross-fertilization between the elements has not been recognized. There persists a compartmentalizing of the elements. In particular, such roles of prayer as energizing pastoral ministry and as making reflective sense both of ministry and the tradition are hardly considered. Prayer is considered as a significant element within the formation process, but never as the very matrix in which ministerial formation in all its dimensions take place.

Significant documents since 1992 include Congregation for the Clergy, *Directory on the Ministry and Life of Priests* (1994) and *The Priest and the Third Christian Millennium: Teacher of the Word, Minister of the Sacraments and Leader of the Community* (1999). Four recent studies in the Catholic Church also reveal the need for both a more focused and a more integrated approach to nurturing a life of prayer in seminarians.

Hoge and Wenger, in *Evolving Visions of the Priesthood* (2003), report a survey of 1,200 US priests. Invited to make recommendations to seminaries, a forty-two-year-old priest reported: 'I . . . recommend . . . more of an emphasis on prayer . . . the priests that tend to fail – to burn out – tend to be priests who neglect their prayer.' A sixty-one-year-old priest, ordained in 1965, commented: 'I don't think I was ever taught to meditate . . . After I got out of the seminary, somebody asked me to teach them to pray. Nobody ever taught me to pray.' Another priest, ordained in 1972, asked: 'How do you make a person realize the importance of prayer and its connection to ministry before you're really involved in ministry? . . . Lay people want to see priests who . . . have a passion for God . . . in my mind, you're only going to get that passion as you see the need for prayer and ministry.' Hoge's *The First Five Years of the Priesthood* (2002) reports its survey among over 500 newly ordained priests who strongly recommend the development of a stronger prayer life during seminary.

Research in the UK includes Timms, *You Aren't One of the Boys: Authority in the Catholic Priesthood* (2001). This reveals a need for more human development in formation. One bishop remarked: 'I think there is too much emphasis on academic development in seminaries. I would have greater emphasis on personal development, human development.' Louden and Francis's study *The Naked Parish Priest: What Priests Really Think They're Doing* (2003), reporting a survey among 1,400 Catholic priests in England and Wales, is more optimistic: 68 per cent affirm 'my seminary training prepared me well for developing a spiritual life'.

Formation in the Anglican tradition

Education for the Church's Ministry (known as *ACCM 22*), a seminal and influential document (Advisory Council for the Church's Ministry: 1987), represents the first, tentative use of formational language. It was to be sixteen years until the Church of England attempted to clarify its understanding of ministerial formation in the publication *Formation for Ministry within a Learning Church* (Archbishops' Council, 2003). This section attempts to map the evolution of thinking that led to the 2003 report.

ACCM 22 (1987) represents a watershed in Anglican thinking about theological education and the beginning of what Nicholas Sagovsky has called a 'quiet revolution in Church of England training for ministry' (ABM, 1992). It marks the end of a centrally determined syllabus for theological colleges based on the General Ministerial Examination, and a devolution to the colleges of the responsibility to devise creative theological programmes, guided by responses to three major questions: 'What ordained ministry does the Church of England require?'; 'What is the shape of the educational programme best suited for equipping people to exercise this ministry?' and 'What are the appropriate means of assessing suitability for the exercise of this ministry?' Three parameters for theological education are outlined: 'Interpretation of the Christian tradition for today', 'The formation of Church Life' and 'Addressing situations in the world'. The paper seeks to present a clear rationale for theological education, noting that the existing syllabus neither specified desirable qualities in candidates to be developed, nor allowed sufficient time for critical reflection. In his preface the then archbishop of Canterbury Robert Runcie highlights the theme of formation: 'Ministerial training, if it is to be successful, must attempt to integrate the intellectual, spiritual, moral and practical . . . the necessary *formation* for the ministry' (ACCM, 1987: 9). The report states:

> It should be the fundamental aim of theological education to enable the student to grow in those personal qualities by which, with and through the corporate ministry of the Church, the creative and redemptive activity of God may be proclaimed and realised in the world . . .
>
> (ACCM, 1987: 45)

The language of formation is used in two major ways in the development of this theme. First, reference is made to the need of candidates 'to be conformed to the very form of God's being for mankind in the world' and 'the inquiry [into scripture and tradition] must serve the goal of discovering the form of God's creative and redemptive activity in the world and learning to participate in it in the present' (ACCM, 1987: 45, 51). Characteristics of the 'form' of God's involvement in the world are not here explored: the phrase evokes Phil. 2: 6–8, the form required by God's *kenosis*. This resonates with a key emphasis in *ACCM 22*, the participation of the ordinand in the costly self-giving of God in his mission in the world.

Secondly, the report refers to formation in wisdom: 'Theological education should therefore seek to form the ordinand in this wisdom and habit of life as a "virtue" bestowed by the grace of God' (ACCM, 1987: 47). It talks of forming this virtue through a personal discipline set within the corporate search of the Church for wisdom, and asks: 'In what does this formation consist?' Traditional processes of instruction are not enough: students are called to

> know the God who presents himself in truth ... [they] should be provided with circumstances which permit careful thought and meditation, where the demands for immediate relevance and utility are suspended for a time. At the same time, they endeavour to be conformed personally (spiritually and practically) to what is found to be the truth, leaving no great distance between 'the head' and 'the heart'.
>
> (ACCM, 1987: 48)

This important statement opens up new opportunities for the role of prayer in training. It calls for both space and time in reflective prayer.

The report reveals both the potency of the formational language and also its potential for confusion: it has a third use of the term in referring to 'the Formation of Church life ... deep inquiry into the conditions of the Church's life as called by Jesus Christ and living from the energy of the Holy Spirit' (ACCM, 1987: 52). The report contains seeds and germs of ideas, but leaves unanswered such questions as: what is the relation between prayer and what it calls the 'deep enquiry' of theological education? What is the relation between prayer and engagement with God's work in the world? How does prayer contribute to 'formation in wisdom'? Certainly *ACCM 22* marks the beginning of a paradigm shift towards a more dynamic model of training, in contrast to former rather static approaches, revealing a new attentiveness to holistic perspectives.

In *Integration and Assessment* (ABM, 1992) the Church of England took significant steps forward in its understanding of ministerial formation. It sought to set out discernible patterns and trends in the courses' and colleges' responses to *ACCM 22* and to provide a catalyst for further thinking about the process. Prior to its publication, the ACCM Occasional Paper *Theology in Practice* (1988), together with a conference in 1990 on this, formed a further seedbed of ideas. Rowan Williams, as chairman of the Committee for Theological Education, called the Church

> to look to a model of theological formation that allows some productive 'conversation' between different frames of reference and accounts of experience, traditional and contemporary, 'interior' and practical, so as to help nurture an integral personal vision, a discipline of informed reflection – 'wisdom' rather than skill alone.
>
> (ACCM, 1988: 5)

This was echoed by Austin Smith, who at the 1990 conference

> expressed anxiety that insufficient work is being done with students on the interior life. He noted a principle from apostolic action, namely that 'you gave what you assimilated and contemplated' ... A student is engaged in praxis/action, meaning that the student should be helped to learn, reflect and interiorize, and then take action which sets off further reactions.
>
> (ABM, 1992: 15)

Integration and Assessment utilizes two key words in preference to formational language. First, 'integration' becomes a central concept, especially in relation to the problems of self-contained compartmentalization of subjects, the attendant fragmentation of theological study and an inner fragmentation sometimes faced by the student himself or herself. The search for integration, healing the divide and dichotomy between different elements, is described through the metaphor of interweaving of interrelated strands within the fabric of theological education into one whole tapestry. Four types of integration are commended: between different subjects in the curriculum; between theory and practice, study and placements; between a student's prior, pre-training experience and that of the college/course; and inner reconciliation and coherence within the student: 'The student's construction of a total picture will also include personal development, spiritual growth and the formation of themselves in readiness for ordained ministry' (ABM, 1992: 51). The language of integration entails a fitting together of different parts of the jigsaw; a making of connections between prayer, theology and ministry. It is concerned with the issues of wholeness, coherence and integrity in the minister's life.

The second favoured concept is that of interaction. In contrast to 'one way systems of learning which moved essentially from under-standings of God's purposes in tradition to life' (ABM, 1992: 22), the idea of interaction opens up the possibilities for a dynamic inter-play between, for example, experiences encountered in placements and the forming of theological perspectives. As the report notes, such interaction and interplay can be unpredictable and risky:

> The word *interaction* suggests that strands can relate to one another, with-out losing their identity, and that the relationship is one in which the strands have mutual influence in a dynamic, rather than static way . . . there may be tension and even contradiction in these relationships.
>
> (ABM, 1992: 49)

The concept of interaction is full of potential in the task of reflecting about the significance of prayer and ministry. The idea of a two-way movement or ebb and flow between contemplation and action, for example, opens a way to understand prayer both as influencing min-istry profoundly and being changed by the practice of ministry. It allows for the unpredictability of both prayer and action, and com-plements the more healing concept of integration, where there is some coming together and encounter between prayer and action that may lead to the creation of a sense of inner unity and purpose.

Mission and Ministry: the Churches' Validation Framework for Theological Education (ABM, 1999) builds on the progress in think-ing and practice since *ACCM 22* and revises the process of validating courses and colleges. It is an ecumenical document, written in con-sultation with the Methodist and United Reformed Churches. In particular it commends the use of a set of 'Agreed expectations of ordinands' – qualities and skills to be achieved in the period of initial training (ABM, 1993). These criteria now included a creative approach to the spirituality required of candidates. Warning against the danger of stereotyping and against the danger of isolating prayer from life or experience, and recognizing the influence of culture, race and social background on the expression of spirituality, the guidelines for selectors note:

One indication of a maturing spirituality is a growing awareness of the presence of God in all aspects of experience and a discerning of God's activity within one's own life and the life of others. . .Bishop's Selectors should try to discover how the candidates' spirituality and prayer lead to a difference in their daily life, to participation in the work of God in the world and to growth in personal holiness.

(ABM, 1993: 89)

This is a significant statement, highlighting the role of prayer in terms of awareness and discernment, communicating a sense that prayer leads to increased consciousness of and alertness to God's presence. The advice also introduces a key concept relevant to this research – the difference prayer makes in living and perceiving. *Mission and Ministry* calls for these criteria to become agreed expectations for candidates in training: 'The emphasis is on their formation as suitable persons for ordained or accredited ministry, not simply on gaining discrete areas of skill or knowledge' (ABM, 1999: 41). It juxtaposes four key elements to be developed in ordinands: personal commitment to Christ sustained by Scripture, spirituality and prayer life; personal self-understanding; discipleship; and maturity and ability to face change and pressure. It does not explore the possible links between these: research is needed to explore the interaction and interplay between them. How, for example, can prayer enable a person to face change and face stress? What role does prayer play in self-understanding and understanding of vocation? *Mission and Ministry* leaves such questions unanswered, but does represent another step forwards in the Church of England's understanding of formation, calling for ordinands to develop a 'habit of prayer in an appropriate style which engages with their life, ministry and work' (ABM, 1999: 68).

The publication in 2003 of *Formation for Ministry within a Learning Church* (*Hind Report*) marks a major shift in Anglican thinking towards making formation the key paradigm of theological education. In 2001 a working party was asked to undertake a thorough review of theological training in Britain, publishing its interim report *The Structure and Funding of Ordination Training* (Archbishops' Council, 2002) and it is instructive to note significant developments in thinking between the two reports as a result of the consultation process.

Formation becomes 'an overarching concept'

A rather personalized and ambiguous understanding of formation was advocated by the *Interim Report*. It said: 'Ordination training is concerned both with personal formation and with the knowledge and skills needed for ministry' (Archbishops' Council, 2002: 22), while elsewhere, in its draft benchmarking statement for deployable clergy, it identified as the three areas to be developed knowledge/ understanding, skills and spiritual and ministerial formation.

The 2003 *Hind Report* registers a shift in understanding, from seeing formation as only one element in the training process to accepting it as the central model:

> It is also important not to understand formation as being concerned solely with questions of spirituality and discipleship which is then added as a third element alongside 'education' (=academic study) and 'training' (=learning skills for ministry). Rather 'formation' should be seen as the overarching concept that integrates the person, understanding and competence.
>
> (Archbishops' Council, 2003: 29)

There remains an unresolved tension in the thinking of the *Hind Report* between a definition of formation which is predominantly functional in its approach to ministry and one that relates to a more ontological understanding. Thus the report can say, on the one hand (pp. 37, 38): 'We regard ministerial formation as development towards the role of particular responsibility for enabling and ordering the Church's life, under God', stressing that 'candidates put themselves at the service of the Church and participate in a process of being *conformed* to the public role'. On the other (p. 58), it seeks to achieve a balance between the three domains of *knowing* (understanding the Christian tradition), *doing* (developing skills for ministry) and *being* (defined in terms of 'growing in faith, discipleship, prayer and vocation'.) Yet it begins (p. 29) to identify elements that might contribute to a theology of formation, recognizing the divine dimension and alluding to the work of the Holy Spirit: 'it is a creative process initiated and sustained by God'.

The role of prayer in formation

The *Interim Report* allows little space for considering the role of prayer in formation, but it does call on students to 'be able to demonstrate a faithful and developing spirituality and life of prayer consonant with their changing role and growth in learning'

(Archbishops' Council, 2002: 43). This suggests a relationship between prayer and the learning process. It is developed further in the *Hind Report* where a possible interplay between prayer and self-awareness is suggested: 'Ministers will be able to evaluate their prayer life and spiritual development in the light of the wider tradition of prayer of the Church; evaluate how their growing awareness of self and others impacts on their ministry' (Archbishops' Council, 2003: 58). A theme of the proposed new framework for ministerial education is

> the making of connections at a deep level between a person's evolving understanding of faith, the life of prayer and Christian practice, through a range of stimuli including the faithful reading and study of Scripture, the Christian theological tradition and the experience of Christian life and witness.
>
> (Archbishops' Council, 2003: 39)

This opens up the possibility of prayer dynamically interacting with ministry and encourages a dialogue or conversation between prayer and experience.

However, the *Hind Report* allows little discussion of the place of spiritual formation and has been criticized for advocating an overly academic approach to training. Even prayer is nominally given a credit rating (Archbishops' Council, 2003: 58, 59)! It struggles to recognize and assess the import of spiritual formation, and does not indicate an appreciation of the ways in which prayer might reveal itself in changed attitude or perception. The difficulty in relating a fluid and dynamic concept as formation to prescriptive academic requirements is revealed in the debate over competencies.

Survey of Anglican theological colleges and courses

How widespread is the use of the formation paradigm in the Church of England's theological training establishments? What understanding of formation is revealed? Is there evidence of a convergence of understanding between the different traditions of the Church? For an understanding of the spread of formational approaches, such significant questions need to be posed to the training institutions of the Church of England.[2]

---

[2]   This study does not include the diocesan training schemes for Local Ordained Ministry.

The methodology engaged to pursue these questions involved the scrutiny of forty-six documents: for each institution, the hard-copy 2002 edition of the college/course's prospectus was compared with its 2007 online prospectus. Particular attention was paid to stated aims and objectives to discover the educational philosophy and approach to theological education, to see if this explicitly employed the paradigm of formation. These documents give the public face of the theological institutions and aim to express clearly and succinctly their values and vision. The five-year timescale for comparison of evolving documents is short but this was a time of ferment in theological education with the publication of the *Hind Report* and it is possible to identify certain shifts of emphasis in this period.

There are eleven Anglican theological colleges in England, of which six are broadly in the evangelical tradition[3] and five broadly in the catholic tradition.[4] Of the five catholic colleges, two utilize the formation paradigm as the central expression of their philosophy and rationale. The College of the Resurrection, influenced by its parent body the Benedictine religious community at Mirfield, in its *Prospectus 2002* states:

> Formation is not a kind of drill nor is it like a production line. Literally, it is about allowing the beauty that belongs to each of us come to the surface – the beauty of the image of God in us ... It will always require disciplined commitment, patience, attentive listening, waiting quietly on God. Two or three years at College [are] a specially focussed time for attending to the formative work of the Spirit who is constantly re-making us that the likeness of Christ may be seen in us.

St Stephen's House, Oxford, explains its educational approach in terms of three dimensions of formation: academic teaching is complemented by pastoral, spiritual and liturgical formation. No definition of formation is offered but the college *Prospectus 2002* states:

> Eucharist, Office and corporate silence provide the framework in which all that we do takes place, whether pastoral, academic or spiritual, work or

[3] Cranmer Hall, Durham; Oak Hill, London; Ridley Hall, Cambridge; St John's College, Nottingham; Trinity College, Bristol; Wycliffe Hall, Oxford.

[4] College of the Resurrection Mirfield; Ripon College, Cuddeson; St Stephen's House, Oxford; Westcott House, Cambridge; in addition, Queen's Foundation, Birmingham, describes itself as an 'ecumenical college in the liberal catholic tradition'. In addition, a diaconal formation programme was based at the Bishop Otter Centre for Theology and Ministry, Chichester, during the period 1995–2005.

relaxation. We believe that theology is properly undertaken within a life of prayer; trying to know God is more important than trying to know about him.

Between 2002 and 2004 Ripon College, Cuddesdon, moved from a training paradigm towards a formation paradigm in its public documents. 'Ministerial formation', not mentioned in the 2002 prospectus, becomes a prominent theme, with the focus on individual spiritual development. It offers:

> A training programme which aims at preparing the whole person for mission and ministry in the contemporary church. We therefore aim for academic excellence integrated with spiritual formation and collaboration in mission and ministry . . . The College encourages personal spiritual formation with a pattern of regular corporate worship.
>
> > (*www.rcc.ac.uk*, 2005. However, the latter two
> > sentences were dropped in the 2007 edition)

This emphasis on the 'personal spiritual formation' is also a feature of some the evangelical colleges. None of the six uses formation as the main, overarching paradigm, preferring the language of training and equipping. One uses formation language side by side with training language: Cranmer Hall 'aims to provide resources for formation and training for the church in mission . . . our particular stated priorities within the whole task of formation are worship, mission, communication, Christian leadership' (*www.dur.ac.uk*, 2007). In September 2002, Trinity College created 'ministry formation groups', stated in the *Prospectus 2002* to 'support the task of ministry and vocational formation in a context of friendship, support and shared nurture'.

There is evidence that a reluctance to use the language of formation is disappearing. Oak Hill in 2007 (but not in 2002) states it is 'Committed to Anglican Formation' and even mentions liturgical formation. Wycliffe Hall, Oxford, nowhere uses formational terminology, either in its 2002 prospectus or 2007 website, yet it appointed a 'Tutor in Spiritual Formation and Christian Worship'. The 2005 job description states:

> Spiritual formation, as we see it in our context, is designed to foster 'the godly wisdom and habit of life of a representative Christian person. It addresses the need for ministers of the Gospel to be whole people whose inner life is integrated with their outer ministry. It aims in a holistic way to bring tighter biblically-based theology, service, prayer, learning, mission and relationships in family, church and the world, as inter-connected

aspects of a person who is living their whole life under the direction of God.

The language of formation is here found attractive because it emphasizes possibilities for wholeness and the reconciliation of diverse aspects of ministry.

None of the twelve ecumenical non-residential, regional ordination courses, as they existed in 2007 prior to their rebirth and reconfiguration in regional training partnerships, used formation as the sole or predominant paradigm, but one-third of them used it in conjunction with the language of training.

The North Thames Ministerial Training Course subtitled itself 'ministerial formation for grown-ups'. It was designed 'to promote the personal development and ministerial formation of Christian men and women for ordained and other ministries'. It gave clues about its understanding of formation: 'our aim is to prepare [students] by informing their growth in the sacramental identity which arises from their participation in God's calling of his Church to priestly ministry' (*Prospectus 2007: Aims* from *www.ntmtc.org.uk*). Year One was entitled 'Theological Foundations for Theological Formation.'

The West of England Ministerial Training Course emphasized the vocational character of its training. Its *Ordination Course, 2002*, stated: 'students are expected to continue their spiritual and personal development alongside ministerial formation . . . the programme includes quiet days, a retreat experience, regular worship and activities to develop self-awareness. Students are actively encouraged to find a spiritual director or soul friend.'

The Northern Ordination Course in its 2002 *Prospectus* spoke of its 'commitment to lively, relevant and rigorous formation of women and men for the churches' ministry' and attended to 'personal and corporate formation in Christian living'. Here is a rare reference to the formation of the learning community: formation, where used, often denotes a more individualistic sense. In its 2008 website, the Northern Ordination Course, uniquely among the courses, uses the phrase 'spiritual education'. It states: 'Theological education in its broadest sense is the aim of the course. This includes: academic, vocational, personal and spiritual education and takes place within the context of an ecumenical, worshipping, Eucharistic community' (*www.thenoc.org.uk*).

The Southern Theological Education and Training Scheme alone had explicit and prominent references to the formation process.

Formational language permeated its three primary aims of educating, training and forming. To describe its objectives it utilized in its *Course Handbook 2002–3* the three categories of knowing, doing and being: 'knowing' entails being educated to 'analyse the personal, social, cultural and institutional practices by which people are formed in daily life'; 'doing' involves being trained to 'discover possibilities for Christian formation'; 'being' involves being 'formed and equipped to embody and express the ways of God in the life of the Church in the world'.

The prospectuses consulted in this survey contain indicators or clues about the institutions' self-understanding and practice.[5] The survey of colleges and courses reveals patchy but increasing use of formational language in the period 2002–7. It is employed in a sometimes imprecise way. There is evidence of the tension, identified in the *Hind Report*, between seeing formation as an overarching concept, on the one hand, and viewing it solely in terms of spiritual growth. Its absence does not necessarily imply inattention to the role of spirituality. For example, St John's, Nottingham's *Prospectus 2007* makes no reference to the formation of ministers but gives as its first core value: 'Our aim is to enable people to grow in relationship with God, so all courses offer you the chance to learn about spirituality and to grow in grace.' Where it is used in an 'umbrella' sense, its inclusion denotes an attentiveness to issues of wholeness and integration. While two colleges in the catholic tradition, both with a strong sense of community, have clear perceptions about its significance, it is also becoming more attractive to evangelical colleges, where it focuses on personal and individual growth. There are signs of a growing convergence in its applicability to spiritual maturity, but colleges prefer the language of training and education. Regional courses favour the language of training 'reflective practitioners': for example, South East Institute for Theological Education, *Prospectus 2005*, is typical in its words:

> At the heart of the training programme for all students . . . is the model of the reflective practitioner who is able to draw on their experience of mission and ministry within the church, step back from the immediate in order to think through the questions of faith and service more fully, re-engage in life and worship from a fuller and more theologically informed perspective.

[5] The empirical research in Part II complements this survey: four staff members are interviewed *in situ* on visits to the institutions.

However, such documents rarely refer to the possible place of prayer in this.

The new regional training partnerships (RTPs) which are evolving throughout 2008 reveal a wide range of approaches to formational language. It is to be observed that, though RTPs emerge from the report *Formation for Ministry within a Learning Church*, the opportunity to use the term 'formation' in their generic title itself was passed over in favour of the more functional language of training.

The Lancashire and Cumbria Theological Partnership states as its aim both 'the development of the necessary basic ministerial skills for beginning ministry' and 'the development and formation of both the person and their character as they prepare to begin public ministry' (*www.cbdti.org.uk*). It adds that it aims 'to ensure that those who minister are firmly grounded in the faith of the Church of God in order to visibly be people of prayer'.

The Southern North West Training Partnership uses the language of learning and preparation: 'The aim of the Learning for Mission and Ministry Programme is primarily to prepare men and women for accredited and authorized ministry in order that they might participate in the mission of God in the world' (*www.snwtp.org.uk*). This mission reference is echoed by the South West Ministry Training Course, which is subtitled 'Formation for Christian Ministry'. It aims 'to form women and men for an ever-deepening participation in the mission of the Triune God' (*www.swmtc.org.uk*).

The Eastern Region Training partnership (*www.ertp.org.uk*) largely restricts itself to the terminology of 'Christian education and training'. The South Central Regional Training Partnership, in its Statement of Intent, states as its purpose: 'We support the transformation of lives and the discovery of gifts by building theological confidence, and creating more effective ministry and more mature discipleship. We do this through formation, education and training, serving the whole people of God in the world' (*www.cofe.anglican.org*). The West Midlands Regional Training Partnership seeks to balance training and formational language. Its founding covenant states:

> Training has in mind the forming of the whole person for ministry, which means giving attention to prayer and spiritual preparation for discipleship, as well as growth in knowledge, understanding and relationships. It is essential that formation has in mind the preparation of disciples to live for God's Kingdom in difficult times of transition.
>
> (*www.hereford.anglican.org*)

It can be seen that within the new RTPs formational language has yet to command widespread use: some seem wary and shy away from it, but others embrace it enthusiastically. There is sometimes explicit attention to the holistic character of education, but often spirituality and the practice of prayer is separated out from the learning process as a distinct element – a creative role within learning does not yet seem to be envisaged.

Questions for reflection

✦ What do these traditions say to your present educational practice or to your experience as a learner?

✦ What insights do you think each tradition offers to understanding the process of ministerial formation?

✦ How does each tradition question us?

✦ How would we want to question each tradition?

4

Perspectives on formation in the Free Church and Orthodox traditions

Formation in the Free Church traditions

The Methodist Church in Britain formally committed itself to the formation paradigm for ministerial training in its 1999 conference and its training department was renamed the Formation in Ministry Office. This followed the adoption of the report *The Making of Ministry* produced by a working party charged with revisiting principles of theological education (Ministerial Training Policy Working Group, 1996). The report proposes two central ideas in relation to ministerial formation, that of 'basic identity' and 'seamless robe'. *The Making of Ministry* states:

> If worship and mission are the key elements in the Church's life, the needs of ministry in the Church and the world are going to be constantly changing and ministers . . . will continually need to rethink their role . . . ministerial education becomes a matter of how a basic identity and commitment can be engendered which can be expressed in a number of changing ways in response to particular contexts.
>
> (Methodist Church, 1996: 32)

As Wakelin (2005: 17) puts it, 'to grow in grace, to have earnest purpose, to be fit for ministry – this is formation, not simply developing skill in academic Theology and then trying to apply it to practical ministry'. In Methodist thinking, formation has to do with the formation of *basic identity*, a rich but problematic word, with many different psychological connotations.[1] It is developed within

---

[1] Methodist colleges also stress the place of identity formation in their prospectus. For example, Wesley House, Cambridge, states; 'Training as a presbyter focuses

four key relationships: with God ('indirectly through the Bible and the theological traditions of the churches and directly through spiritual experience'), with the created order, with others ('individuals, communities and institutions') and with self – a concept not explained. How, then, does formation nurture a sense of ministerial identity? 'Training for this life involves a rigorous and prayerful process of acquiring understanding and applying theoretical knowledge . . . developing self-awareness whilst undergoing affective change' (Methodist Church, 1996: 32).

This is explored further in the Methodist Church's discussion document *Vocational Discernment and Formation* (Methodist Church, 2003b). This offers a definition of formation as 'developing the appropriate character, outlook and predispositions of a presbyter or deacon (both as an individual and as a member of a collegial body in an order of ministry) and the credibility to be a representative person in the Church and the wider world' (p. 8).

It suggests that there is a dual process at work: formation both in discipleship and in ministry. There are two 'strands' within the shaping of ministerial identity, the personal and the public – development in faith as a Christian person and growth into ministry with an increasing public role. Thus *basic identity*, in the Methodist view, is formed in the interaction and interplay between person and role. The process of formation, then, functions in relation to its *telos*, which is expressed in a model of ministry. In *Church and Ministry: A Theological Framework* the roles of the presbyter are summed up as 'presiding, overseeing, coordinating and superintending' (Methodist Church, 2003b). For views on the Methodist understanding of the presbyterate see Methodist Conference (2002) and Luscombe and Shreeve (2002).

Methodism develops its approach from the foundation of its rich Wesleyan tradition of holiness and sanctification: Wesley, whose heart was 'strangely warmed' in his Aldersgate conversion, defined perfection as 'love governing the heart and life, running through our whole mentality, words, and actions' (Backhouse, 1988: 55; see also Flew, 1968; Wynkoop, 1972). Contemporary understandings of this process increasingly recognize the place of the affections within a learning that takes account of human vulnerability. The Methodist

upon forming an identity as a ministry of word and sacrament . . . Diaconal Training emphasizes forming an identity as a member of the Methodist Diaconal Order' (*www.wesley.cam.ac.uk*).

approach to training acknowledges a debt to Maier's concept of 'transformational learning':

> For knowledge to be utilizable in practice, cognitive learning has to be accompanied by affective change. This involves relinquishing old conceptions and living with the discomfort of uncertainty whilst new ones are formed. At the same time it involves stepping back from previously determined emotional or intuitive responses and living with the pain of vulnerability whilst more appropriate responses are created. It is therefore a deeply spiritual experience of that grace which enables both heart and mind to be transformed as a warm heart and cool head are brought into contact with each other.
>
> (quoted in Methodist Church, 2003a)

The second major theme in Methodist thinking is the imperative of maintaining a unified continuity in formation, which is expressed in terms of the metaphor of the 'seamless robe': 'the training of Presbyters, Deaconesses and Deacons should be seen as a seamless robe covering the period from candidature to supernumeryship [including the stages of foundation training, pre-ordination training, probation, reception into full connexion]' (Methodist Church, 1996: 33). The fear is of 'tears in the robe' or the disruptive effect of discontinuities in the candidate's formation of identity: it is recognized that the formation process crucially involves the crossing of thresholds, the experience of handling transitions, the experience of liminality.[2] Recognizing the danger of compartmentalizing the stages of training, the Methodist Church proposes a 'single trajectory' for training. At the same time, it acknowledges that there is a necessary role for discontinuities in the formation process, with the letting go of former roles and the facing of a different set of expectations, both themselves seen as formative experiences.

Thus the Methodist Church in Britain regards the formation paradigm to be not only significant but central to its thinking about clergy and lay training. It highlights the need to develop a clear sense of ministerial identity, and emphasizes the need for continuity and wholeness in the training process that will necessarily have different phases. It does not have a developed sense of the role of spirituality in the process, but hints at a place for 'reflective meditation'.

---

[2] An anthropological concept explored, for example, by Turner (1995). He identifies three stages: separation from normal life; a marginal phase likened to the experience of the womb, tomb or desert; aggregation, re-entering society in a new role.

Other Methodist writers have also underscored the need to develop thinking in this area, revealing parallels in different contexts. Nickerson (1987), from an American perspective, writes: 'There continues to be vagueness and perplexity about what spiritual formation really means and whether it is faculty responsibility. A primary barrier is that few faculty have done significant research in this area.' Robin Pryor (1994: 14), from an Australian standpoint, observes:

> The classical core courses of theological education are an important but incomplete approach to ministerial formation, emphasizing as they do the cognitive over the affective, knowledge of traditional and contemporary ways of speaking *about* God, as distinct from traditional and contemporary ways of speaking with God. Academic communication . . . is emphasized at the cost of personal and shared communion with the One about whom we theologise . . . As a result, the prayer and worship life of candidates is too often marginalized and individualized, isolated from the mainstream of theological curricula, and left to limp along under the onslaught of lectures . . .

The US Methodist writer William Willimon (2002: 215) points out that ministerial training will be profoundly countercultural and, noting the complementarity of instructional teaching and prayer, draws attention to ministers' key role as teachers:

> Because this faith is countercultural . . . discipleship requires the formation of people who are able to resist the powers and principalities . . . Through the words and practices of the church, such as tithing, worship, forgiveness, prayer, devotional reading, and self-denying service, the church deconstructs the socialization and spiritually stultifying conditioning of the world . . . For all these reasons, a primary pastoral task must be teaching.
>
> (See also Hauerwas and Willimon, 1989)

The United Reformed Church (URC) offers a contrasting approach within the family of Free Churches. It has been cautious about formational language. In an interview with the author, a member of the URC Training Committee comments:

> There are still some anxieties about the term 'formation'. Viewed as a holistic term emphasizing the development of the whole person, it is acceptable. But if it is understood as moulding, there is a negative reaction against the idea of being formed into a particular mould. Formation is perceived to be elitist if it goes with an idea of ordained ministry that is somehow separate from the ministry of all God's people. The URC is very cautious about ontological understandings of ministry.

The Church's Training Committee echoes this reserve:

> The use of the word 'formation' is increasing in the culture of the United
> Reformed Church. However, it does cause some concern in some quar-
> ters where a preference for the use of the term 'theological education and
> training' still resides. This might be related to another point which is that
> the conception of ministry betrayed in the [Hind Implementation] cur-
> riculum documents does indicate differences of understanding.
>
> (United Reformed Church, 2003)

The URC Training Committee is concerned to safeguard its
Reformed understanding of ministry arising from the doctrine of
'the priesthood of all believers' and fears that the use of formational
language in relation to ordained ministry could be elitist (see Tucker,
2003). The Church has recently stressed the 'Gospel imperative' that
training should be accessible to all people without distinction: this
was one of its six principles presented to the URC General Assembly
2004 (United Reformed Church, 2004). It stresses that the minister
has a role in equipping the ministry of all, rather than being a representative of all, or even a representative of Christ:

> The idea that the minister is a pointer to Christ is perhaps more helpful
> that the commoner view that the minister is the representative of Christ, a
> view that tends to lead implicitly to the idea that there can be only one
> minister in a congregation.
>
> (United Reformed Church, 1994: 33)

Reluctance to use formational language does not imply any inattention to the place of spirituality, though its relation to other aspects
of training might be considered in terms that stress partnership rather
than integration. Lesslie Newbigin, chairing the 1982 Review Group
on Ministerial Training, wrote: 'The study of theology and the growth
in personal devotion should go hand in hand. Students should learn
to pray to the God whom they think about and think about the God to
whom they pray' (United Reformed Church, 1984). More recently,
attention has been given to the potential of the language of education:
'We look to the growth of community and of individuals as the Spirit
liberates and the reading of scripture inspires. Both community and
individuals can be "led out" or "brought forth" (from the Latin word
educere) in ways they could not have imagined' (United Reformed
Church, 2004). But it is to be noted that neither prayer nor spirituality
are mentioned among the six principles for theological education
presented to Assembly.

However, as Rice (1991: 10) points out, there is an urgent need to educate ministers in the neglected historic riches of Reformed spirituality:

> No one can be part of a church within this [Reformed] tradition for very long without meeting the suspicions that seem to be aroused by the subject of spirituality. This resistance is the probable result of several factors, not least of them a lack of appreciation of their own tradition itself . . . Because Reformed Protestants do not recognize and are not taught that there is a spiritual tradition within their own heritage, they have frequently had no basis to integrate their own experience into their faith or church life.

Increasingly, there are resources available which integrate historic and contemporary Reformed spirituality: see, for example, Foster (1980 and 1992), Peterson (1993), Smith (1992); Whitney (1991).

Formation in the Orthodox traditions

Chalcedonian churches

> You must not think of Orthodox training in terms of Anglican or Roman seminaries. It is completely different. There is great variety, with many different patterns. The main aim is always to initiate the candidate into the Mysteries.

So explained an educator in the Greek Orthodox Archdiocese of Thyateira and Great Britain. What sort of patterns of training are common? In the UK, as elsewhere in the Orthodox tradition, candidates are elected by their congregation. Some will study at the Institute for Orthodox Christian Studies in Cambridge which exists 'to provide theological education that encourages intellectual and spiritual formation in the Orthodox Christian Faith' (*Prospectus*, 2002). Others may participate in the bachelor's or master's programmes at either of the two major theological schools in Greece which are part of the universities of Athens and Salonica. Others will commit themselves to personal study and to being mentored by experienced priests in Britain, especially for the conduct of liturgies. In the US, the major Orthodox seminary reveals clearly the distinctive Orthodox approach. St Vladimir's Seminary, New York, states:

> The seminary is convinced of the importance of strengthening and deepening the spiritual life of all the members of the community . . . As vital to the seminary as its classrooms and library is its chapel, the focus of its life

of prayer, for a true center for theological education and reflection must be grounded in prayer . . . All aspects of its life are moulded by an understanding of theology which seeks to engage the whole person, shunning that compartmentalization and fragmentation which so often characterize higher education.

(*www.svots.edu*)

The Dean explains:

A seminary is different from other educational institutions . . . St Vladimir's is not just another graduate school . . . trade school or professional school, whose goal is the training of competent practitioners. While we do have to be concerned about the academic and practical preparation of our seminarians, we also have to be concerned about their spiritual growth.

(Erickson, 2002: 311)

An Orthodox parish priest looking back on this training reflects:

It is only now, after years of parish service, that I fully understand the importance of what the seminary tries to pass on. The academics are important, but they are not ultimate. The most vital tools with which it equips us are not subject to academic testing, but only to the testing of God's Judgement. They are the life of liturgical and private prayer . . .

(Merick, 1988: 71)

One can compare the approach of St Tikhon's Orthodox Theological Seminary, Pennsylvania, which functions in relation to its adjoining monastery in which it calls 'a symbiotic and synergistic relationship'. It has a clear vision of the nature of theological education:

Theological knowledge can never be seen as merely the acquisition of academic information about matters ecclesial and theological. On the contrary, by its very nature, all theological knowledge is rooted in the soul of man, from whence his intelligence springs, and in the relationship that exists between man and his Creator. In this lies the great insight of the mystic theologians. True theological education is thus, first of all, the acceptance of the highest spiritual knowledge – the indwelling of the Holy Spirit.

How, then, does the practice of prayer fit into this vision?

The knowledge of God the Holy Trinity is, at once, the object of theological enquiry and also its means, or methodology. Through the simple act of beginning every discourse or study with prayer, the theological school proclaims that its first – and ultimately, its only goal – is to teach the student to draw nearer to God. The only certain way to accomplish that goal is by means of study that begins and ends in dialogue with God.

(*www.stots.edu/seminary*)

As Archbishop John Shahovskoy put it:

Theological education is extremely valuable and has a great importance but only if through the entire structure of the theological school genuine faith shines through. Seminaries must not only educate but also *form* the pastor . . . Knowledge *about God* is but a way to the knowledge *of God*.

(1966: 39, 40)

Non-Chalcedonian churches

In the Ethiopian Orthodox Church theology and prayer are linked in a unique way through the use of poetry in theological reflection.[3] The candidate is first instructed in a doctrinal or hagiographical theme. He is then dismissed with the task of making a theological composition (in the evening he identifies the musical form to be used for this). The next day the student finds a place of solitude and composes a poem on the set theme. This entails an intense process of internalization and meditation in which the student assimilates the topic and reveals his understanding through the composition. This theological song is offered during the liturgy and assessed by experienced priests or singers: this will contain both 'wax' and 'gold' elements according to the quality of the interpretation.[4] In addition to developing this skill in theological reflection through poetry, there is close attentiveness to developing the character of the candidate by spiritual disciplines. As one theological educator at the monastic school of Debre Libanos put it to me: 'What is needed in the trainee priest is not only deep knowledge of the tradition but also deep character . . . the sort of person he is. Rich or poor, tall or short, what matters most is the heart.'

In the Coptic tradition, as in other Orthodox churches, priests and bishops are trained in the monasteries. In an interview with

---

[3] The Ethiopian Church has three forms of training: Holy Trinity Seminary run on western lines in Addis Ababa; local schools, such as at Lalibela, specializing in music, literature and poetry (called Qene Bet); monastic schools such as that at Debre Libanos. These three were visited in 2004 as part of this research.

[4] The designations derive from the use of wax mould containing gold jewellery: the *qene* poem should have two levels of meaning, an outer or obvious meaning and a message which is inner or profound. This is described in Ethiopian Orthodox Church (1997: 92–4) and in Binns (2005: 103–13).

the author, one monk-teacher of the world's first monastery of St Anthony, Egypt, explains:

> Each candidate will have a spiritual father in addition to the Abbot. This is his spiritual guide who leads him into the traditions of prayer. Meditation is like savouring fruit in the mouth – we *live* the scriptural text all day, going deeper with it. Those who hear the words of teaching need to open their inner ears, to hear inwardly. When you are teaching them, you are spreading seeds – the heart receives these, but the seeds will not grow inside them without prayer. Prayer is the water that helps the seeds of knowledge to grow and come to fruition. What matters is not the one who plants the seed, but the One who gives inner growth. And without water we cannot live! Without prayer, knowledge stays on the argumentative level of the intellect: prayer takes knowledge to a deeper level. Prayer grows the seeds because it takes them into a relationship with God, which we describe like the *Song of Songs* as a relationship between Lover and beloved.

In the Armenian Apostolic Church, prayer was said to form the 'backbone' of training in the seminary. In an interview with the author one student from Sevan Seminary explains:

> There are two ways of looking at prayer. One way is by following the curriculum that has been set out for us: Morning and Evening Prayers and the Liturgy, and using prayers assigned for us, like the student's prayer in the morning which asks God to guide us and help us in our knowledge. The other way of prayer is our own personal prayer, which really forms the spine of our training – it's the anchor to which we can hold throughout both our spiritual and academic life here.

The student went on to say how such prayer life can be supported: 'The priests are available to encourage us but also there is a responsibility on the part of the students to help each other. The older seminarians sometimes share their spiritual experience with the younger ones. And that means even more than academic lectures.' A wide range of resources is needed to underpin the seminarian's prayer life:

> We read of course Armenian classics like the writings of Gregory of Narek and Nerses Shnorhali.[5] But it is also important to learn from the spiritual writings of other churches. They help you to see yourself, and your prayer life from another culture's perspective.

---

[5]   See Samuelian (2002) and Kudian (1986).

In the Syriac Orthodox tradition of theological education prayer plays a key role. Sometimes different forms of learning are distinguished, as a superior of a Syriac monastery in Kerala put it when interviewed: 'There are two types of knowledge and two ways of knowing. On the one hand there is the academic, bookish learning of the study. But there is also a theological understanding you reach through intuition, through prayer.' However, these do not have to be polarized in this way. In the traditional model of priestly training in the churches of the Syriac tradition in India, an apprentice model where a candidate learned about priesthood from a recognized *malpan* or teacher by sharing the life of a small household, sometimes the bishop's house,[6] liturgical prayer and silence were woven into the rhythm of the community. In the modern model of seminary today, the chapel is given an equal weighting with the classroom, as the vice-principal of Kottayam Malankara Seminary, Kerala put it:

> The most outstanding feature of the Orthodox Seminary is the fact that students spend at least three hours a day in chapel. Rising at 4.45 a.m., they have a fixed time in chapel for silent meditation each morning, as well as the Offices of the canonical hours.

Two distinctive themes emerge from the Byzantine Orthodox and Oriental Orthodox tradition. The first can be called liturgical formation, and concerns the relationship of theology and worship. The principle of *lex orandi lex est credendi*, 'the rule of prayer is the rule of belief' (belief is revealed in worship), underpins the Orthodox view of worship as a 'learning event'. The Divine Liturgy, the Eucharist, both shapes its participants and educates them in an eschatological vision of the Kingdom. The works of Alexander Schmemann (1966a, 1966b, 1974) have brought this perspective to the West. More recently, Petros Vassiliadis (2000: 15) has written of the Orthodox perspective:

> Ever since the beginning of medieval scholasticism, and even after the Enlightenment, theology was defined as a discipline which used the methods of Aristotelian logic. Rational knowledge was, and in some case is still, considered the only legitimate form of knowledge. Theological education, thus, gradually shifted away from its eucharistic/liturgical framework, i.e. away from its ecclesial, community, local context. The

---

6   The ancient bishop's house in Paramulla is called 'the Old Seminary'. This model is sometimes called *gurukola*: formation at the family or house (*kola*) of the *guru* or teacher, where students would stay for a few years.

rational understanding of God and humanity had in fact led to a *knowledge*-centred and, especially in the West, to a *mission*-oriented theological education.

He argues that in contrast to Western traditions which might be called pragmatic and practical, the Orthodox tradition has struggled to preserve a liturgical and eschatological dimension to theological education, once widespread in the Church in the first millennium. In Orthodox practice, theology takes place within the framework and parameters of the Eucharistic liturgy, at once grounding students in the experience of *koinonia* and lifting them up to a cosmic vision of the New Creation. Thus worship is in no sense an 'add-on' or even a preliminary to study but rather the very matrix in which theological study and the experience of God takes place. The idea of the Eucharist as constitutive of the Church as an eschatological community has been powerfully restated by Zizioulas (1988); see also McPartlan (1993) and Wainwright (2002).

The second distinctive Orthodox theme can be called 'mystical formation': this term is not used by Orthodox writers but seeks to encapsulate the Orthodox conviction that silence and contemplation are not only the true source of theology but also play a profoundly transformative role in theological education. A classic statement of the place of contemplative prayer in theology is offered by Vladimir Lossky:

> We must live the dogma expressing a revealed truth, which appears to us as an unfathomable mystery, in such a fashion that instead of assimilating the mystery to our mode of understanding, we should, on the contrary, look for a profound change, an inner transformation of spirit, enabling us to experience it mystically. Far from being mutually opposed, theology and mysticism support and complete each other. One is impossible without the other.
>
> (Lossky, 1957: 8)

For Lossky, mysticism is defined as 'acquired experience of the mysteries of the faith' (p. 236). It involves the practice of contemplative prayer, meditation on the Scriptures or dogmas, and will always include that 'apophaticism which constitutes the fundamental characteristic of the whole theological tradition of the Eastern Church' (p. 26).

Of particular relevance to this study is the way Orthodoxy views prayer as transformative. This is developed in terms of divinization/*theosis* or transfiguration: 'To see the divine light . . . as the disciples saw it on Mount Tabor, we must participate in and be transformed by it, according to our capacity. Mystical experience implies this change in our nature, its transformation by grace' (Lossky, 1957: 224). It entails 'forgetfulness of self, the full flowering of personal consciousness in grace' (p. 231), but Lossky acknowledges that it is very difficult to describe this experience or find a proper vocabulary for it.

More recent writers have argued strongly for the healing of the divide between spirituality and theology. Metropolitan Emilianos Timiados writes:

> Spirituality is needed to restore the sense of mystery and awe often lacking in theological education . . . Irrespective of improved programmes and academic systems, the central focus of theological education remains the reality of our awareness of God . . . To keep up the vitality of future theologians it is indispensable to back them up spiritually, pastorally, nurturing them with daily spiritual discourses by a competent guide of profound sanctity.

He goes on to ask: 'How far have students (during their studies) succeeded in making a real contact with Christ, experiencing the loving presence of Christ in addition to the *gnosis* they have?' (Timiados, 1985: 20).

Timiados is fully representative of the Orthodox approach in his appeal to the Fathers as somehow 'normative' for current practice: 'For the Fathers in general, theology is wholly a grace of God. God . . . is not a discernible object to be investigated, rather his life is a spiritual presence to be encountered. Theology then, is exclusively defined as a spiritual initiation.' (Timiados, 1985: 21).[7]

Thus, it can be said that the Orthodox tradition resonates with many of the concerns expressed in different terminology in the theological education debate. It understands itself as preserving the approach to priestly training of the patristic period, and clearly echoes elements both the *paideia* and *ascesis*/monastic types considered above. As Orthodox educator Jessica Rose puts it:

> From an Orthodox Christian perspective, it is impossible to think of human beings in any other way than as an integration of body, mind and spirit . . . It follows that education is not primarily a matter of absorbing

---

[7] He makes reference to Simeon the New Theologian, Gregory Nazianzus, Cyril of Alexandria. See also Arseniev (1979); Matthew the Poor (2003).

information and skills, important though they may be, but of restoring an awareness of ourselves as physical *and* spiritual beings.

(Rose, 2005: 70)

Conclusion to chapters 3 and 4

From the survey undertaken above in chapters 3 and 4, there emerges evidence that a shift is taking place, from the traditional language of training and education towards greater utilization of the terminology of formation. This is not just a change in semantics, but represents the embracing of a new dynamic model of learning that resonates with ancient concepts and yet challenges some inherited patterns of training. It represents a reframing of theological education, a different perspective – as Banks (1999) put it, a 'reenvisioning'. Since the 1980s the new paradigm has been emerging, even in diverse traditions, and can be said to represent a movement towards a convergence of thinking in more holistic terms about the task of theological education. What emerges as significant is the way the formation paradigm can function in relation to varying ecclesiologies and theologies of ministry and in diverse settings and contexts. It is also clear that, while most traditions explicitly acknowledge a role for prayer within formation, none speak with accuracy or precision about what range of roles it might fulfil within the process.

Questions for reflection

✦ What do these traditions say to your present educational practice or to your experience as a learner?

✦ What insights do you think each tradition offers to understanding the process of ministerial formation?

✦ How does each tradition question us?

✦ How would we want to question each tradition?

5

Emerging themes, contemporary issues, research questions

Introduction

In this chapter, we see how each of the six historic models and four ecclesial traditions considered thus far raises its own concerns in respect to contemporary theological education. The models and traditions thus stand in a dialogical relation to current practice and give rise to issues which help shape the specific questions which will be used in this empirical investigation with practitioners, the newly ordained clergy and their tutors (noted below, with the tutors' questions in brackets). The issues raised resonate with both the Theological Education Debate in the 1980s and 1990s, initiated by Farley (1983) and facilitated in the US by the Association of Theological Schools (texts in Astley, Francis and Crowder, 1996), and with more recent US deliberations such as the Lexington Seminar (Warford, 2004). These have been taken forward in the UK by the debate around the *Hind Report*. The issues coalesce around five major themes which lie at the heart of ministerial formation.

Formation develops through transformative practices of prayer

The historic models and ecclesial traditions considered above reveal the importance of a variety of spiritual disciplines, but little research has been undertaken thus far into their effectiveness in relation to ministerial formation. Individual disciplines include the use of silence, the study of Scripture, and the use of a spiritual director. Communal disciplines include the Daily Office, the common

Eucharist, as well as other community disciplines like shared meals and the common life. We saw how the Roman Catholic tradition adopts a prescriptive approach to spiritual disciplines within the seminary, specifying what is required in *Ratio Fundamentalis Institutionis Sacerdotalis* (1970) and in *Spiritual Formation in Seminaries* (1980). Both the Catholic and Orthodox traditions speak in terms of liturgical formation to express the formative power of worship on candidates. The present research seeks to identify patterns of prayer that are considered helpful in the formation process. In particular, the *ascesis* tradition raises this issue: *What spiritual disciplines, both individual and communal, most support and enable ministerial formation?*

From Augustine's *monasterium clericorum* to latter-day seminaries and colleges, formation can be said to take place within the interplay or interaction between the individual and the community. The Augustinian and *seminarium* models invite us to reconsider the role of the community today in relation to ministerial training, especially the desirability of residence in the semi-monastic community of the seminary or theological college. The *Hind Report* questions the need for extended periods of residence (Archbishops' Council, 2003: 39). Others have written of the relevance of a communitarian spirituality:

> To arrive at a life lived for others and an integrated life with others, a life of communion and mutual love, one needs a Christian asceticism. This is the highest form of personalization because it means living a life in the image of the Trinity. If we want to have a total formation of the person it is not enough to have academics, traditional ascetics . . . What is necessary and essential is a true communitarian life . . .
>
> (Cola, 1991: 38)

However, the *ascesis* tradition also raises the issue of *anachoresis* – the part that withdrawal or detachment from the world should play in formation. What place should *anachoresis* hold in today's training: is there an appropriate degree of solitude, silence and retreat that is in fact essential for the making of priests?

A rereading of Basil and other pioneers of the monastic life requires us to ask what spiritual disciplines (Foster, 1980, and Whitney, 1991) are most needed today in the training of priests and Christian leaders? Stephen Sykes asks:

> which aspects of the inherited tradition must be continued today and in what form and why . . . there are some vital continuities which are in search of realisable form in the contemporary world. Paramount among these is continuity of commitment. The monastic ideal strove to

be a concrete realisation of Jesus' invitation to single-minded discipleship
... monasteries preserved the tradition of complete dedication in public
institutional form.

(1994: 14)

He concludes: 'What separates us from the medieval period is an
appetite for spiritual athleticism.' Research is needed to identify
which forms of *ascesis* are most fruitful and necessary today.

Research questions arising from issues about disciplines of prayer

1. What opportunities for experiencing different types of prayer did
   your college/course provide? (What types of prayer-experiences
   are encouraged or taught in your college/course?)
2. Which types of praying were most helpful to you and why?
   (What opportunities are provided for experiencing and understanding different types of prayer?)
3. Please describe the forms of praying which are helping you in
   ministry now and say how they are helping you.

Formation unites theology, experience and prayer

This theme emerges in four of the traditions examined, which each
raise different but related issues. In the last twenty years, theological
reflection on *praxis* has become a key feature of training for the
ordained ministry: indeed, the goal is often stated in terms of producing 'reflective practitioners'. Different models have been
developed, building on the pastoral cycle which originated in the
midst of struggles in Latin America (see, for example, Bevans,
2002). Prayer within this process has been described as 'an incarnate
contemplative prayer as the way to perceive and detect the Reign [of
God] in the obscurity of history' (Casaldaliga and Vigil, 1994: 177).
One of the greatest challenges facing theological educators today is
in communicating models of theological reflection that can be used
effectively by clergy and lay leaders in parish settings: Pattison,
Thompson and Green (2003) uncover resistance to the task of theological reflection in parish ministry. Van der Ven (1998b) has argued
convincingly that such are the processes of change affecting society
and Church that it is imperative to develop a model of ministerial
training that is centred on reflection in and on ministry. He states
that 'the pastor's spirituality is considered to play a constitutive part

in the [training] program' but he fails to show how prayer fits into the process of theological reflection and this calls out to be thoroughly researched (1988b: 232). Green (1990: 140) gives some clues:

> the thorny issues and tangled problems, which crystallize during the spiral of theology, can and should become the raw material of our prayer life ... each phase of the cycle of theology ... will require prayer, spiritual sensitivity and courage. So, as the group first confronts the theme in the experience phase and when it then teases out the theme in the exploration phase, all that will be a form of prayer, so that it will be difficult to discern just where prayer begins and where theology ends, since they will be incorporated into the very fibres of a seamless robe of *praxis*.

All this suggests many questions for research. What does it mean to be 'contemplatives in action' (the phrase is credited to Nadal in Gutiérrez, 1988: 6)? If reflection in and on *praxis* lies near the heart of training for ministry, what is the role of prayer in this? Can meditation become a form of perception, enabling one to see the world differently? How can meditation clarify issues in theological reflection? The present research attends to these relationships and explores how prayer might provide a space and a means for theological reflection where new perspectives, perceptions and insights can be gained. A *praxis* issue to be considered by the empirical research crystallizes as: *If theological reflection on action is a dimension of ministerial formation, involving making sense of the struggles of ministry, what is the role of prayer in this?*

A key concern is the very nature of theological enquiry. The place given by Christ to silence and reflection in the training of the disciples has been noted. Within both the patristic tradition and later Orthodoxy the term *theoria* emerged as significant in terms of a contemplative understanding which brings together both contemplation and *gnosis* – theology as knowledge of God (though we have also noted the apophatic tradition of divine unknowability). One recent Orthodox writer has put it:

> *Praxis* and *theoria*, the active and the contemplative life ... should not be envisaged as alternatives, nor yet as two stages that are chronologically successive – the one ceasing when the other begins – but rather as two interpenetrating levels of spiritual experience, present simultaneously in the life of prayer.
>
> (Ware, 2000: 103)

Clement's ancient concept of *theoria*, including both knowledge of God and love for God, may yet help us in our contemporary search for understanding the role of prayer in theological education. An *Orthodox* issue emerges: *In what ways can participation in worship and prayer enable a kind of knowing that unites* theoria *and* gnosis?

The *paideia* model raises the query: what, precisely, is the *gnosis* which ministers in training should be seeking? Kelsey (1992: 72) puts it thus: 'Theological schooling as *paideia* is ruled by a religious interest to know God by *gnosis*, an immediate intellectual intuition ... compatible with ... contemplative understanding; discursive understanding; affective understanding.' Banks (1999: 19), pointing to the need for prayer in the cognitive process, also expresses this in experiential terms: 'It is faith's internal process of becoming reflective, and as such is based on our human capacity for intuitive knowledge of divine things.'

The concept of *paideia* also invites us to take another look at the role of the teacher in theological education. The teacher is to be bearer of the tradition, not only instructing the student, but also helping to create the conditions in which makes possible the learner's immediate intellectual intuition of God; as Kelsey (1992: 73) puts it, the teacher becomes midwife, helping one come to *gnosis*. Battle (2002: 167) develops the theme: 'A new image came to mind: teacher as mediator of transformation. Such transformation in the classroom is a movement from pretence to authenticity ... I formulate the vocation of theological teaching through the transformative movement of prayer.'

Battle aims for the practice of 'continuous prayer' in the classroom, in the sense of an alert attentiveness to the Holy Spirit. He argues for a prayerfulness to permeate even an academic setting, in order that a process of communal discernment can take place. The present research therefore attends to the perceptions of the theological teacher, as well as to the insights of the student.

The recurring concern about the character of the knowledge to be sought is central to any evaluation of the scholastic model. The *scientia* tradition, we noted, with its study of theology as a separate discipline and its divorcing of scholarship and *ascesis*, raises the issue of the relationship of prayer and theology in an acute form: to what extent is theology a *habitus* – a fundamental capacity to know God himself? Since Farley initiated the Theological Education Debate with his seminal *Theologia* (1983), renewed attention has been given to the concept of *habitus*. Charles Wood (1985: 79) puts it thus:

The theological *habitus* sought is not a 'habit' in the popular modern sense . . . It combines a sense of 'capacity' with a sense of 'disposition' . . . Perhaps 'aptitude', with its combination of 'ability' and 'inclination', comes closer now to conveying the sense of what *habitus* than does 'habit'.

The *Hind* task group is even more explicit: 'This approach is grounded in an understanding of theology as *habitus* which lays the stress not upon the acquisition of knowledge and skills, but upon the development of people of faith within communities that shape Christian living' (Archbishops' Council, 2006: 60).

The *scientia* model, then, throws up major questions that lead us to the heart of the matter. If theology is more than seeking to articulate knowledge about God, if it involves relationship with God, a fundamental orientation or capacity to know God, what part can prayer play? Is it to be regarded as pietistic devotion that complements serious theological study, or does it, indeed, have a more pivotal role, the very source and origin of theology? The *scientia* model raises this major issue for the research: *What is the role of prayer in relation to the task of theology?*

In the US, the Lexington Seminar, bringing together the insights of more than thirty-five diverse seminaries since 1999, has touched in this issue briefly. Sumney (2004: 139) writes:

the first step is to demonstrate to our students that intellectual work is in fact a spiritual work and that it is central to being a pastor. [Some] students who expected something very different . . . saw academic and intellectual endeavours as distinct from, if not opposed to, spiritual growth.

In the UK, the *Hind Report* brings these issues to a head. It was widely perceived to overstate the need for candidates to be academically accredited and qualified. Its proposal that all clergy reach the level of bachelor's degree before being appointed to a post of first responsibility was decisively rejected by the General Synod in July 2003 on the grounds that it elevates academic qualifications above other more personal requirements for ordained ministry. Noting that an increasing number of university centres already play a role in theological education, the report seeks to strengthen the role of university theological departments in initial ministerial education through the establishment of regional training partnerships.

More controversially, the *Hind Report* attempted to apply a system of credit rating not only to academic subjects but also more personal standards of achievement. These 'benchmarks' (Archbishops' Council, 2003: 58ff) were presented as 'a statement of expectations for ministerial education' encompassing 'knowing' (content of the Christian tradition), 'doing' (skills for ministry) and 'being' (spirituality and sense of vocational identity). These originated in the higher-education level descriptors used in university theology and religious studies departments, and sought by this means to indicate an equal weighting between theological study and prayer. They were widely criticized and dropped from further documentation, but help raise the issue of how proper recognition can be given to the place of prayer in the overall schema of training.

Thus the proposals before the Church of England in the *Hind Report* contain many tensions and unanswered questions about the relationship of theology and spirituality. The *Hind Report* quotes approvingly some words from the 1968 *Bunsen Report* about the desirability of 'the deepening of a man's prayer and commitment and self-knowledge, in a way that is integrated with his growing knowledge of theology' (Archbishops' Council, 2003: 37). As we noted, the report identifies the importance in learning of an interplay between theology and prayer:

> the making of connections at a deep level between a person's evolving understanding of faith, the life of prayer and Christian practice, through a range of stimuli including the faithful reading and study of Scripture, the Christian theological tradition and the experience of Christian life and witness.
>
> (Archbishops' Council, 2003: 39)

The first follow-up document to the *Hind Report* (Archbishops' Council, 2006: 74) talks about the integration of five different kinds of learning: personal, affective learning and development of self-understanding; development of generic skills like critical thinking, collaborative working; disciplinary learning such as biblical studies, doctrine, ethics; performance practice including preaching and pastoral skills; contextual learning/theological reflection on practice.

However, while calling for an integration of these five types of learning, there is still no clarity about how spirituality impinges on other areas, or what, precisely, its role might be in learning. Thus from the *Anglican* tradition this issue emerges: *If ministerial formation entails the 'making of connections at a deep level between a person's evolving understanding of faith, the life of prayer and Christian practice' (Hind*

Report, p. 39), *how does prayer function in this process of interaction and perception?*

Research questions arising from issues about prayer and theological reflection/doing theology/making connections/ contexts

1. What do you think about during prayer?
2. What feelings do you associate with the different types of prayer you described above?
3. What relationship, if any, do you see between prayer and theological reflection? (What role do you see for prayer within the process of theological reflection/doing theology? How is this role of prayer taught and practised?)

Formation involves development of ministerial identity and growth in virtue

A third theme emerging from the historic and ecclesial traditions is ministerial formation as a process of personal transformation, entailing both the development of ministerial self-understanding and the growth of ministerial qualities.

This theme emerged especially from two traditions, ancient and modern. First, in the *paideia* model we noted that Clement of Alexandria wrote of the role of the teacher in terms of 'training in virtue'. Other patristic writers echo this concern for the ethical nature of theological education: for example, Basil of Caesarea speaks of the need to nurture *diathesis*. John Chrysostom allows for the place of personal struggle within this quest for priestly virtue, while Gregory of Nyssa emphasizes the dynamic character of *paideia* in his concept of *epektasis*. In his study of the ordained ministry in the fourth century, Greer reminds us:

> It is, of course, not enough to speak of character or virtue. We must explain what we mean by these words; the fathers of the church probably had a far clearer view of what they meant than we do . . . the active life of virtue depends upon the contemplative life and the religious vision of God.
>
> (1992: 51–2)

At the heart of *paideia* is the issue of the shaping or moulding of character and its relation to prayer. In recent times many of the concerns of *paideia* have been explored (Neuhaus, 1992, and Kelsey,

1988) in terms of 'moral formation' or 'character formation'. The use of the term 'character-formation' can be problematic, because 'character' has a range of philosophical and psychological connotations. Its psychological sense denotes 'structuredness of personality', emphasizing not so much a process of change as what abides as consistent and reliable in personality. In philosophy, 'character' has been used from Aristotle to St Thomas as a 'settled set of dispositions to act in certain ways' (Kelsey, 1988: 62–75). In Catholic teaching, a priestly character is understood in terms of an indelible ontological imprint upon the soul of the priest imparted in holy orders. A recent restatement of this is in Congregation for the Clergy (1994). Anglican canons also state 'no person who has been admitted to the order of bishop, priest or deacon can ever be divested of the character of his order' (Canon C.1,2).

Preferable to such 'character' language is the more dynamic language of growth in ministerial qualities (ABM: 1998; Archbishops' Council, 2003). This echoes the pastoral epistles in identifying personal attributes and inter-personal skills necessary for ministerial office (qualities of a bishop and deacon in I Timothy 3 and Titus 1). There has been renewed attention to the issue of character through the revival in 'virtue ethics' among theologians and moral philosophers (Trull and Carter, 1993; Gula, 1996; Hauerwas, 1981). The Methodist writer Willimon offers a definition of character as the 'basic moral orientation that gives unity, definition and direction to our lives by forming our habits into meaningful and predictable patterns that have been determined by our dominant convictions' (quoted in Bridger, 2003).

In *Shaping the Future: New Patterns of Training for Lay and Ordained* there is a movement, too, towards recognizing character-formation as crucial: 'At all stages of the formational process the report of 2003 envisages that character (being, spirituality, vocation) is being transformed in Christ . . . for the sake of deep knowledge [*metanoia*/practical wisdom]' (Archbishops' Council, 2006).

However, some object to the shaping of character being defined as the aim of ministerial education. As Hall (1988: 53–79) argued at the seminar sponsored by the Associated Theological Schools on 'theological education as character formation', such a focus may reflect the narcissism and self-indulgence of our age and is 'on the verge of subverting the very faith-tradition that it has been designed to comprehend'. He finds that it does not sit easily with the Gospel's call to self-forgetfulness, though he himself resorts to the language of building 'qualities of spirit' in ministry candidates, mentioning specifically the need to develop personal integrity, depth of understanding and courage to risk new ideas. Hall's argument leads him to the point where he acknowledges the necessity of prayer in the educational process: 'Of course the wisdom that is required of the theological community cannot be gained solely by means of disciplined intellectual activity . . . It is also a matter of prayer' (Hall, 1988: 67).

Hall laments the dualism that splits mind from spirit, which arises when reasoning takes place in the classroom and prayer is confined to the chapel: 'Under this arrangement, theological education only mirrors the bifurcation of mind and spirit that is close to being the core of the malaise of our society' (Hall, 1988: 67). He concludes by calling for theological education that ensures that 'the core academic activities of our institutions are grounded in some depth of spiritual engagement'. The *paideia* tradition encourages us to consider, then, the complex interplay between the role of prayer and the formation of character. It raises the issue: *If the development of 'priestly character' and virtue is a dimension of ministerial formation, what is the role of prayer in this?*

The major ecclesial traditions consider this matter in relation to developing appropriate models of ministry for the contemporary world. The Methodist Church, we noted, sees formation in terms of developing 'basic identity'. The use of the phrase 'ministerial identity' is not without its difficulties, for 'identity' carries a variety of anthropological, philosophical and psychological meanings. This is both shaped in the interplay between person and role, and crystallized in a model of ministry, which expresses and sums up the distinctive features of the presbyterate. This brings to the research a *Free Church* issue: *If ministerial formation involves the acquisition of a strong sense of ministerial identity (uniting person and role, within an evolving model of ministry), how does prayer contribute to this process?*

The Anglican tradition has traditionally favoured a Christological model of ministry. Some have argued recently (Greenwood, 1999) for ministry to be worked out within a Trinitarian model, which has space for the themes of mutuality, collaboration and interdependence in ministry. The Roman Catholic Church develops its thinking about formation in terms of a strongly Christological model of ministry. It speaks of a priest's increasing *identification* with Christ, an ever closer resemblance to him, becoming a real and faithful image of Christ, shepherd and priest. Thus it sees ministerial formation in terms of configuration to Christ – not in the general way required of all Christians, but specifically to Christ as head and shepherd (John Paul II, 1992: III). Karl Rahner (1968) emphasizes that the whole of the human person is brought into relation with this new sense of identity: 'You are only what you should be as a priest, if you bring your whole life into your vocation . . . Your life-work is to establish an ever closer intimacy between yourself and your office.' These models raise the key formational concern of developing self-understanding in the minister or priest.

What seems to be missing in the traditions is a theological anthropology. None of the major historic or ecclesial traditions examined develops formation with an explicit model of the human person. Thus even the Catholic Church's basic document on formation can say, without further explanation: 'Spiritual formation should take in the whole man. Grace does not take away nature, but raises it to a higher level' (Congregation for Catholic Education, 1985: para. 51). The *paideia* tradition is a student-centred model of theological education and takes the personal development of the student seriously, though the danger of individualism or elitism remains, despite *paideia* being considered historically a corporate activity. Important queries are thrown up. What understanding of personhood is in view in ministerial formation? What anthropology is in sight? What assumptions about human nature are being made? Can ideas drawn from Platonic anthropology have any currency today?[1]

The recovery of Trinitarian theology in the churches has enriched contemporary approaches to Christian anthropology, which springs from the idea of the *imago Dei* in the creation account: 'Let us make humankind in our image, according to our likeness' (Gen. 1: 26). Recent writers emphasize that the *imago Dei* denotes primarily the human capacity for relationship, mirroring the interrelatedness, mutuality and communion of the Trinity itself: (see Boff, 1988; Schwoebel and Gunton, 1991; Zizioulas, 1985). Older commentators interpreted this in term of humanity's domination of the earth (Wolff, 1974). The account in Genesis depicts Adam, made in 'the image of God', walking with the Lord God in the garden in the cool

---

[1] Compare Tracy's (1988) attempt to rehabilitate the platonic notion of 'soul' in terms of 'a subject-in-process' tending towards 'differentiation in consciousness' and 'participation in the divine'.

of the day. The formation paradigm is grounded in the conviction that the human person has a fundamental and essential capacity for communion with God and that this must be a key determinant of theological education. As Habgood reminds us, this relational sense of identity is expressed most poignantly in the sacrament of baptism. He puts it succinctly: 'our personal formation depends on our relationship with other persons. We make each other. We discover ourselves over against the other' (1998: 227, 221). Such perspectives bring a necessary critique to those traditions of ministerial formation which emphasize the individualistic dimension. Recent philosophical explorations of personhood also stress its essential relational aspects. McFadyen (1990: 70) maintains: 'The sense of oneself as a subject, a person, is not individually but socially acquired. The way others have related to, regarded and intended one as a subject is individually appropriated as a distinct personal identity.' Cautious of isolated individualistic interpretations of the person, McFadyen emphasizes the role of others within each social context as most formative of personal identity (compare Ward, 1990).We noted that some colleges and courses, for example, talk only in terms of personal formation. Attention to the communal context of formation is vital in the present research.

Philosophical approaches also raise the issue of the extent of human responsibility and freedom in the formation process. To what extent can a candidate freely choose to advance his or her formation – or create barriers to it? To what extent is formation a divine – human synergy? Such concerns are present in the New Testament. Paul, in calling his readers to cultivate 'the same mind that was in Christ Jesus' – developed in terms of a kenotic form or *morphe* – urges: 'Work out your own salvation with fear and trembling; for it is God who is at work in you' (Phil. 2: 12).

This issue is especially pertinent to the question of the role of prayer in personal transformation within the interplay between the individual and the institution, the public and the private. The present research seeks to explore how the experience of prayer can help the minister cope with the tensions and stresses of the passage into authorized ministry. It may uncover a healing role for prayer in handling stress and coming to terms with the struggles and demands of ministry as the newly ordained copes with moving across the threshold into a new public role which carries many expectations – a transitional experience of liminality.

Research questions arising from issues about prayer and identity/character/change

1. How do you feel you have changed as a person as you have grown into the roles of ordained ministry? (What changes do you expect to see in candidates during their training period at the course/college?)
2. How does your practice of prayer contribute to this process of change? (How do you expect the practice of prayer to contribute to this process of change?)

Formation is orientated towards mission in the world

Cautions have been noted about the use of formation language: in particular, Free Church concerns that it might encourage an elitist view of ordained ministry or unhealthy introspection. This raises the whole issue of the *telos* of ministerial formation, sometimes stated as forming clergy (see, for example, 'The idea of the Catholic priesthood as the proper end of priestly education', in Congregation of Catholic Education, 1985). But ministerial formation as a concept must function in relation to ecclesiology and missiology. If former patterns of training focused on serving the institution of the Church, contemporary ministerial formation functions in relation to new models of the Church in mission. In the historical survey, it was noted that Schleiermacher, needing to justify the place of theology in modern university, found himself advocating the need for knowledge and skills relevant to the practice of ministry (in parallel fashion to the need for doctors to acquire medical knowledge and for lawyers to understand the law). Ministerial formation thus must have an outward-looking focus and resonate with current challenges to mission within today's culture.

Overemphasis on the need to acquire skills has attracted criticism, and sometimes is evaluated negatively. When the *Hind Report* in its first draft advocated benchmarks and developed a framework for clergy standards in terms of academic credits (Archbishop's Council, 2002: 42–4) Dr Andrew Moore (2002) pointed out:

> When we look at the report's 'Draft Benchmarking Statement for Deployable Clergy' (5.11), it is clear that it has drunk deeply from Schleiermacher's well. The tone and content suggest that ordinands will not so much be inducted into a tradition of sacred learning as into a set of skills and methods, dominated by the ideals of uncommitted intellectual neutrality and professional competence.

However, in the final edition of the *Hind Report* (Archbishop's Council, 2003) these benchmarks were rewritten in terms of 'expectations' in which 'knowing' and 'doing' are supplemented by 'being': complementing professional standards with renewed attention to the person, vocation and prayer-life of the minister. These were subsequently changed again in the implementation document to 'learning outcome statements' offered as parameters for the new curriculum and based on the selection criteria used in the discernment of candidates: vocation/ministry, mission/evangelism, faith, quality of mind, relationships, leadership and collaboration, spirituality, personality and character (Archbishops' Council, 2006: 67ff).

There has been some tension in recent Anglican documents as they have struggled to find the best nomenclature for this: reference is made to 'personal qualities', to 'expectations', to 'criteria', and to the difference between what is measurable and what is immeasurable (Archbishops' Council, 2003: 55). The language of 'competencies' plays its role, and has been increasingly utilized in secular employment (ABM, 1998). One might compare the use of competencies in National Vocational Qualifications where competence is defined as 'the ability to carry out your work role or job, by doing the tasks within it and having the skills, knowledge and understanding of these tasks, so that they can be performed to the standards required by the industry you work in' (quoted in Board of Education, 1996: 13).

Some educators, noting the trend of the *Hind Report* towards a standardization of professional behaviour measured in competencies, advocate the complementary approach of nurturing 'capacities'. Recalling Augustine's teaching that 'the soul is in the image of God, in that it is capable of God', Riem (2003: 78) observes: 'With capacity language, developing ministry can be seen as a dialogical process, where growth happens as heart and mind are widened, and deepened and slowly changed by engagement with the Other.'

The publication in 2003 of *Guidelines for the Professional Conduct of the Clergy* decisively put before the Church a professional model of ministry and training, claiming: 'The criticism that a code of practice amounts to a concession to managerialism must be seen to be misplaced' (Bridger, 2003). The professional model raises in an acute manner a central issue for this research: the tension between a functional view of ministry, which stresses necessary tasks and skills, and a more ontological view of ministry which attends to the being of the minister, personal development and identity, where ordained ministry is understood as a sacramental sign uniting the person and prayer.

Indeed, a professional model raises fundamental issues about the role of prayer in ministerial training. As Hall (1988: 63) comments:

> Over the course of three or four years, the candidate has acquired the knowledge and skills which fit him or her for 'professional ministry', as this has been enshrined in the conventions of this or that ecclesial community; but the very possession of this 'know-how' may have deprived the candidate of many of those qualities of character that, from the perspective of biblically-informed faith and theology, at first commended him/her: the sense of personal unworthiness, inadequacy to the task, humility *vis a vis* the tradition . . . anticipation of discovery, awe before the unknown . . .

Positively, this model raises the possibility of asking whether the practice of prayer itself can be seen as involving a set of skills essential for the work and witness of the Church today. From the *Wissenschaft* tradition emerges this issue: *In what sense can skills in prayer be seen to be a 'professional' requirement for ministers, especially in relation to the Church's contemporary mission?*

Recent studies, exploring the 'spirituality' of those outside the Church, have highlighted the necessity for clergy and evangelists to have skills in leading seekers and enquirers into an experience of Christian prayer. While recommendations have been made that clergy and leaders are trained to develop experimental 'fresh expressions of church' (Archbishops' Council, 2004), research has shown that many people are seeking a spiritual experience which, from an evangelistic point of view, can be directed and guided towards God: 'We need more "contemporary mystics" . . . who are dedicated to unpacking the hidden treasures of Christian spirituality and teaching Christian leaders how to facilitate styles of worship that engage with contemporary spiritual hunger' (Croft and Frost, 2005: 118). Thus, the present research seeks to uncover what prayer-skills are needed today for contemporary evangelism.

Research questions arising from issues about prayer and mission

As you think of the mission of the Church in today's world, what particular skills in prayer do you think are necessary for the ordained?

(As you think of the mission of the Church today, what particular skills in prayer do you think are necessary for the ordained?)

Formation entails a dynamic process of integration

We noted that ministerial formation encompasses and integrates the dimensions of human, spiritual, intellectual and pastoral formation. This fifth theme coalesces around the complex word 'integration'. It emerges in several traditions and crystallizes in the issue raised by the Roman Catholic tradition: *If formation entails an integration between its different dimensions (human, spiritual, intellectual, pastoral formation), what is the role of prayer in promoting this integration?*

What is at issue here is the interrelatedness of aspects of formation: moving from 'coordination' to complex interpenetration, cross-fertilization and coherence. This leads to the heart of formation as a holistic process uniting aspects which have historically been kept separated or compartmentalized. The theme of integration emerges wherever there are perceived to be 'fault lines', 'gaps' or failures in 'joined-up thinking'. For example, Archbishops' Council (2001) identifies a range of 'gaps' including the lay/clergy divide in access to theological education and the gap between ministerial review and training . There is a danger of equivocation in the use of the word 'integration' as if it is a panacea to cure all ills. Nevertheless, the theme of fragmentation is also a recurring one, surfacing not only in Farley's study (1983) *Theologia: the Fragmentation and Unity of Theological Education* but also in several recent studies of pastoral ministry (Society of Martha and Mary, 2002, and Warren, 2002). Thus it becomes a key formational issue to be addressed through the empirical questions. The search for integration concerns restoring unity, identifying continuities and healing dichotomies. It concerns:

- the separation of discrete theological disciplines within the curriculum;
- the gap between theory and practice;
- the separation of the seminary or theological college from the world;
- the discontinuity between the ordinand's prior experience in the world and ministerial training;
- the break between pre-ordination training and the post-ordination phase (reunited and reconfigured in the *Hind Report* as one process of initial training);

• the failure to relate the doing of theology and the practice of prayer.

Within the historical sources, perhaps Benedict comes closest to expressing how a wholeness can emerge from the interrelatedness of different aspects of community life, with his *Rule* bringing together in one organic unity the commitment to solitude and the commitment to community; time for work, prayer and study; balancing activity and stillness, action and contemplation; attending to the needs of body, mind and spirit; the dynamic vow of *conversatio morum* in dialectic relation with that of *stabilitas* (see de Waal, 1997). Benedict commends a close attentiveness to such integration (Klimoski, 2004).

Related issues emerge from the *seminarium* model, which we saw derives from the idea of the nursery or seedbed – the metaphor of the planting of seeds that come to fruition through an intense process of cultivation. A nursery or greenhouse aims to foster growth in a controlled way, monitoring its own climate: thus this model entails the danger of colleges becoming remote 'hothouses' or fostering a rarefied, detached environment for learning. The key question here concerns the proper context for nurture: what distinctive roles does the intentional community of the training institution play in the formation of the candidate, and what other settings are essential for the making of the minister, including the setting of mission? The *seminarium* is a static place, a segregated, settled community with clearly defined boundaries; indeed, it is often a cloistered, monastic type of community. But recent thinking is towards a more dynamic pattern of interactions which involves 'movement between communities and settings': 'Formation takes place in a range of settings, and not just in the intentional communities of training institutions. It takes place in Christian life in the world; in the parish or church setting; in college, course or scheme, both in their gathered and dispersed modes' (Archbishops' Council 2003: 39). Research into the role of prayer in training needs to be sensitive to this acute question of context for growth and learning and be ready to entertain a diversity of modes of learning.

Thus the issues of spirituality in the seminary centre around integration: what forms of prayer are helpful in the process of training and to what extent is prayer integrated into learning or kept separate, in a different compartment, from learning? What is the

relationship between the college chapel and the classroom? Is fostering a 'devotional life', as some traditions put it, enough? Does this
become an escapist piety or an empowering spirituality? The *seminarium* tradition raises this issue for research: *What emerge as the most
significant contexts for ministerial formation?*

More recently, within the different traditions, the integration of
elements has been explored through varied metaphors: the undiv-
ided 'seamless robe' of Methodist tradition, or the interweaving of
different strands into one fabric of ministry or tapestry of theological
education as described in the Anglican text *Integration and
Assessment*. It spells out what cohesion is sought:

> Integration is understood to take place in the student's own awareness or
> self-understanding. The student becomes aware of a fitting together of
> the disparate elements in the training process, including previous experi-
> ence. This will include bringing together the subject matter and arriving
> at a method for achieving coherence. The student's construction of a total
> picture will also include personal development, spiritual growth and the
> formation of themselves in readiness for ordained ministry. Such a type
> [of integration] looks for the integration of knowing, being and doing so
> as to result in a complete integration.
>
> (ABM, 1992: 51, 52)

There is a hint that 'spiritual growth' may play a part, but no developed idea of what part prayer might play in the process.

The theme of integration, it has been noted, is revisited in the
Hind Report. It notes:

> The three domains ['knowledge and understanding'; 'spiritual and minis-
> terial formation'; 'ministerial skills'] are described separately *only* to
> ensure that the importance of each domain is clearly recognized. In terms
> of the development of an individual or the design of a syllabus their inte-
> gration is of primary importance.
>
> (Archbishops' Council, 2003: 56)

It recognizes that the formation paradigm opens up a way to unite
these elements: 'formation should be seen as the overarching concept that integrates the person, understanding and competence'
(Archbishops' Council, 2003: 29). The formation model thus has
the potential to bring to ministerial training a wider perspective,
attentive to the whole person, not standing alone but in relation to
his or her particular context.

The four categories of formation within the Roman Catholic tradition prompt the consideration of new issues. To what extent does

human formation (sexuality, relationships) impact on ways of praying (spiritual formation)? How do ways of praying contribute to the minister's journey towards wholeness? What part can the emotions play in this? To what extent can intellectual formation be creatively reunited with the practice of prayer? How can pastoral formation be shaped by the practice of prayer? If the healing of fragmentedness and the search for integrity become a goal within ministerial formation, how does prayer contribute to this?

Research questions arising from issues about prayer and formation

1. What use of the language of ministerial formation did you encounter in your course/college? (How is the language of ministerial formation used in your course/college?)
2. How helpful do *you* find the language of 'formation' in describing the changes taking place in you in the training period? (How helpful do you personally find the language of formation?)
3. How do *you* understand the term 'formation' in relation to ministerial training? (What is your understanding of 'formation' in relation to ministerial training?)
4. How would you describe the role of prayer in your ministerial formation? (How would you describe the role of prayer in formation?)
5. What changes or improvements, if any, would you recommend for developing the practice of prayer in theological colleges or courses? (What changes or improvements, if any, would you recommend for developing the practice of prayer in theological colleges or courses?)
6. Finally, looking back over your experience of formation and the role of prayer in it, how would you describe your understanding of the role of the Holy Spirit in this? (How do you understand the role of the Holy Spirit in formation?)

Questions for reflection

✦ Consider your own response to the research questions above, whether as a teacher or student.

✦ What is your own understanding of formation, at this point?

✦ What is your initial reaction to the five themes we will be researching: transformation through prayer; reuniting prayer and theology; nurturing identity and virtue; resourcing mission; bringing coherence to theological education and ministry?

Part II

**The Role of Prayer in Formation:
Findings and Reflections**

6
Theological and empirical approaches to prayer

Introduction

In this chapter we examine the foundations on which the empirical research of this book will be built. The chapter is in three parts. First, we examine theological approaches to prayer. Secondly, we explore empirical and psychological approaches. Thirdly, we look at the design issues and methodology which shapes the present research. But first we must grapple with the slippery concept of spirituality itself.

Spirituality: the problem of definition

'It appears that spirituality is one of those subjects whose meaning everyone claims to know until they have to define it' (Sheldrake, 1991a: 32). As Professor Sheldrake cautions, spirituality has become an elusive word to define. In recent years, the word has been utilized in ever wider contexts, far beyond the confines of Church or even religion: indeed, the rise in the use of spirituality to denote some kind of personal experience of awareness seems proportionate to the decline of the institutional Church (Archbishops' Council, 2004: 9). A national study of college students' search for meaning and purpose typifies current usage of the term: 'Spirituality . . . captures those aspects of our experience that are not easy to define or talk about, such as inspiration, creativity, the mysterious, the sacred, and the mystical. Within this very broad perspective, we believe spirituality is a universal impulse and reality.'[1] Does spirituality allude only to

---

[1] 'Spirituality in Higher Education: A National Study of College Students' Search for Meaning and Purpose', on *www.spirituality.ucla.edu/about/spirituality.html*.

some ephemeral, elusive dimension of human existence or is it possible to redeem its use for scholarly research? What can we learn from the history of the term?

The word *spirituality* translates the Latin *spiritualitas*, corresponding to Paul's use of *pneumatikos*. In his theology, Paul expresses the believer's new life in Christ as 'life in the Spirit' *kata pneuma*, 'according to the Spirit', contrasted with life outside Christ which is *kata sarx*, 'according to the flesh', where 'flesh' denotes not body or physicality but 'life not ruled by God' (Ziesler, 1990: 79). For Paul, 'all who are led by the Spirit of God are children of God' (Rom. 8: 14). The earliest recorded use of *spiritualitas*, in a text once attributed to Jerome, conveys this same sense: 'So act as to advance in spirituality.' It was only in the twelfth century that *spiritualitas* began to be used in contrast to *corporalitas* (bodily) or *materialis* (matter). In France in the seventeenth century the word *spirituality* began to be used more widely of the spiritual life, referring to practices of prayer or devotion; ultimately it entered the English language in this sense of 'means towards Christian perfection' in the early twentieth century through the translation of Pierre Pourrat's *La spiritualité chrétienne* (Downey, 1993).

In recent years scholars have pointed to the transformational or transformative character of spirituality in a sense that is directly relevant to this study. Schneiders writes that 'spirituality as an academic discipline studies the transformative Christian experience as such', while McGinn goes further and calls mysticism 'a process of personal transformation'(Waaijman, 2002: 455–6). Waaijman considers spirituality as a process of transformation taking place within the divine–human relationship (Waaijman, 2002: 426).

A definition of spirituality that entails divine/human encounter is offered by the former Anglican officer for Evangelism: 'By *spirituality* is meant our understanding and experience of how encounter with God takes place and how such an encounter is sustained' (Warren, 1995: 19). But such a definition does not go far enough, for it stops short of suggesting that such encounter changes people, makes a measurable difference to their lives. The late Methodist scholar Gordon Wakefield stresses this: 'Spirituality concerns the way in which prayer influences conduct, our behaviour and manner of life, our attitudes to other people (Wakefield, 1983: v). Two major areas of empirical exploration are opened up by such definition: first, the experience of prayer itself (disciplines, practices and ways of praying); and, secondly, its impact and outward effect on Christian thinking and living.

Theological approaches to prayer

The *Revised Catechism* defines prayer as 'the lifting up of heart and mind to God' (General Synod, 2003). The Roman Catholic Catechism (Catholic Church, 1994) also uses this phrase in its definition, attributing it to the seventh-century John Damascene. It identifies five types of prayer: adoration, confession, thanksgiving, intercession/petition, listening to God/seeking to know his will. The Psalms traditionally encapsulate and express all the major types of prayer in the Judeo-Christian tradition. They include both community prayer and individual prayer: lament, complaint, questioning of God, praise and expression of trust and confidence, wisdom poems reflecting on moral or religious dilemmas (Broyles, 1989). The present research seeks in particular to be alert to four dimensions of prayer.

The role of the Holy Spirit in formational prayer

Exploration of theological dimensions of formation leads to the search for a theology of prayer, to consider the question: what is God doing in prayer? The Pauline writings link the themes of the Spirit, prayer and the search for wisdom:

> I pray that . . . the Father of glory may give you a spirit[2] of wisdom and revelation as you come to know him (*epi-gnosis*), so that, with the eyes of your heart enlightened, you may know . . . what is the immeasurable greatness of his power for us who believe.
>
> (Eph. 1: 17–19, cf. Col. 1: 9–12)

Here God is celebrated as the source and fountainhead of *sophia* and *apokalupsis* (revelation). As Lincoln says: 'revelation continues to be given by God through the Spirit to all believers to enable them to understand the disclosure of God's secret . . .' (Lincoln, 1990: 57). Of the use of *epi-gnosis*, Coggan comments: 'This is knowledge with a difference . . . intellectual knowledge by itself is not enough . . . More than the intellect is called for. Knowledge must be brought

---

[2] As Muddiman notes: 'As not infrequently in the Pauline letters, it is difficult to decide whether to spell spirit with an initial capital, referring to God's Spirit, or with lower case as a quality or capacity of human beings' (2001: 85).

into the sphere of spiritual experience' (1970: 130). The Ephesian writer later prays explicitly for the Holy Spirit: 'I pray that, according to the riches of his glory, he may grant that you may be strengthened in your inner being with power through his Spirit' (Eph. 3: 16).

In Paul's thought, it is the Holy Spirit who enables both wisdom and prayer in an unfathomable process in the depths of the human person: 'The Spirit helps us in our weakness; for we do not know how to pray as we ought, but that very Spirit intercedes with sighs too deep for words' (Rom. 8: 26). Swete observes: 'The Spirit is seen here in the most intimate relations with the human consciousness, distinct from it, yet associated with its imperfectly formed longings after righteousness . . . The mystery of prayer stands here revealed, as far as it can be in this life' (quoted in Ramsey, 1977: 73).

Ziesler (1989: 223) puts it thus: 'The Spirit vivifies everything for Christians, even their prayers: "spiritual" life too needs to be guided and enriched by the Spirit of God.' Paul describes a divine–human synergy in prayer: 'When we cry "Abba! Father!" it is that very Spirit bearing witness with our spirit that we are children of God' (Rom. 8: 15, 16). This mysterious interpenetration can be expressed in terms of the mingling of the human waters of prayer with the divine flow or current of wisdom, holiness and power.

For Simeon the New Theologian (949–1022), the greatest exponent of a theology of the Holy Spirit in the eastern tradition, the Spirit is the very key that opens the doors of understanding: 'It is the Holy Spirit who first opens our spirit . . . If the Holy Spirit is called the key, then it is above all through and in him that our spirit is enlightened . . . and illuminated by the light of knowledge' (Catechesis XXXIII, quoted in Congar, 1983: 97). Simeon has harsh words for those who do not explicitly seek the experience of the Spirit in learning:

> We think we will receive the full knowledge of God's truth by means of worldly wisdom, and fancy that this mere reading of the God-inspired writings of the saints is to comprehend Orthodoxy . . . How ridiculous! . . . Who . . . could ever know the hidden mysteries of God . . . without the revelation which comes through the Lord from on high? These are mysteries which are unveiled through an intelligible contemplation enacted by the operation of the Holy Spirit . . .
>
> (Symeon, 1996: 113–14)

In relation to the way we learn, it seems appropriate to speak of a different way of processing data, an appropriation of truth at a deep level. Certainly, there can be no detached study; as von Balthasar puts it:

> Intimacy with the Holy Spirit thus cancels out the spectator's uninvolved objectivity, with its external, critical attitude to truth, and replaces it with an attitude that one can only describe as prayer. This prayer is total; it encompasses our beholding and our readiness to be beheld, our receiving and our self-giving . . .
>
> (1986: 79)

While a theology of the Spirit is largely absent from contemporary church documents that deal with theological training, ordination rites do contain explicit references. The Anglican *Common Worship Ordinal* states: 'You cannot bear the weight of this ministry in your own strength but only by the grace and power of God . . . Pray earnestly for the gift of the Holy Spirit.' Ordination itself is essentially an *epiclesis:* 'Send down the Holy Spirit upon your servant . . . for the office and work of a priest in your Church.' The *Veni Creator* asks for the seven-fold gifts of the Spirit to grow within the lives of the ordained: the gifts of wisdom, understanding/insight, counsel and power, knowledge and the fear of the Lord.

Prayer as discernment

John's gospel gives hints and clues about discernment when it describes Christ's prayerful communion with the Father in terms of glimpsing his will: 'The Son can do nothing on his own but only what he sees the Father doing . . . The Father loves the Son and shows him all that he himself is doing' (Jn 5: 19, 20). Such a model of prayer in terms of communion and obedience is highly significant for the practice of Christian ministry.

The Ignatian tradition provides insights regarding the discovery of discernment in prayer which develops this alertness (Sheldrake, 1991b). Hassel (1984), writing out of the Ignatian tradition, identifies four levels of awareness in prayer which are useful to bear in mind in the course of empirical research:

1. First level, the sensuous-superficial. This includes surface impressions gained through the five senses and swings of mood; he assigns vocal prayer and outward disciplines to this level.
2. Second level, the physical-vital: the power of pains or pleasures, fatigue or energy, which he links to active, reflective meditative types of prayer.

3. Third level, the psychological-psychic: 'the deep sorrows and the pure joys of this level totally permeate a person's being and consciousness' (Hassel, 1984: 8). Here Hassel locates more profound prayer-experiences of fear, doubt, security or fulfilment and a kind of prayer that might unite the feelings with the imagination.
4. Fourth level, where the 'prayer of simplicity' or 'simple being' sustains the pray-er throughout the upheavals of life, providing a continuity and stability beneath extremes of joy or sorrow, testifying to a sense of God's faithfulness. This, says Hassel, is the level at which one can discern the significance of what Ignatius called consolations and desolations.

While these levels may be an oversimplification, they challenge the researcher to penetrate beneath the surface in order to uncover the profounder aspects of prayer and their effects in the pray-er.

Prayer as thinking and perception

There is a small literature on the theme of prayer as a perception and as a way of knowing. Moltmann (2001: 200) contrasts two approaches in epistemology. In modern scientific methods, he maintains, we know in order to achieve mastery, to gain possession of our subject, whereas

> Meditation is in fact an ancient method of arriving at knowledge which has not been pushed aside by our modern activism . . . meditation is preeminently a way of sensory perception, of receiving, of absorbing and participating . . . The act of perception transforms the perceiver . . . Perception confers communion. We know in order to participate, not in order to dominate.

Macquarrie (1972: 30) understands prayer as thinking: 'Prayer is a fundamental style of thinking, passionate and compassionate, responsible and thankful, that is deeply rooted in our humanity . . . To pray is to think in such a way that we dwell with reality, and faith's name for reality is God.' For Macquarrie, prayer helps to heal the human experience of fragmentedness and individualistic isolation, enabling the pray-er to see the world as a whole: 'prayer enables us to see things in perspective . . . Prayer changes our vision of the world . . . Prayer interprets the world' (1972: 34). For Gibbard (1970: 15) 'prayer is an exploration of reality and a reflective engagement in life . . . seeking truth is a kind of prayer'. Hiller (2000) following the German theologian Gerhard Ebeling in seeking to reconnect theology with human experience, proposes a theological theory of cognition in which prayer facilitates a discernment process enabling both knowledge of God and self-knowledge.

Prayer as receptivity

The research seeks to be alert to the movement in Christian prayer from active discursive thinking, associated with meditation and reflection, towards contemplative prayer that aims to be open and receptive to divinely given insights and the experience of communion with God. This corresponds to the movement in the prayer-journey delineated, for example, by such classic writers as Teresa of Avila (Kavanaugh and Rodriguez, 1979; for a modern application see Humphreys, 1992). In her *Interior Castle* she distinguishes various possible stages in the prayer-journey, and notes the transition from prayer characterized by routines and devotional practices (the 'Third Mansion') to what she calls the Prayer of Recollection and the Prayer of Quiet ('Fourth Mansion'), which is prayer beyond words, concepts and analytical thinking, testifying to the apophatic tradition of prayer.

Writing of 'infused contemplation', John of the Cross describes those who experience such mystical prayer:

> They liberate themselves from the impediment and fatigue of ideas and thoughts, and care not about thinking and meditating. They must be content simply with a loving and peaceful attentiveness to God ... contemplation is nothing else than a secret and peaceful and loving inflow of God, which, if not hampered, fires the soul in the spirit of love.
>
> (Kavanaugh and Rodriguez, 1991: 382; for an Anglican restatement see, for example, Northcott, 1962: 165–82)

The research aims to be sensitive to these mystical dimensions of prayer once characterized as 'the art of union with Reality' (Underhill, 1991: 2). See also the useful article 'Mysticism and the mystical: the current debate' (Howells, 2001).

Empirical/psychological approaches to prayer

William James in his 1902 *Varieties of Religious Experience* invited research in this area. He wrote:

> [Prayer is] every kind of inward communion or conversation with the power recognised as divine ... Prayer ... is the very soul and essence of religion ... the very movement itself of the soul, putting itself in a

personal relation of contact with the mysterious power of which it feels the presence.

(James, 1971: 444)

James's work promoted a view of prayer as a purely private mystical experience unrelated to behaviour or life, a view maintained in a rare but significant study of prayer in the 1930s by Heiler (1937).

Major reviews of prayer research confirm a dearth of empirical studies in this area (Brown, 1994). Finney and Maloney (1985: 104) concluded: 'Nowhere is the longstanding breach between psychology and religion more evident than in the lack of research on prayer. Few studies exist in spite of the fact that prayer is of central religious importance.' Prayer hardly features even in such a major work as Beit-Hallahmi and Argyle's *Religious Behaviour, Belief and Experience* (1997).

In their 2001 survey Francis and Evans identify four areas in which there has been limited research: first, the practice of prayer, including prayer as a coping strategy, petitionary prayer; secondly, the development of patterns of prayer during childhood and adolescence; thirdly, study of the so-called objective results of prayer, looking for changes as a perceived result of prayer (for example, longevity, improvements in health); fourthly, subjective and therapeutic effects of prayer on those praying, such as identifying a correlation between the practice of prayer and quality of life or the reduction of stress. They recommended: 'Future studies need to distinguish between different understandings of prayer and to map the place of different understandings of prayer within individual lives' (Francis and Evans 2001). The present research attempts to uncover what forms of praying are significant in the lives of the interviewees. From recent studies and monographs it is possible to identify six aspects which are of relevance to the present research.

Types of prayer

Poloma and Pendleton (1991) identified four kinds of prayer: colloquial prayer or 'conversations with God'; meditative prayer; petitionary prayer; and ritual or set prayers. In 1992 David, Ladd and Spilka, in their paper 'The multidimensionality of prayer' (reported in Brown 1994: 161), developed a set of scales to measure confession, petition, thanksgiving, ritualistic prayer, meditation as self-knowledge and knowledge of God, good feelings, self-improvement as a result of prayer, intercession and habits of regular prayer. Such studies alert the researcher to the variety of prayer types likely to be encountered, but need to be complemented by the theological perspectives below (compare Thouless, 1971: 90ff).

Structures of prayer

In their study of prayer among young people, Janssen, de Hart and den Draak (1989) identified seven structural elements in the practice of prayer: need (motivation to pray); action (dialogue/address); direction (God); time of day; place; method (including bodily posture, use of words or silence); reported effect (help, trust, blessing, understanding, reflection). Such 'structures of prayer' are kept in mind in the present research as it seeks not only to identify prayerforms in use but also to name the reported changes that take place in the course of praying.

Cognitive and affective aspects of prayer

Ladd and Spilka (2002), following a typology suggested by Foster (1992), identified eight factors prevalent in prayer: self-examination and tears/sadness ('Inward, self-connection'); sacramental and silence ('Upward, human/divine connection'); petition, intercession, suffering, radical/'bold prayer' ('Outward, human/human connection'). However, two significant omissions can be noted. They allowed no place for prayer as theological reflection, and no role for inner struggle or wrestling with God which has been a well-attested part of the Christian tradition (Mayes, 2002). Significantly, they conclude that future studies of prayer should be more sensitive to prayer as both thinking and feeling, and attend to the emotional or affective dimensions of prayer as well as to the cognitive. This observation shapes questions in the present research, which include open enquiry into feelings and thoughts: 'What do you think about during prayer? What feelings do you associate with your experience of prayer?'

Prayer and perception

Rowan Williams describes contemplative prayer as involving 'the project of reconditioning perception' (1991: 156). Watts and Williams in their study *The Psychology of Religious Knowing* are cautious about assigning a directly cognitive role to prayer. They take issue with Phillips's *Concept of Prayer* which emphasizes, from a philosophical point of view, the effects of prayer on the one who prays (for example, increased self-knowledge):

Indeed it is doubtful whether the 'acquisition of knowledge' is at all an appropriate way to describe the cognitive changes that take place in prayer. Prayer is probably better described as the *reinterpretation* of what is in some sense already known than as an exercise in the acquisition of knowledge.

(Watts and Williams, 1988: 115)

For Watts and Williams (1988: 113) prayer is 'an exercise in the interpretation of experience' and they find attribution theory helpful in understanding this process, in which religious people attribute events to God. As Brown puts it: 'To decipher inner thoughts is therefore part of the practice of prayer and more recently of psychotherapy' (1994: 63). This resonates with prayer as discernment, a theme that will emerge in the empirical data.

A. and B. Ulanov, in *Primary Speech: A Psychology of Prayer*, describe prayer as 'primary speech' in the sense that in prayer a person can talk freely with unguarded honesty of his or her deepest desires, fear, fantasies, misconceptions and confusions: 'This is what depth-psychologists call "primary-process thinking," that level of our psyche's functioning that leads straight to the workings of our souls' (1982: 2). For them prayer is the naked exposure of the soul to God, which entails an experience of transformation they describe in terms of transfiguration:

This means we are living now in rearranged form. We are the same persons and yet radically different . . . The theme that dominates our lives now is the effort to correspond with grace. We want to go with the little signs and fragments of new being given us in prayer.

(1982: 122)

Thus prayer entails the risk of change, in which, little by little, perceptions are revised, self-acceptance grows and contradictions, if not resolved, become better understood (compare the arguments of experiences of God as perception in Alson, 1991). This approach alerts the researcher to the possibility of all kinds of perceptual changes in the prayer experience.

Hermeneutical issues

Van Knippenberg (2000) draws attention to four hermeneutic levels that play a role in the description of prayer or configuration of a personal narrative on prayer:

1. unarticulated experiences and events, which have not yet been explicitly formulated in terms of time and space;

2. a 'story in itself' about personal experiences like an internal private diary that makes sense only to the participant;
3. a 'recalibrating' or 'reconfiguring' of the story in interaction with the narratives of others;
4. an ability to assess one's experience against the background of the tradition or collective narrative.

This is a helpful reminder that the prayer experience passes, as it were, through different levels of consciousness and interpretation before it can be described to an interviewer. Watts and Williams, recognizing the difficulty of individuals' articulating 'raw insights' gained in prayer, note that a process similar to that in psychotherapy is needed: a movement towards 'symbolization' (articulate conceptualization): 'characteristically it is those experiences that are most difficult to symbolize that provide the most powerfully therapeutic insights' (1988: 72).They note that the apophatic way, the *Via Negativa*, in Christian mysticism also points to the limits of human language in describing divine realities.

C. F. Davis (1989: 147) reminds us that all experience is interpreted within 'a continual interplay between concepts, beliefs, events, reflection, the creative imagination, and other cognitive and perceptual factors'. Every subject makes sense of their experience, for themselves and in communicating their experience to others, through 'perceptual sets' influenced by language, culture and context. Nevertheless, she is emphatic: 'The fact that an experience has been 'interpreted' in terms of a specific conceptual framework or mental model (religious or otherwise) cannot in itself make that experience evidentially suspect' (1989: 148). The researcher needs to be alert to the thought-world of the interviewee, and appreciate that the interviewee's interpretations actually add understanding to their experience.

Personality and prayer
Studies have centred on applying Jungian theory to prayer, as in Duncan (1993) and Morton T. Kelsey (1977). In *Spirituality and the Four Jungian Personality Functions*, Bunker (1991) identifies four different ways of praying based on Jung's functions of intuition, sensation, thinking and feeling; (see also Michael and Norrisey, 1991). In *The River Within: the Search for God in Depth*, Bryant (1978) applies Jungian insights to spiritual growth and maturity,

concluding that the practice of prayer brings greater coherence and direction to life.

More recently, attention has been given to the impact of sexuality and sexual orientation upon ways of praying (Thatcher, 1993; Stuart, 1997; compare Sheldrake, 1994 and Nouwen, 1986).While investigation of these dimensions lies beyond the scope of the present study, the researcher should cultivate a respect towards aspects which reveal the mystery and complexity of the human subject. The present research seeks to be alert to the complex interrelation between personality and prayer.

Design issues and methodology

There are six features of the present research among a sample of newly ordained clergy about the role of prayer in their training and ministry and within their experience of formation.

Tradition of enquiry

This empirical research is located broadly within Weber's *Verstehen* ('understanding') approach. Weber commended this approach to social scientists as a basis for understanding human behaviour, identifying two key elements in the process: *erklärendes Verstehen* seeking to uncover an individual's motivation for action (the 'why?' question) and *aktuelles Verstehen* seeking to identify the meaning people associate with their actions (the 'what?' question). He stressed the need to become familiar with people's 'commonsense constructs' – the terms they use to make sense of behaviour within their own thought-worlds (Bryman, 2004: 13).

This approach has been criticized as being over-optimistic in terms of what relationships are possible or desirable between a researcher and his or her subject and the desire to 'see through their eyes'. Shields (1996) observes: 'The "empathetic aspect" of *Verstehen* silences the other by masking difference.' However, within the context of the Christian community, it is to be hoped that a relationship of mutual understanding is indeed possible within the necessary balance of the researcher's objective detachment and involved attentiveness towards his or her subject. *Verstehen*'s key aim resonates strongly with that of the present research: to hear the voices of the subjects and to seek to appreciate the meanings they attach to prayer/formation experiences within the contexts both of the college/course and the parish.

Adopting a *Verstehen* approach leads to the choice of qualitative research methods. Quantitative methods such as the use of a questionnaire would not be able to uncover the subtle or hidden dynamics of formation in any depth – these need to be probed in the context of a semi-structured interview which respects the otherness of the person while attempting to appreciate the person's motives and actions. This research seeks to approach the other in terms of 'stepping onto holy ground' where the personal, inner experiences of prayer can be sensitively explored.

Inductive exploration

This part of the research has the character of inductive exploration. Van der Ven (1998a: 115) summarizes induction as 'the observation, directed by reflection, of phenomena in the empirical reality. This involves the discovery and naming of classes of phenomena, the discovery of patterns in the phenomena, and the uncovering of comparative, correlative and causal relationships between the phenomena.' In van der Ven's terms (1998a: 125) the present research is explorative-descriptive. It seeks to be descriptive in the sense of conveying an accurate picture of prayer/formation; it seeks to be explorative in the sense of discovering significant factors at play in the process of prayer/formation.

Here there is no theory to be tested: rather a reality to be investigated. The data collection method utilized is that of the semi-structured interview, one hour long, with a set of open-ended questions, framed around the five themes identified in chapter 5. This instrument gives scope for exploring issues while maintaining the discipline of a common consistent approach which enables comparison of responses across the five themes. This instrument is also designed to solicit a wide range of comments on formation by providing space and freedom within the interview for the asking of supplementary questions as the interviewee opens up the subject (Berg, 1989: ch. 2).

In his significant textbook on spirituality research, Waaijman (2002) identifies four major lines of enquiry to be pursued:

1. descriptive research: delineating different forms or expressions of prayer;

2. hermeneutic research: interpreting 'spiritual texts';
3. systematic research: distinguishing different themes in spirituality;
4. mystagogic research: attending to self-descriptions, accounts of spiritual experience and spiritual biography.

This study focuses on Waaijman's first and fourth approaches, seeking to identify ways in which various experiences of prayer bear fruit in different ways, including aiding theological reflection, interiorization and assimilation of theological ideas and perception and insight; the development of character and the healing or reconciliation of woundedness in the minister.

Ethical issues

A letter of approach explained clearly the purpose of the research and procedures to be used, invited participation and consent, and assured anonymity of person and institution. A consent form was signed by participants agreeing to the interview being tape-recorded, transcribed and stored securely for the purpose of research, and the use of quotations from the interview in the text of the book on the understanding that confidentiality will be safeguarded and any proper names changed.

Validation procedures

Validation was sought: interviewees were given a copy of their transcribed interview within twenty-four hours of its taking place (it was transcribed in the evening of the same day from the tape-recording, when impressions and field notes taken were fresh in the researcher's mind). Interviewees were invited to confirm veracity or to add additional comments to clarify points. In addition, a triangulation method was used where possible: interviews with students and tutors of the same institution were compared to identify resonances. All interviews were checked against the published views of their training institution as it is available in the course/college prospectus (triangulation, as described in Bryman, 2001: 131).

Data analysis procedures

Content analysis was developed using a manual approach, which was chosen as being most appropriate to this scale of data, rather than using a computer tool. There were four phases.

First, after the interviews had been transcribed, every data bit or phrase was given a numerical code and a category list was developed, with categories grouped within the five main themes.[3] Secondly, the occurrences were tabulated on an Excel spreadsheet, so that the frequency of phrases could be scored and relationships between phrases used could be identified. Thirdly, colour coding was added to the transcriptions for major themes emerging, using the search facility on Word. Fourthly, the main themes from each transcript were copied and pasted onto a kind of matrix (the text transferred using different fonts to differentiate different speakers) to enable close comparison of varying answers to the questions and to make possible the identification of shades of meaning within clusters or themes (Riley, 1990; Dey, 1993). It was necessary to maintain an alertness to the dangers inherent in interpretation of data, especially a temptation among researchers to impose ideas onto the data (Bryman, 2001; Cartledge, 2003): the content analysis aimed, above all, to let the results speak for themselves, as we shall see in the following chapters.

Sample interviewed

The target population was the post-ordination clergy group (Continuing Ministerial Education years 1–4) of a southern diocese: those leaving college or course and ordained in the period 2002–5. A purposeful sampling was employed to reveal a range of different perspectives on the issues.[4] The sample was chosen to include, within a cross-section of the target population, these main variables: tradition/churchmanship; gender; age; college/course; full-time/part-time; stipendiary or non-stipendiary ministry (NSMs). Eleven interviews were conducted, with seven clergy and four staff members from a range of training institutions. Of the seven newly ordained clergy, four were female and three male; four were NSMs (two being available for almost full-time ministry, two in full-time employment) and three stipendiary. In addition to staff from a Catholic and an evangelical college, and a regional course, the sample included a staff member involved in the training of permanent deacons, to see if there were any different perspectives on formation from the diaconal

---

[3] The advantages and limitations of coding are discussed in Bryman, 2004: 189.

[4] What is needed, Glaser and Strauss point out, is not so much a representative sample, as a number of interviews sufficient to 'saturate' the categories being developed, cited in Bryman, 2004: 117.

ministry. Generalizations cannot be posited from a sample of this size; however, the comments of the sample, especially in reference to how colleges and courses can be improved, carry their own weight. The sample reflects the growing diversity (of age, prior occupation, spiritual histories, backgrounds) among candidates for the ordained ministry (Gilliat-Ray, 2001).

clergy (ordained 2002–5)
(a) female, single, 20s, Catholic, Catholic college, stipendiary
(b) male, married, 50s, central, course, NSM
(c) female, single, 40s, Catholic, course, stipendiary permanent deacon
(d) female, married, 40s, 'central' (she defined her tradition as 'evangelical-Catholic'), course, NSM
(e) male, married, 20s, evangelical, evangelical college, stipendiary
(f) male, single, 60s, Catholic, course, NSM
(g) female, married, 40s, evangelical, evangelical college, stipendiary

staff members/tutors
(h) female, 40s, course
(j) male, 40s, Catholic college
(k) female, 50s, evangelical college
(m) male, 40s, course

These letters denoting the different interviewees will be used throughout the following chapters, as we report the discoveries of the empirical research.

Questions for reflection

✦ How would you define spirituality?

✦ How would you express the relationship between prayer and cognition?

✦ Do you accept that prayer might be a form of perception?

7

Life-giving waters: towards a pneumatology of formation

There is a river whose streams make glad the city of God (Ps. 46: 4)

Introduction to chapters 7 to 10

The aim of chapters 7 to 10 is to report the findings of the empirical research and offer some theological reflections: to pursue a conversation between the theological tradition (represented in the historical models and ecclesial traditions of training and formation and theological, biblical and spirituality resources, east and west) and the empirical data. These chapters seek to identify elements that can contribute towards building a theology of formation, exploring the questions: what is happening theologically in formation and what is the role of prayer in this? What can we affirm about the role of the Holy Spirit in formation, and what kind of transformations can be identified in the process?

Findings

We begin by identifying core spiritual experiences and disciplines, following the first theme of ministerial formation: *formation develops through transformative practices of prayer.* The interviews revealed a variety of prayer-practices, both within the colleges and courses and within present parish ministry, which fall into five categories, and their transformative potential will be recognized as our chapters unfold.

The Office and communal prayer

All except two evangelical interviewees testified to the significance of the Daily Office, in both the pre- and post-ordination phases. The discipline of structured days shaped by the liturgical framework of the Offices inculcated the importance of regular rhythms of prayer which were valued in the early years of ordained ministry.

However, assumptions were made in some colleges about the value of the Offices. One interviewee put it:

> I think it was a missed opportunity really. They were very good in terms of structuring prayer into the 'timetable' each day – the chapel demands were very strict in terms of Morning Prayer, Evening Prayer, Eucharist, Compline . . . All these were set in stone and attendance was expected – even a compulsory time for silent meditation was provided. And yet, with all this prayer going on, it was never really discussed what anyone might do with it or, rather, the different ways one might approach or engage with it. I always thought this was a huge shame. People ended up with the routines, but how they engaged with them was left up to them, perhaps to work out with their spiritual director. (a)

One interview saw the use of a fixed form of Morning Prayer in the college as betraying a lack of creativity and sensitivity to individual differences:

> One thing it would be good to have is more variety on a practical basis . . . rather than Morning Prayer in a set form . . . We need to recognize just as there are different ways of praying within a congregation, so in College people respond in different ways and need a variety of different sorts of prayer, on a morning by morning basis . . . We're not all fed by Morning Prayer! (g)

Colleges and courses inculcated disciplines which are not always easily transferable to parish life, where there are different sorts of stresses and pressures on time. Some felt the Office in parochial ministry burdensome, creating its own pressures:

> At the time, I didn't think the Offices were the most helpful, because, to learn a discipline is really tough. It's alright when you're at College, in that structured environment, where it routinely happens, but when you're at home, or in the parish setting it's helpful when you can make it happen, it's not helpful when you have to juggle it, with all the tensions . . . (d)

Other forms of communal prayer were experienced, especially in the college setting: the evangelical tradition valued fellowship groups, where informal prayer could be offered for one another, and 'prayer-triplets' where prayer-ministry in a charismatic sense can be offered to one another (g).The Catholic colleges wished to emphasize the totality of the community experience in both prayer and in sharing a common life: the interpersonal aspects of formation.

Eucharist

The Eucharist was appreciated by those both in the central and Catholic traditions, both in college and parish settings. The Catholic colleges stress Eucharistic formation, a staff member saying: 'I believe the regular participation in the Eucharist is formative, especially given its importance in ordained ministry, and not least because of the way in which what the Church does at the Eucharist models its life' (j). Within the parish, the Eucharist provides for some a place of profound affirmation of priestly identity.

> There is a deep sense of being God's tool, of being his channel, particularly when celebrating the Eucharist . . . In the context of the Eucharist, there is a movement which in a physical sense begins the moment I begin to robe; the physical appearance and the way I carry myself – in an attitude of prayer and praise, embodying the body of Christ – representing Christ to the people and the people to Christ. I feel more and more as if I am living from the centre of the Eucharist – from the centre of the broken Body as a source of blessing and healing rooted in the life-giving power of God. (d)

Meditation/reflective prayer

A wide variety of prayer-practices share the common characteristic of providing a space for silent reflection. The traditional distinction between meditation and contemplation blends into one. The meditative use of Scripture was a common practice in college, course and parish: described in phrases like: 'chewing the Word', 'savouring the Word'; *lectio* or 'reflective reading of texts', 'meditation on Bible texts'. There was evidence that meditative techniques from different sources are widespread, including Ignatian meditation (taught at several colleges and courses represented in the sample), the Jesus Prayer and Celtic spirituality. But there was little scope for experimentation in the pre-ordination training with some more creative forms of prayer, which came to be valued in ministry: contemplative prayer-walks in creation, sculpture and the use of clay, music and art:

> I like to be creative in prayer, but only once in my two years at college did I get a chance to explore prayer in painting. We could have explored

dance in prayer, for example. Huge opportunities aren't taken up. You realize, afterwards, that many people are gifted in this. It comes down to giving more resources to us so we can feed the sheep – that's what we're called to do. (g)

This issue of inattention to personality differences will recur below.

The research revealed a wide appreciation of the place of silent reflective prayer in parish life: its many fruits are considered below. Yet few of the interviewees mentioned being taught silent reflective prayer at college or on a course: indeed, this seems to be a serious omission. Interviewees mainly referred to silence in respect to reflective thinking (see below). There were notably very few references to the prayer of adoration.

Solitude

Closely associated with the issue of silence in prayer was the discipline of solitude. Few colleges provided opportunities like retreats and quiet days – those that were provided were much appreciated. In ministry clergy valued space to be alone, recognizing both its benefits and dangers: 'The Daily Office I tend to say at home on my own. On my own I can create more space within it, for listening' (b); 'You have to take on board responsibility for your own formation in many ways . . . no one has ever asked me if I say Evening Prayer on my own . . .' (a).

A recurring theme in the interviews was that solitude is neither escapism nor isolationist, but rather can enable a profound way of communion and solidarity with the world:

> I feel connected, both across to others now, but also down through the centuries . . . in that sense of praying with the saints, and with the whole of heaven, including the angels. And I love praying in the church and knowing that one's participating in and contributing to the prayers of the centuries . . . being part of that continuity. In stillness I feel connected. There's definitely a connection with the world around, the physical world - I go for prayer walks in the woods - even to the earth, a feeling of that ground beneath your feet. Making connections with the world, the human world, like thinking of the troubles, for example, overseas. (d)

Continuous prayer

This leads to a wider consideration of the contexts and timing of prayer. Many interviews spoke of continuous prayer through the day of ministry, of praying at all times, especially before and after demanding pastoral situations. One NSM priest (b) testified: 'To pray continuously – certainly in working life – when you're facing someone who really is in difficulty . . . is really praying for the insight about how to deal with that situation.' Another, (c), put it: 'Prayer isn't just "hands together, eyes closed" or going through a shopping list of petitions but is an offering of ourselves as we proceed thorough the day.'

For one, such recurrent prayer maintains the very focus and aim of ministry:

> Prayer is at the centre . . . prayer before leading services, during sermon preparation, before delivering sermons, prayer on the way to visiting someone. There's a huge sense that deep down, the only thing I have to offer is being God's hands, eyes, ears, and so on. If I'm not that, I'm not going to be able to help anyone. Prayer keeps this vision alive. (g)

Thus the setting for prayer is not only the place of retreat but the place of engagement. As one tutor put it: 'I wouldn't want to put prayer into a very interior box and say it's just about what you do in a quiet corner. It's about the openness we show to God in our neighbour, in worship, in reading, in everything – it's that listening ear' (m).

It is not clear how far college or course equipped ministers for such a practice of prayer. This may come from training in theological reflection, as we see below, or from instilling the rhythms of prayer into candidates, as one person notes: 'I'd want to see prayer as almost becoming what you do all the time . . . praying without ceasing. Making prayer a regular rhythm in life hopefully leads to the feeling that everything that you do becomes a prayer in a sense' (a).

Several interviewees used vivid metaphors to describe how prayer relates to the experience of ministerial formation: 'Prayer is the gateway to God's hand in shaping you, to open up the channel for this formation to take place' (b). 'Without prayer my ministerial formation couldn't happen. I think of Herbert's poem ['Prayer']: "the soul's blood", "something understood." It's that breath that gives life' (d). One tutor put it succinctly: 'Formation can't happen without prayer. It's vital, because formation isn't self-improvement, it's allowing God to work in you, and prayer opens up this possibility' (h).

In what ways, then, does this varied practice of prayer actually advance the process of ministerial formation? What kind of transformations takes place during the practice of prayer which are deemed indispensable to formation? A powerful metaphor emerged in the research which can stimulate our theological reflections:

> We need to see prayer as the thing that undergirds everything, the hidden stream from which everything comes from and goes back to, a way of being . . . Prayer is a stream running through formation, and it is that stream which gives it life. (a)
>
> prayer is like that hidden stream: how do we make courses so that there is that hidden stream running through Jerusalem, through the heart of the city? (m)

Reflections

The metaphor of the hidden river of prayer

This metaphor of prayer as a hidden river will guide our reflections. It is apposite for three reasons. First, the river of prayer is a symbol of divine creativity and re-creation. Formation itself is a metaphor drawn from the natural world, speaking of a creative process at work in the landscape both physical and spiritual, and the metaphor of the river of prayer complements this.

The use of metaphors in theology has been rehabilitated after a period in which they were considered ineffective in theology. As Avis (1999: 102) has argued: 'All the significant assertions of theology are expressed in a language that is irreducibly metaphorical.'

McFague (1982) recognizes the heuristic potential of metaphor in theology. From a different perspective Brueggemann (2001) points to the creative use of imagery in the Old Testament prophets, making possible the emergence of an alternative perception of reality. The limits of metaphor and its provisionality must be recognized alongside its potential for communicating insights (Gunton, 1988).

The use of metaphor to describe prayer respects the mystery and elusive character of prayer. From a literary perspective, Countryman (1999a: 28) notes how metaphor and lyric poetry play a part in enabling experiences associated with prayer to be explored, offering 'a point of comparison and perhaps illumination . . . an opportunity to discourse about the hidden, interior realities of spirituality'. The image of the river of prayer will be employed here as a means of enabling an imaging or visualization of invisible forces: it will sum up in pictorial language some of the issues to be explored, aiding the communication of ideas in a postmodern world that favours the image over the metanarrative (Grenz, 1996). It is hoped that such use of metaphor will have 'added value', not only illustrating but illuminating: aiding description but also encouraging insights. Stimulating the use of the river image have been Michael 2000; King and Clifford, 2000; Graebner, 2003; Tweedie, 1867.

The language of formation is, as Kelsey (1988: 64) points out, a hylomorphic term, utilized scientifically of the shaping of matter. Used in relation to theological education, it implies that at the heart of training is the raw material of a person's life, on which God and human agents act in a creative way. Most of all, the language of formation communicates the need for the candidate to undergo a series of *changes* in his or her inner life, an evolution. It implies a *process* of change.

The language of formation is potentially richer than that of training/education, precisely because it allows for a divine role in the shaping of priests: the *Hind Report* describes ministerial formation as a 'creative process initiated and sustained by God' (Archbishops' Council 2003: 39). This evokes the accounts of creation: 'the Lord God formed man of dust from the ground, and breathed into his nostrils the breath of life; and man became a living being' (Gen. 2: 7). In the Servant Songs of Isaiah, the prophetic teaching combines the language of formation with that of vocation: 'Thus says the Lord, he who created you, O Jacob, he who formed you O Israel . . . I have called you by name, you are mine' (Is. 43: 1). Formation recalls the language of Psalms 139: 13–15 about God's secret moulding of the person in the womb. Ephesians puts it: 'We are God's work of art' (2: 10, Jerusalem Bible). The formation paradigm allows the ever creative God to be the key agent of formation, from beginning to end, and recognizes that formation is not a purely human process.

The research will discover that prayer has several creative functions within the formation process. The Bible begins and closes with rivers of water, bespeaking creation and new creation: 'a stream would rise from the earth and water the whole face of the ground, then the Lord God formed man . . . a river flows out of Eden to water the garden' (Gen. 2: 6, 7, 10; cf.1: 1). In the Apocalypse 'The Lamb will guide them to the springs of the water of life' (Rev. 7: 17). The vision concludes:

> Then the angel showed me the river of the water of life, bright as crystal, flowing from the throne of God and of the Lamb through the middle of the street of the city. On either side of the river is the tree of life . . . producing its fruit each month; and the leaves of the tree are for the healing of the nations. (Rev. 22: 1, 2)

The river is at once a primordial and eschatological image of the divine life.

Secondly, the hidden river symbolizes the mystery of prayer. Like a hidden spring or underground river, prayer is often unseen, unrecognized, elusive but having powerful influences. Christ highlights the hiddenness of true prayer in the Sermon on the Mount, contrasting it with the false paraded prayer of street corners: 'Whenever you pray, go into your room and shut the door and pray to your Father who is in secret' (Matt. 6: 6). The word used for secret is *kruptos*, denoting something hidden or concealed. The author of Colossians asserts: 'Your life is hidden with Christ in God' (Col. 3: 3). Prayer as a secret river remains something that cannot be measured or quantified. It is something essentially mysterious, but rises to the surface and reveals its presence in a number of different expressions.

Thirdly, the river is an image which reflects diversity and flexibility. As rivers have different characteristics as they flow through the terrain, from incisive fast-flowing torrents to meandering ponderous currents, so prayer goes through various phases and embraces different intensities. The diversity of prayer encompasses turbulence and confusion as well as contemplative peace.

It is also to be recalled that the river is only part of the ecosystem. It has a significant part to play in the shaping of landscape but remains one factor amongst many. Prayer too fulfils important functions within the ecology of formation but is not the whole story, pointing to a diversity of human factors and resistances that come into play. As a river will course through different geologies (the great biblical river of the Jordan itself flowing along a fault line) so prayer will encounter both resistance and weakness.

A recurring theme in the empirical research was the conviction of those experiencing formation that it is essentially a process of transformation wrought by the Holy Spirit. An evangelical minister testified: 'formation is going on at the deepest level . . . the Holy Spirit is the agent through which the change is happening . . . He's the key to the whole thing' (e). A tutor put it: 'formation isn't self-improvement, it's allowing God to work in you, and prayer opens up this possibility' (h). This prompts the search for a pneumatology that will make theological sense of the process of formation and the role of prayer in it.

The image of water in the Scriptures is predominantly concerned not with cleansing but with giving life. This is often associated with the work of the Holy Spirit. To the woman at the well Jesus promises: 'the water that I will give will become in them a spring of water gushing up to eternal life'. The woman represents all of humanity in her cry: 'Sir, give me this water' (Jn 4: 14, 15). Witnessing the Temple ceremony celebrating God's renewing waters, Jesus cries out: 'Let anyone who is thirsty come to me and let the one who believes in me drink. As the scripture has said, "Out of the believer's heart shall flow rivers of living water."' John adds: 'Now he said this about the Spirit' (Jn 7: 38, 39).

The three dimensions or domains of formation suggest one way of exploring this theme theologically. The Church of England is moving ahead in its evolution of theological education on 'the understanding that Initial Ministerial Education, in both its pre- and post-ordination phases, is a rich process of formation that weaves knowing, being and doing, or understanding, character and practice' (Archbishops' Council, 2006: 67). This echoes the *Hind Report's* view that 'Formation should be seen as the over-arching concept that integrates the person, understanding and competence' (Archbishops' Council, 2003: 29). Three aspects of the work of the Holy Spirit thus emerge.

The transformation of knowing: a river of wisdom

The search for wisdom was identified in the *Hind Report* as the key guiding principle to shape theological education. Daniel Hardy's words were accepted as providing such a focus: 'Theological education needs a clear conception of its distinctive thrust . . . the *goal*, I think, is an inhabited Wisdom . . . active in responding to the issues of present day life' (Archbishops' Council, 2003: 42).

The empirical research uncovered deep yearning for such wisdom. Two tutors comment:

> Silence enables recollection and reflection . . . The real hope is that recollection will enable learning to produce an increase in wisdom. (j)

> What we're looking for is a growth in wisdom, confidence, authority . . . and that's a gift of the Holy Spirit. (m)

Clergy too linked the search for wisdom with the Spirit's role: 'I speak of the Spirit of God, Spirit of wisdom, Spirit of life . . . The Spirit of God inspiring, challenging, informing, refining' (d).

The Johannine and Pauline traditions point towards the role of the Spirit in this. John's Gospel suggests a Christian pedagogy in which the Holy Spirit is understood as *the* teacher of disciples: 'The Advocate, the Holy Spirit . . . will teach you everything' (Jn 14: 26). As Lincoln (2005: 397) puts it: 'part of his work as Advocate for the disciples in their mission to the world is to give them the requisite insight into Jesus' teaching . . . unfolding [its] significance for the new situation in which the disciples find themselves.'

John develops this further: 'When the Spirit of truth comes, he will guide you into all truth . . . He will take what is mine and declare it to you' (Jn 16: 13,14).[1] The Spirit 'both reiterates what Jesus has said (cf. 14: 26) and says more (16: 13). What more he says is all the truth and all God's truth (v.15)' (Smith, 1999: 298). As Westcott observes: 'The Spirit makes the Son known in his full majesty by gradual revelation, taking now this fragment and now that from the whole sum of truth' (1902: 231). Brodie (1997: 498) observes here 'an advancing process of revelation'. Temple (1970: 280) sums up its significance for Christian epistemology: 'The disciple is not to clamour for the solution of perplexities or for intellectual mastery of divine mysteries. What knowledge he has in this realm is his because the Spirit has declared it to him; and for the Spirit's declaration he must wait.'

In Paul's thought the Holy Spirit has a revelatory role, in relation to wisdom (1 Cor. 2: 7,9,10). For him, the Holy Spirit works at a very deep level – as Barrett (1968: 75) puts it: 'The Spirit thus enables inward apprehension of profound divine truth.' Kinn (2004: 14) observes: 'Paul's point is that the Spirit alone is capable of revealing the mystery of God, since only the Spirit has intimate knowledge of God.' Paul contrasts divine *Sophia*, manifest in Christ crucified (1 Cor. 2: 2) with worldly wisdom that cannot grasp God's upside-down ways. As Dunn reminds us (1998: 267), 'wisdom' functions primarily in relation to Paul's Christology. He is advocating a particular way of approaching the study of divine things. As Horsley (1998: 57, 58) reminds us, this is forged in the context of polemic against the 'sophisticated' elite of Corinth. Wisdom especially denotes God's plan of salvation. Paul is insistent on the task of 'interpreting spiritual things to those who are spiritual' (1 Cor. 2: 13). Christians must be *didaktois pneumatos* – 'taught by the Spirit',

---

[1] There are intriguing parallels with Qumran. As Sanders (1975: 355) observes: 'In the *Manual of Discipline* the spirit of truth illuminates the mind . . .; in the FG the Spirit of truth has a didactic function (16: 13)'.

for divine truths are 'spiritually discerned' – 'investigated spiritually' in Barrett's translation (1 Cor. 2: 14). Paul suggests in this passage the basis for a Christian pedagogy or pattern of learning that is explicitly and self-consciously alerted to the role of the Spirit. He concludes with the claim 'We have the mind of Christ' (1 Cor. 2: 16).

This has particular resonances with ideas of formation. Calling for a 'sharing in the Spirit' (Phil. 2: 1), Paul urges his readers to have the mind of Christ which he explores (through an early Christian hymn) in terms of the form or *morphe* of Christ. Christ's *kenosis* is described in terms of a movement from the form or shape of God to the form of a servant or slave. As Ziesler (1990: 45) puts it: 'Christ offers not so much an example to be followed as a pattern of life to be entered.' The story of Wisdom's descent may lie behind this language. Paul calls his readers to live within a divine–human synergy: 'work out your own salvation . . . for God is at work in you' (Phil. 2: 13). Thus, in his perspective, the Spirit enables a distinctive way of learning that is open to divine wisdom and a conformation to the form of Christ.

The quest for wisdom has been a theme that has occupied recent writers (MacIntyre, 1985; Porter, 1994; Cocksworth, 2003). Ford (1997: 72) calls attention in this information age to our sense of being overwhelmed by an excess of information and data. The challenge is to dare to swim in the river or ocean of wisdom:

> we have to swim in wisdom. If we try to stay in control through information, knowledge and skills, keeping our feet safely on the bottom of the ocean, we drown. So we see an educational system drowning in information, knowledge and skills and rarely even attending to the question: how can we learn and teach wisdom?

He seems to echo the cry of Eliot (1974):

> Where is the life we have lost in living?
> Where is the wisdom we have lost in knowledge?
> Where is the knowledge we have lost in information?
>
> ('Choruses from the Rock')

In ordination training we have seen a movement from cramming for papers under the old General Ordination Examination to the plethora of modules in present-day diplomas and degrees. Less is more: candidates for ordination need to develop disciplines of learning wisdom rather than all the knowledge they may or may not need for the practice of ministry in the years ahead. As Louth (2004) points out, the danger is that if knowledge becomes viewed as an object of consumption, the one who knows becomes consumer rather than contemplator. However, such sentiments are vulnerable to critics who sense in them an obscurantist anti-intellectualism, and must be balanced with a case for *necessary* knowledge.

Writing from a scientific philosophical standpoint, Mary Midgley challenges all educators and students in the fundamental question of her book *Wisdom, Information and Wonder: What Is Knowledge For?* She argues that since the rise of the professions, a body of knowledge has been valued as the goal to be sought, sometimes leading to narrow and isolated specialisms and the 'fear of facing the large questions' (1989: 19). Knowledge is not for storage but for living: 'If thinking is our professional concern, the wisdom and wonder are our business: information-storage, though often useful, is just an accidental convenience' (Midgley, 1989: 253).

For the priest, the goal becomes not acquisition of information but inhabited wisdom. Hardy argues that wisdom is not an abstract, elusive substance-like notion or hypostatization that somehow lies behind all things. He points out that in both the Hebrew tradition and Pauline writings wisdom is to be located and lived within the materiality and particularity of the demands of daily life in society where it functions in terms of reproportioning or reordering reality through the discernment of God's presence and kingdom in the world. For the Christian, wisdom is incarnated and lived in the 'alienations of life' (Hardy, 1996: 244f). Thus wisdom encompasses the three domains of ministry, not only knowing, but being and doing, as one clergy in the research put it: 'The Spirit of wisdom, the Spirit of life . . . takes me from that place of *being* and commitment into that place of *doing*, enabling transformation "by the power of the Spirit"' (d). Thus wisdom dissolves the boundaries and has the potential to integrate into a unity of discernment elements which are sometimes split off from one another. This is the meaning of 'inhabiting wisdom' or nourishing in Christian leaders a *habitus* which is sometimes hinted at in the *Hind* documents (Archbishops' Council, 2006: 60) – a spiritual maturity and depth that is trained in discerning God's ways.

The transformation of being: a fountain of holiness

A second domain of formation in which the Spirit brings transformation is the area of 'being'. In the *Hind Report* this encompasses attention to the person of the minister, growth in self-awareness, spiritual development and understanding of vocation. It includes dedication to 'a deepening pilgrimage of faith in the Holy Spirit' (Archbishops' Council, 2003: 57).

In the empirical research, several clergy understood their experience of formation in terms of a growth in Christlikeness. This was summed up by one tutor: 'The reason I believe in formation is because I believe we are made in the image of God and renewed in that image, and we achieve the likeness of Christ' (m). The Pauline writings employ the language of continuous transformation into Christ: 'Do not be conformed to this world but be *transformed* by the renewal of your mind' (Rom. 12: 2). Paul is clear that this is a work of the Spirit: 'Reflecting the glory of the Lord, we are *being changed* into his likeness from one degree of glory to another; for this comes from the Lord who is the Spirit' (2 Cor. 3: 18). The Greek word used is related to *metamorphosis*, denoting a process of fundamental change. This is Paul's vision: 'Though our outer nature is wasting away, our inner nature is being renewed every day' (2 Cor. 4: 16). This allows a transcendent dimension in ministry: 'we have this treasure in earthen vessels to show that the transcendent power belongs to God and not to us' (2 Cor. 4: 7). Paul teaches that the Christian's calling and vocation, indeed destiny, is 'to be *conformed* to the image of his Son' (Rom. 8: 27). As Ziesler (1989: 227) puts it: 'Bearing his image is being like him, and representing him.' The Greek idea *summorphosis* means 'to be formed or fashioned like, to be shaped like'. Inner lives are to be reshaped according to the pattern of Christ; personal resources and aptitudes to be realigned to the template of Christ. This is growth in Christlikeness, especially in those virtues required for priesthood and leadership.

In terms of the Anglican *Ordinal* (General Synod, 2003) this invites a reshaping of priests' lives on the model of Christ the Good Shepherd: 'They are to set the example of the Good Shepherd always before them as the pattern of their calling.' This is not simply a pastoral role, but a sacrificial role and a leadership role; 'he goes before them . . . he lays down his life for the sheep' (Jn. 10: 4, 11). This is not only revealed in outward and external action, but springs from the very centre, the very core of the priest. So there is a key relation between mission and interiority, between outer life and inner life. The Anglican *Ordinal* maintains a careful balance between function and being, between the duties of the priest and the call to 'stir up the gift of God that is in you'. As Moberly (1969: 261) put it:

> There are not only priestly functions . . . there is also a priestly spirit and a priestly heart – more vital to true reality of priesthood than any mere performance of priestly functions . . . those who are ordained 'priests' are bound to be eminently leaders and representatives of this priestliness of spirit.

The development of priestly character relates to the empowerment of others for ministry. It is not concerned with the status of the priest but with the mission of the priest and the inner resources which underpin this. Willimon (2000) identifies courage as a key quality to be developed in today's clergy. In *Calling and Character: Virtues of the Ordained Life*, he is critical of the way in which clergy have become a respectable profession accommodated to the spirit of the age: 'We seem to have a high proportion of those who wish to keep house, to conform, and too few who like to play, confront, disrupt, revise, and foolishly envision' (2003: 99). He calls on theological educators to seek to form clergy who can dare to be subversive, unsettling in their prophetic and countercultural witness.

Such a Spirit-driven process of transformation in the character and being of the minister invites exploration of how the formation process is a particular expression of what has traditionally been termed sanctification or growth in holiness. Indeed, the *Hind Report* affirms:

> A key pursuit for ministerial training should be a holiness that seeks to maintain the integrity and effectiveness of the Church . . . a key theological theme that should inform training is that the ordained ministry should be marked by the holiness that Christ gives to his Church.
>
> (Archbishops' Council, 2003: 33)

Such a holiness needs to be worked out within two paradoxes. First, there is the dialectic between separation and engagement. The root meaning of the Hebrew word for holy, *qadesh*, is 'to separate' or 'to be set apart for a divine purpose'. It is the opposite to 'what pertains to ordinary life'. In the New Testament such a meaning is carried over into the Greek *hagios* (Purkiser, 1983: 18). This sense of separation and the call 'to be holy as I am holy' (1 Pet. 1: 15) stand in paradoxical relation to the Gospel call for engagement with the world. The Incarnation holds the two elements together, and Jesus prays that his disciples will be 'in the world but not of the world'

(Jn 17: 15–16). There will be an other-worldliness in the midst of the world. We have seen this dilemma revealed in models of priestly training: notably in the seminary which sought to be set apart from the world. How can the paradox be lived?

Modern writers have struggled to hold the two ideas together. Matthews (1996: 95) talks of a 'muddy mysticism'. Casaldaliga and Vigil (1994: 174ff), from a liberationist standpoint, write of a 'political holiness' that is committed to seeking signs of the divine kingdom in the midst of a world of oppression. For clergy, this is revealed in the ebb and flow of prayer and action, stillness and activity.

Secondly, how justifiable is it to set forth clergy as exemplars of holiness? The ideal of holiness and the pursuit of sanctification can lead to a dangerous perfectionism among the clergy. Wesley taught about holiness in terms of perfection and perfectionist language has also been used in the older Catholic manuals on priesthood. This research has revealed some indications of a tendency among the clergy towards compulsive overworking, stressful patterns of ministry, the fear of failure and the inability to relax (compare Society of Mary and Martha 2002; Sanford 1982). The dilemma is that priests find themselves caught between the reality of their humanity and the highest standards of holy living. Such higher standards for the clergy, first set out in the Pastoral Epistles, have been inculcated by many traditions of formation. For example, seminarians have been urged to emulate certain ideals of Christ the priest within an identification model of formation (Schuth, 1989: 149). In order to avoid burn-out, priests not only need to work out the call to holiness within a healthy and realistic appreciation of their humanity, they also need to re-focus on the fact that such sanctification is predominantly the work of the Spirit, a gift and grace. A rediscovery of theological education in terms of *paideia* would prompt attentiveness not only to the character and being of the priest but also to a pneumatology which makes sense of character transformation.

The transformation of doing: the energy of the Spirit

A third domain of transformation within the formation process is within the doing of ministry, developing the skills necessary for worship, pastoral care, mission and leadership. In what ways can the Holy Spirit energize and animate formation? The Lukan tradition within the New Testament provides clues for a pneumatology of ministry. The Spirit of God energizes and makes possible the liberating ministry of Jesus (Lk. 4). In Luke, the Holy Spirit comes to Jesus when he is at prayer (Lk. 3: 21–2) and Jesus teaches his disciples to pray for the Holy Spirit whom the Father longs to give in response to our searching (Lk. 11: 13). The Risen Christ promises the apostles: 'You shall receive power (*dunamis*) when the Holy Spirit comes, and you shall be my witnesses' (Acts 1: 8). Stronstad (1984: 80) says: 'In this dominical saying Luke gives his readers the key to interpreting the purpose of the gift of the Spirit, not only to the disciples on the day of Pentecost but also throughout Luke-Acts . . . the gift of the Spirit always results in mission.'

In the empirical research, clergy referred to the Holy Spirit in dynamic terms ranging from the poetic (f: 'He is the strong wind which propels you') to the practical (c: 'He's someone who kicks you up the backside and gets you to do the difficult things you want to put off'). Theologians freely use metaphor to describe the empowering of the Spirit. Moltmann (2001: 283) is inspired by Meister Eckhart's depiction of the Spirit of God as a great underground river which rises to the surface in springs and fountainheads:

> Out of God, blessing and the energies of life spill over onto the whole of creation (Ps 65: 9); from this fountain people receive 'grace upon grace' (Jn 1: 16). Jesus talks about . . . 'a spring of water welling up eternal life' (Jn 4: 14). The 'well of life' is not in the next world, and not in the church's font: it is in human beings themselves. If they receive the life-giving water, they themselves become the wellspring of this water for other people.

Moltmann (2001: 285) commends what he calls 'mystical metaphors' to explore the experience of the Spirit: 'In the mystical metaphors, the distance between a transcendent subject and its immanent work is ended . . . the divine and human are joined in an organic cohesion.'

John Taylor, in his seminal book on the Holy Spirit (1972: 44–5), also points us towards the life-giving waters of the Spirit.

> Baptism has so often been treated simply as a *rite de passage* which, having been passed through, is left behind, that the church has largely forgotten to see in its waters the symbol of that element in which the Christian lives and moves and has his being, namely the Spirit himself. He does not leave those waters behind but lives on in their meaning.

He goes on

> We must allow the awesome archetypal resonances of the water symbol to fill out our understanding of our baptism and of that life in the Spirit which it represents . . . The Holy Spirit is totally primordial. His is the elemental force beyond all other forces . . . the force of love.

Paul alludes to such river or current: 'God's love has been poured (*ekkechutai*, lit. streamed forth profusely) into our hearts through the Holy Spirit that has been given to us' (Rom. 5: 5). This river of the Spirit energizes and animates formation and ministry.

As Gutiérrez (1984: 37) says, 'spirituality is indeed like living water that springs up in the very depths of the experience of faith'. The streams of the Spirit flow imperceptibly within the river of prayer. Such life-giving waters are the key to ministerial formation.

Questions for reflection

✦ How do these findings resonate with your educational practice or with your experience as a learner?

✦ What strikes you most about them?

✦ To what extent do you find yourself agreeing or disagreeing with the reflections?

8

Dark waters: formation, prayer and the experience of inner change

Save me, O God, for the waters have come up to my neck . . . I have come into deep waters, and the flood sweeps over me.

(Ps. 69: 1–2)

By the rivers of Babylon, there we sat down and there we wept.

(Ps. 137: 1)

Findings

This chapter explores the empirical evidence clustering around a further major theme in formation: *ministerial formation involves development of ministerial identity and growth in virtue.*

Formation was recognized by most of the participants as a process of personal change. It was recognized that the use of the language of formation enabled close attention to issues of personal development, in contrast to a focus on gaining competencies. What sort of change was experienced, and how does prayer contribute to the process?

The role of prayer in forming a ministerial identity and shaping a model of ministry

Formation emerges as the interplay between the uniqueness of the candidate and the inherited expectations associated with the ministerial role. There is a need for self-acceptance, for coming to terms with one's gifts and limitations, and this involves reaching an understanding of how one's personality fits with the role so a confident sense of ministerial identity can flourish. A tutor brings this perspective:

Alongside the academic progress, you would be looking for some sort of inner change. I would say that the main change is moving from seeing ministry in terms of *doing* to seeing it in terms of *being*. When people begin, they often have the tasks of ministry in mind. But they learn that formation is about accepting who you are and bringing who you are into vocation and ministry. I know some people see formation more negatively, especially when formation seems to be forced on you, like pressing you into a particular mould. But that's the exact opposite of the way I see it: formation is allowing the person you *are* to come out in ministry. (h)

This entails embracing both a public role and a theological role, in terms of learning to act *in persona Christi* or as representing Christ in a particular way. All traditions agree that formation entails a growth in Christlikeness and a maturation of the fruits of the Spirit. As we noted, catholic traditions would want to emphasize this more specifically: 'Formation is being transformed into the image of Christ in respect to your particular vocation. So diaconal formation is growing into the likeness of Christ the servant' (h).

A Catholic college brings a paschal perspective to this process of change:

> Formation is about moving out of our current selves into our true selves, via the Cross. We are formed into Christ – 'until Christ be formed in you' as Paul puts it in Galatians. This involves conformation to Christ in the power of his Cross and Resurrection. It can be an uncomfortable process. Ministerial formation can involve helping square pegs to fit round holes. This is an unpalatable message today. This is like knocking the edges of pebbles. I think this is a very unfashionable thing today! (j)

Complementing this, an evangelical sees the role of prayer in this process in terms of reflection and relationship:

> Prayer is recognizing that I need God to be at work in me, as change happens, and that the change is being directed by Him, so I'm changing in a right way. Prayer helps – in learning to be dependent on Him, through that process. Also the reflective, meditative time – taking a step back and thinking 'what's happening? How is God changing me? Or, how is the role changing me?' – allows reflecting about that and praying about it. Prayer is keeping that closeness to God as the change happens and helping you to make sure it's good change rather than any change which is not so good. (e)

Prayer can also be a place of profound affirmation where identity and vocation and motivation are strengthened:

Certainly not each time I pray, but in prayer generally, particularly where there's times of stillness, there's a deep sense of being loved, a deep sense of being called to love, and a deep sense of being equipped to love. That's why it's so essential. It's the very breath of life, actually. (d)

For one person, prayer fulfils an essential role in keeping in view a model of ministry which has the humility to recognize its dependence on God:

Prayer is the core of it. I mean, you can have change and development in any aspect of life, but unless it's done in relation to God then I question where that is going – what is the *telos* of the process of change? If you don't make sure that you're always keeping God at the core, and that dynamic relationship with God at the core, then it's very easy to begin valuing things for their own sake. That is especially dangerous in this job . . . (a)

Formation and the transition into a public role

The experience of crossing the threshold from being a private citizen into becoming a public figure has been described as that of liminality (see above, chapter 4). It can be a demanding process in which space for reflective prayer can enable a certain coming-to-terms with a bewildering variety of expectations and the need to clarify boundaries:

There's also been a period of adjustment for me. I've found it quite hard, initially, being a more public figure and I'm still getting used to it . . . Also being treated differently by people, because of the position you hold. And the whole issue of getting into a leadership role as well – being that sort of figure – adjusting to that, is a big change. (e)

What role does prayer play in this process of making sense of ministry? One tutor puts it eloquently:

I think that without returning to the Centre of things, without returning to the Source of all life, we will simply run out of steam, get choked up with all sorts of good ideas and never know which one is the best idea, and there will probably be a dissociation of roles, where we can no longer say who we are. The thing about prayer is that it has to be an activity of the heart, and the heart is the centre of our being . . . So prayer of whatever type, has to be the centre if we want to stay in one piece. (m)

Pain and vulnerability in formation

Female clergy were more prepared than male clergy to speak of the personal cost of formation. A female tutor puts it thus:

> Formation is about accepting what you are and who you are and prayer gives you a space to do this. Sometimes it includes facing inner pain. I think it's so important to be honest in prayer about our feelings and thoughts, and bring them to God, and not staying at a superficial level. (h)

She goes on:

> Formation can't happen without prayer . . . because formation isn't self-improvement, it's allowing God to work in you, and prayer opens up this possibility. Prayer is the experience of God helping the candidates move on in the journey. This prayer can make things uncomfortable and formation may at times mean having to let go of things we find very hard to let go of. I feel echoes here of Jacob wrestling with God.

One aspect of this painful process of transition is the perceived need to let go of one's past confidences.

> There is a sense in which formation inevitably involves an unmaking and remaking. Some candidates, especially the older ones, find it deskilling sometimes, especially if they had a previous career. Part of formation is, I hope, that we teach new skills. It is more difficult for older candidates to be vulnerable and to acknowledge the need to go back to first principles. That can be unpopular. But those in their twenties seem to be more open. (j)

This can certainly be experienced by candidates as unnecessary pain:

> It's been the hardest five years of my life [two years in college, three since ordination]! The whole system is a struggle. I haven't grown; rather I've struggled not to go backwards. Prayer is my life-line. There's an inference in the system that people's life prior to coming to college is valueless. I have struggled with that and lifted my frustrations to God – it's the prayer that keeps me sane. (g)

Some are able to see this more positively: 'It has been a difficult journey at times. It's seeing how every experience can build on the previous experience, and bringing to the life of this parish things that I've experienced in my previous parish and job' (c).

The sense of loss is not only the loss of privacy, but also the loss of self-determination, as candidates learn that they are no longer their own, but belong in a new sense to the institution and to the people of God. Some curates find that prayer helps them make sense of painful struggles in professional relationships:

> Formation recognizes that this is a journey and also that bad experiences can be formative too . . . bad formation can happen, but also negative experiences can actually lead to good formation, if you're able to reflect on it properly. It comes back to being open to the experience . . . allowing that experience to lead to development. (h)

Prayer can have a profoundly healing effect: 'it's to do with being vulnerable – surrendering to His love and to the intensity of His love for me and the whole world – the hot coal on my lips and in my heart gets close to the essence of what this about' (h).

Only one person had the courage to admit to the cost of *metanoia* in formation: 'I nearly always have a time of personal confession, a feeling of my own inadequacies and failures, and the need for cleansing and new starts all the time – that's very much there as well' (e).

Prayer and stress

The interviews revealed that clergy face many kinds of stress in the parish which threaten the identity and confidence of the minister. Some feel battered and bruised, if not hurt by ministry.

> I think the busier things get, in a way, the more you need to stop and have time for prayer . . . I think I did spend the first few months running around like a headless chicken and in many ways did feel I'd lost direction in terms of *why* I was doing it. It was actually a good lesson to learn that the more you have practically to do, the more important it is actually to make sure that you're rooted in prayer, that prayer becomes a priority, rather than the thing that gets squeezed out. (a)

Prayer, especially types which enable reflective space, can function, unintentionally, as survival techniques for hard-pressed clergy. Several reported arriving breathlessly at Evening Prayer in the parish and finding calm:

> Physically, I may arrive in a rush to get to Church for the Evening Office, and then comes that sitting down, and then the gentle reading of the psalms actually brings a sense of order, in my physical being as well as my spiritual being. That sense of just slowing the pace of life down. (c)

This seems a common experience:

> Sometimes I come to prayer feeling quite flustered – the busyness of life again – and praying helps me to take my foot of the pedal a bit, just to relax, and hand things over to God, recognize that it's not just me doing

this. Prayer helps me hugely with the demands and stresses of ministry – I think it's vital. (e)

He goes on to explain this in terms of reorientation:

> I'm aware that when prayer gets squeezed out then, in myself, I'm not operating in a right sort of way, in a spiritual sort of way. I can slip into a worldly way of doing things, which is just about being busy and getting jobs done and ticking things off the list. So prayer is absolutely vital in that process of re-orientating yourself. (e)

It seems that prayer functions in several different ways in relation to stress. There is the reflective space in which things can be looked at in a new light, placing things within a larger picture: 'I think prayer helps you to put things in the true perspective that they're supposed to be in' (a).

Prayer can also transform stress into a place where vocation can be rediscovered and affirmed:

> I am increasingly aware that my depth of prayer, in all my pain and vulnerability is feeding my calling to enfold others in prayer and communicate God's love for others to them . . . Prayer is about putting myself in God's way, about being refined in His service and love. (d)

Several clergy right across the spectrum of age and tradition spoke of 'unloading' the day's pressures through prayer, and recognized its therapeutic effects. A Catholic in his sixties said: 'I think praying helps you cope with the stresses and strains of ministry. In prayer any problems you have, you realize you're sharing them, so in a sense it takes the load off' (f). An evangelical in her forties gave a candid account:

> Sometimes life and ministry can be frenetic – and after a difficult pastoral situation or difficult visit, extempore prayer would help me offer it to God, or someone praying with me. Especially after an emotional situation, a tough situation, I need to unload it onto God . . . And I bring my frustrations to God too, frustrations from things in the parish. Prayer helps me make some sense of parish life and its demands. . . I need to share with God on a regular basis or I couldn't do it. I think prayer gives me hope. Prayer is the thing that sustains me, and prayer gives me the whole meaning of my life. (g)

Thus prayer can enable the release of pent-up emotions, and the expression of anger when necessary. Several clergy valued the Psalms in particular as a way in which to bring frustrations and questions to God in prayer in an acceptable and time-honoured way: 'Like the psalmist, you can have a good rant and rave but end up blessing God' (d). One spoke in terms of becoming in prayer 'enfolded in God's love, feeling his presence, feeling safe' (b). Two spoke of weeping in prayer: 'Sometimes the prayer is full of tears' (d); 'Tears just came, a real release of something I wasn't conscious of' (c).

Another way in which prayer functions in relation to stress is its role in translating anxiety and concern into intercession. Several found that evensong after a hectic day of ministry afforded a time to surrender back to God the stresses of the day:

> After the formal intercessions in the Office, whoever's leading prays openly and actually brings to God the local situations which have occurred during the day. This is vital for me, because of the really sad situations that I face in the hospital. I have somewhere to offer that back. (c)

But it is not only intercession which carries this healing function in relation to ministerial stress. One tutor spoke of the profound reorientation that comes from contemplation, sometimes parodied as escapism:

> When you're faced with the world . . . you get bogged down with it . . . you allow yourself to be dissipated – and then you come together again; you are drawn into one, you are integrated, re-integrated, by finding once again the source of all being. And so, in a sense, the movement into contemplation feels like a movement away from concerns. But there is a way in which you have to let it all go and let it into the mind and heart of God, in order to pick it up again with one's own mind changed, so that when you go back into the cycle of mission, you are renewed. (m)

Empirical evidence thus testifies to the powerful restorative and empowering function of prayer. It is not clear how far theological colleges prepare candidates for this. Certainly, this function of prayer is never mentioned in descriptions of what is learned about prayer at college. It may be that part-time course prepare better:

> People on our course weren't formed by sharing common meals and so on, but by adversity . . . People were formed by juggling many balls at once, which they couldn't possibly do by themselves, having elderly parents, getting cancer themselves, combining a job, family and study . . . they were under pressure in a way that I never was when I was at theological college. (m)

Prayer as integrating

Another integrating function of prayer is the opportunity it gives to draw together often conflicting or competing aspects of pastoral ministry and bring them back into a uniting vision of ministry where they make more sense. One interviewee spoke of how prayer helps to heal the potential fragmentation:

> If you don't make sure that you're always keeping God at the core then it's very easy to begin valuing things for their own sake. That is especially dangerous in this job because there are so many facets to it – I suspect it's probably quite easy to let prayer (and therefore God) get squeezed out and lose the reason why you're doing things . . . It's a fragmented job in many ways but it all stems from one thing and it's actually remembering that it all comes back to that one thing that is the important aspect. (a)

She went on to explain:

> I think prayer helps you to put things in the true perspective that they're supposed to be in. I mean, you can get sucked into so many day-to-day things . . . hundreds of things to worry about, and it can seem very fragmented, but it's actually a case of thinking, well, it *is* all part of a larger picture, of a wider picture, and that is God, really . . . it's for me to learn to be open to discerning God's will and hearing God's call. If all the fragmented strands of life are gathered up in an individual and corporate relationship with God, then things have a habit of turning out to be less fragmented and strange they otherwise appear! (a)

Prayer and human formation

Though no personality tests or characterizations were attempted among the sample, clear differences emerged in preferences for different kinds of prayer according to individual make-up. It was highly significant that a role for reflective prayer was appreciated by the whole sample, which encompassed people across the introversion–extraversion spectrum. It is possible to discern different personality types by looking at what is said in terms of preferred ways of working and noticing correspondences with Jung's four mental functions of thinking/feeling, sensing/intuition (Briggs Myers and Myers, 1995). Across the sample, the clergy interviewed testified to releasing a full range of emotions in prayer, ranging from anger, frustration and bewilderment to joy, awe and astonishment at God's grace. Clearly, the affective dimensions of prayer were important because they enabled some release and perhaps indicated that some inner change was taking place in the course of the prayer-time. This was especially mentioned by female interviewees, who were also the ones who felt able to use words like 'wholeness' and 'vulnerability'. Otherwise, gender differences did not prove to be significant in terms of the function of prayer.

A theme which surfaced in some interviews concerned the measure of human freedom in the formation process. To what extent can a candidate freely choose to advance his or her formation – or create barriers to it? This question was not directly asked, but some clergy recognized very clearly that they had control both over their formation and prayer-life, and that the training institution had a limited role: 'In a distance learning course, the formation is governed very much by you as an individual really. There's only an occasional input' (b); 'At the end of the day it is the individual's responsibility [in college] to marry the academic study and the reflective prayer and contemplation' (e). The candidate's awareness of responsibility is especially crucial in the post-ordination phase:

> The important thing is to constantly be aware of making sure you are allowing yourself to engage with the process of living 'in formation' – it's quite easy *not* to be in formation! I think at college it feels a very different process than how it feels outside of the college environment. At college, much is imposed on you that other people have decided is important for your formation . . . But this is a different world from the parish, where you have to take on board responsibility for your own formation in many ways. It's an act of actually saying, 'Well, am I going to allow myself to continue to be in formation? and how am I going to do that?' – and I do think it's very very easy not to. (a)

The issue of human freedom in formation emerges not only in the question of taking responsibility for one's own progress. It is also raised in relation to how the candidate might cooperate with God's role in formation, or resist it:

> I hope prayer is moulding me in accordance with God's will. I am opening myself to that moulding process. As I pray, God is moulding me, but not controlling – like a control freak! God respects the material he's working with. Like Henry Moore who would work with a particular piece of stone – he would pay attention to the natural characteristics of the stone, or the wood, and the actual shape would reflect the grain, the physical structures of the material. (b)

Those who see formation in some sense as a divine work speak in terms of a divine–human synergy in which openness and human vulnerability are essential.

Reflections

The experience of pain in ministerial formation

Within the metaphor of the river of prayer, these experiences can be described as 'dark waters', an allusion to the phrase of John of the Cross (1542–91). 'Dark water' is an image the mystic uses in reference to the 'dark night of the soul' which expresses the painful dimensions of formational prayer. Locked in his prison in the Toledo city walls, John could hear few sounds but the rushing waters of the river Tajo below (Matthew 1995: 72). This became an image to communicate the mysterious way in which God flows into human prayer: '*He made darkness and the dark water his hiding place* (Ps. 18: 10–11) . . . the dark water of his dwelling denotes the obscurity of faith in which he is enclosed' (Kavanaugh and Rodriguez, 1991: 177).

John talks of darkness to express two things. First, he explores prayer in terms of venturing into the unknown, where visibility is nil, where one must progress by faith not sight. The darkness refers to a process of radical dispossession that John sees as lying at the heart of prayer. John sees prayer as a movement from egocentricity to God-centredness, as a process in which God seeks to reshape us and convert the ego. What is needed is the renunciation of one's own confidences to enable a total surrender to God. The pain to be faced is the pain of 'letting go' of being in control, the cost of being stripped of our egotistical powers. Follent puts it thus:

> The abandonment of self-mastery and the taking on of a radical dependence on God will necessarily be accompanied by a sense of being undone or being annihilated, yet such an anxiety is quite ungrounded. In fact, the discovery that one can no longer find one's guarantees in oneself may indeed be a sign that progress in the life with God is finally being achieved.
>
> (1994: 97)

This resonates with the 'unmaking and remaking' of formation which has been noted above.

Secondly, the darkness expresses the mystery of God, who is beyond boxes and concepts. For the process of dispossession or undoing of the self, which is akin to New Testament concepts of *metanoia*, is but the preparation for the *inflow* of God's dark waters into the soul. John writes of 'the fortitude this obscure, painful, and dark water of God bestows on the soul . . . after all, even though it is dark, it is water, and thereby refreshes and fortifies the soul in what most suits it – although in darkness, and painfully' (Kavanaugh and Rodriguez, 1991: 435). Significantly, for John, the waters can denote the experience of prayer or the experience of God – he writes of 'the clear water of sublime contemplation and wisdom of God' (Kavanaugh and Rodriguez, 1991: 607). The waters flow together imperceptibly. In his poem 'The Fountain' John celebrates this night-time flow:

For I know well the spring that flows and runs, although it is night . . .
I know well the stream that flows from this spring
is mighty in compass and power,
although it is night.

(Kavanaugh and Rodriguez, 1991: 58–9)

The night of prayer, for John of the Cross, is at once the place of wounding and transformation. Such are the dark waters of formational prayer. Four aspects of the inner pain, coalescing around the question of ministerial identity, can become the raw material for prayer in this way.

First, there is the experience of being deskilled, a letting-go of one's past career and one's identity bound up in it, the loss of past confidences and the entry into 'no-man's land' or a wilderness in training where a sense of vulnerability is acute.

Secondly, there is the pain of bereavement closely associated with this, a sense of dislocation involved where the candidate has to move home and family to college and let go of ties to the former community where one belonged. In beginning ordained ministry, bereavement can be experienced as the loss of privacy as the candidate moves from being a private citizen to public property and a representative role. There can be a loss of self-determination: one is no longer one's own but a servant of the Church (and sometimes of the vicar).

Thirdly, there is pain involved in facing one's 'shadow side' as Jung described it (Monbourquette, 2001). A growth in self-understanding can entail a fresh consciousness of one's inadequacy for an awesome calling. Fourthly, in the practice of ministry there is the experience of stress and the diversity of demands often felt as perplexing or even overwhelming.

As all these are carried into prayer, prayer is experienced as a turbulent place, with eddies, whirlpools, rapids and unexpectedly strong currents. Prayer is now a torrent where boulders, other detritus and rubbish get forced along. The river of prayer becomes a place of attrition and erosion, where stones get their corners knocked off. But prayer can also at the same time be experienced as a place of profound transformation and creativity, where a new identity is being shaped and formed. Waters can break down and build up. This has resonances with important biblical and theological traditions which help to make sense of the experience, in particular, with the archetypal tale of Jacob's struggle in the waters of the Jabbok (Gen. 32: 22–31): it is the struggle of humanity with God.

The story of Jacob's wrestling with God in the swirling, dangerous waters of the Jabbok has become symbolic of the struggle of prayer.[1] From the outset, as von Rad (1972: 325) notes, the story was archetypal and representative: 'It contains experiences of faith that extend from the most ancient period down to the time of the narrator . . . as it is now related it is clearly transparent as a type of that which Israel experienced from time to time with God.' It is the struggle of humanity with God. Jacob wrestled and fought with a stranger, an unknown figure; he later described this encounter thus: 'I have seen God face to face.' It was indeed a divine–human combat.

Amidst the swirling currents Jacob experiences a barrier or frontier becoming a threshold or place of transition. It evokes both the creation account of order emerging from the waters of chaos (Gen. 1) and the Exodus story of liberation where foes were drowned in the waters of the Red Sea and where a barrier became a crossing-place. It also recalls the Old Testament theme of dragons and demons lurking in the dark waters (cf. Job 41: 1, Ps. 74: 14).[2] When seen as an encounter with God, this story casts light on the experience of prayer in formation because it is precisely in the waters of struggle, in the darkness and in the experience of being wounded by God, that Jacob receives his new name and new identity: no longer is he 'Grasper' (Jacob) but 'One who struggles with God' (Israel). This profound affirmation comes in the midst of solitude: 'Jacob was left alone' (Gen. 32: 24). For Jacob this meant a letting go, for the moment, of attachments to people and possessions. He was

---

[1]   The account will be approached in spirit of *interpretive obedience* commended by Brueggemann (1991: 1) involving 'an act of imaginative construal to show how the non-negotiable intentions of Yahweh are to be discerned and practiced in our situation'.

[2]   There is a debate about the extent of the symbolism in the text. Fokkelman (1991: 208ff) sees symbolism in the crossing, the darkness/the sun rising.

prepared to part from family and to stand alone before God. Prayer becomes a place of honesty and naked exposure to God, a place of risk and vulnerability where God is allowed both to wound and to bless. Henri Nouwen (1990: 31) put it thus: 'Solitude is thus the place of purification and transformation, the place of the great struggle and the great encounter. Solitude . . . is the place where Christ remodels us in his own image and frees us from the victimizing compulsions of the world. Solitude is the place of salvation.'

Jacob is brought to a point of brokenness. His running had symbolized his independence, his desire to escape uncomfortable truths and conflicts, his evasion of God and his determination to stay in control of his life. Such running and exhaustion resonates with sometimes self-inflicted stresses which are experienced in the intensity of training and ministry. Now Jacob can run no longer: he can only limp, for God touches him and disables him. He is reduced to a state of new dependency on God himself. This wounding of Jacob represents God's finally melting his wilfulness and paralysing his defiant ego. For the moment, at least, he crumples up: God has the mastery.

In giving Jacob a new identity God affirms the role of struggling in an evolving relationship with him. It is not to be avoided but faced: those who embrace their struggles with God can emerge with a clearer sense of identity and mission. Jacob's experience in the dark waters actually equips him to face the next stage of his journey. As the clergy testify, the torrent of prayer is experienced as a place of profound growth, and ministers become wounded healers: 'For a deep understanding of our own pain makes it possible for us to convert our weakness into strength and to offer our own experience as source of healing' (Nouwen, 1998: 161). As Brueggemann (1982: 271) puts it, noting the significance of Jacob's struggle for ministry: 'This narrative reflects some of Israel's most sophisticated theology . . . God is God . . . Jacob is a cripple with a blessing . . . This same theology of weakness in power and power in weakness turns this text towards the New Testament and the gospel of the cross.'

Formational prayer as a paschal/baptismal experience

During the research, a tutor commented: 'Formation is about moving out of our current selves into our true selves, via the Cross . . . This involves conformation to Christ in the power of his Cross and Resurrection. It can be an uncomfortable process . . . like knocking the edges of pebbles' (j). As Methodist educator Cetuk puts it:

Formation requires a person to die to the self; to give up former ways of being and thinking and believing and relating; to renegotiate one's belief systems about oneself and the world; to replace old ways of being with new, more sophisticated and lasting ways of being that are more appropriate to the new role in society that one is preparing to take.

(1998: 187)

It is in the waters of the Jordan that Christ receives the affirmation of his identity and mission 'as he was praying' (Lk. 3: 21). His descent into the waters and re-emergence foreshadow the crucifixion, burial and resurrection. Mark depicts Christian discipleship as a formative journey paschal in character:

If any want to become my followers, let them deny themselves and take up their cross and follow me. For those who want to save their life will lose it, and those who lose their life for my sake, and the sake of the gospel, will save it.

(Mk 8: 34–5)

Losing one's life entails fundamental dispossession of the self, vulnerability, giving up self-sufficiency. As John reminds us: 'Unless a grain of wheat falls into the ground and dies, it remains just a single grain; but if it dies, it bears much fruit' (Jn 12: 24). Paul in developing this theme in terms of dying and rising with Christ (Rom. 6), points to the heart of formation: 'I have been crucified with Christ; it is no longer I who live, but Christ who lives in me' (Gal. 2: 20). He teaches that it is in the waters of baptism that the Christian participates in the paschal mystery: 'We have been buried with him by baptism into death, so that, just as Christ was raised from the dead by the glory of the Father, so we too might walk in newness of life' (Rom. 6: 4). Baptism entails a radical casting off of the old clothes of faithless living and the putting on of the new life of Christ (cf. Col. 3: 5–14). As the baptismal liturgy puts it:

Through the deep waters of death you brought your Son, and raised him to life in triumph . . . We thank you, Father, for the water of Baptism: in it we are buried with Christ in his death. By it we share in his resurrection. Through it we are reborn by the Holy Spirit.

(Central Board of Finance of the Church of England, 1998)

As Rolheiser (1988: 137ff) reminds us, all Christian spirituality is essentially paschal in character. He contrasts two types of death: a terminal death that ends possibilities and a paschal death that opens one up to a new future. This casts light on the experience of the clergy's prayer in formation. A dying is taking place on different levels, a letting-go. This is experienced at the time as something disorientating and painful. But within a longer perspective, it is possible to discern that this is important and significant change taking place within the transition towards public ordained ministry. The paschal waters of prayer are not, however, to be considered as limited to this transition. Rather, they set the pattern, even paradigm, for prayer throughout ministry. As Perri (1996: 98) puts it: 'Mystical death is required . . . Priests need to contemplate the inner contradictions. By holding this chaos, the grace of God's aggressive and creative hand will refashion the indelible mark.'

Questions for reflection

+ How do these findings resonate with your educational practice or with your experience as a learner?

+ What strikes you most about them?

+ To what extent do you find yourself agreeing or disagreeing with the reflections?

9

The meeting of the waters: formation, prayer and theological knowing

Deep calls to deep at the thunder of your cataracts.

(Ps. 42: 7)

I will pray with the spirit, but I will pray with the mind also.

(1 Cor. 14: 15)

Findings

This chapter explores the empirical evidence that echoes two major themes in ministerial formation: *formation unites theology, experience and prayer* and *formation entails a dynamic process of integration.*

Prayer enables perception/discernment

A recurring theme in the interviews is that prayer, especially the reflective type, enables a different way of looking at reality, and is inseparable from theological reflection. The latter was often taught at theological college:

> But rather than seeing it as something you simply *do*, we were taught to see theological reflection as a way of approaching things and a way of looking at things and interpreting things, which is actually, I would say, almost a way of prayer. It's trying to look for where God is in this and be open to where God is in that, rather than trying to apply God to a particular situation. Prayer and theological reflection are in many ways one and the same – it's the eyes through which you look at things. (a)

Several clergy talked in terms of gaining a new perspective in prayer, seeing things differently: 'Contemplative prayer brings a sense of enlightenment, I'd say. It's seeing a clear way through a particular problem, getting a new insight you hadn't really had before, into the nature of the problem' (b). It becomes second nature or a habitual, instinctive way of reacting, even in the thick of ministry:

> [there's a] subconscious theological reflection going on at all times – like when I hear a child crying out for its mother at the gate – whatever I'm seeing, I will find myself praying and reflecting about it. But I'm probably not good at giving time to theological reflection in terms of the bigger issues, thinking and praying about them more in depth. (g)

It is where there is created a dedicated space for reflection that deeper wrestling and agonizing with issues can take place. But a certain distance is needed:

> Prayer is an enabling thing [in relation to theological reflection] . . . You can't always see where God is or what God might be saying or how he's working, until later – there needs to be a distance between what actually happened – what you're actually reflecting on and actually hearing or seeing God at work. Prayer is about being open to seeing God at work. (d)

In this context, interviewees talked in terms of prayer enabling a process of discernment, in terms of seeing things more clearly, in terms of glimpsing connections not always apparent which help to make sense of ministry. This noticing of connections was taught clearly at several theological colleges, but the role of prayer in it was often left unexplored:

> I don't think they did specifically teach about the role of prayer in theological reflection. I think the link was always there, in how we were taught to think about it and engage with it, but I don't remember it ever being made explicit. (a)

Prayer enables theology 'from the heart'

Significantly, the question of what is the knowledge to be sought recurred in almost all interviews. There was dissatisfaction, even impatience, with theological colleges and courses wherever academic study did not link in to the experience of mission today. The following is typical:

> I guess education, in a worldly sense, is just filling the brain with facts. But actually a Christian education, learning God, learning theology, is so different from that. It's recognizing that only God can do this work. There is a human side of it – there needs to be a desire from your part – but ultimately God needs to come in and be at work. (e)

Where a narrower view of prayer is retained, its role in the doing of theology is limited:

> Prayer can be quite non-intellectual – saying 'thank you' or 'please, God, help me with this' and you may not really be grappling with the concept, which you could be if you were reading a theological book . . . Perhaps theological reflection is more with the brain and prayer is more with the heart. In theological study, you would try to look at it objectively. . .(f)

However, these comments are untypical. Most ministers recognized an essential role for reflective prayer within the task of doing theology, both within the college and in the parish. One testified to a sense of wonder and insight enabled by prayer:

> [Study] did lead into prayer. Especially when we studied the doctrine of the Trinity I discovered something new in my life and that did affect my prayer life in terms of that sense of God's invitation to be part of the Trinity in some way . . . and that's what changed me most profoundly. Instead of being asked 'how do you *understand* the Trinity?' it changed me into learning to *live* in the Trinity and that had an impact on my whole spiritual life and in prayer too . . . I suppose it was one of those 'wow!' experiences in life where you suddenly discover that God graciously invites you into *his* life . . . this living relationship . . . says something about how my spirituality needed to be something that is living and lively and vibrant. (c)

The evangelical tradition was the strongest in clearly contrasting different types of knowledge. One tutor made the distinction between academic knowledge and relational knowledge: 'knowing the Lord personally is clearly the most important thing' (k). A minister from the same college used two contrasting images:

> People sometimes use the phrase *head knowledge* as opposed to *heart knowledge* . . . You can't just read a book and instantly be a different person. It's a case of allowing God to let that change you and make you more like Himself . . . I guess it's the difference between *knowing about God* and *knowing God*, really knowing God in your inner being as opposed to just knowing facts about Him. (e)

He refers to the way in which theology is not a subject that can be studied dispassionately or without personal involvement or engagement. In traditional terminology *scientia* is impossible without *theoria*. He went on to explain how prayer fitted into the learning process:

> I think the more meditative side of things is important here because what I like to do is to reflect on what I've learnt, and then pray. The praying

side is actually forcing me to do the reflecting bit. For instance, in lectures at college – ideally – I wasn't just receiving and then going on to the next thing – ideally I'd want to reflect on what I'd received, pray about it, think it through a bit more deeply perhaps. It's allowing that which I've received with my mind to percolate down, and affect the whole being. (e)

A Catholic tutor put it succinctly: 'There is a difference between learning about theology in an academic way and using knowledge to form and inform your spiritual life' (h).

Five ways in which prayer, both solitary and corporate, could be included in the learning process were mentioned:

1. *lectio*, meditative reading of texts, likened to 'banging the nail in' (m);
2. use of reflective journal, rolling essay;
3. prayer in lectures, at beginning, end or occasionally, in the midst of teaching;
4. use of a theological reflection cycle which explicitly included prayer (one course superseded the basic 'see–judge–act cycle' with a 'mission–identification–interpretation–contemplation' cycle (m);
5. use of handouts commended for prayer (especially where a mixed university group of students did not make possible prayer in the seminar) (h).

The difficulty of teaching spirituality itself

The difficulty of uniting prayer and learning is revealed in an acute form in the very challenge of teaching spirituality. What is provided? Paradoxically, in only rare cases is there opportunity to experience prayer-exercises. Spirituality itself becomes an academic subject, with an emphasis on the study of historical spiritual traditions, with few pointers to how these can be related to the practice of theology or ministerial life. The stress is once again on imparting knowledge of the subject rather than allowing space for its experience. One evangelical college strictly maintains a critical approach, each spiritual tradition examined in the light of the college's dogmatic understanding of salvation, so wherever traditions seemed to imply a 'ladder of prayer' or seeing union with God as the goal of the prayer-process, they were given a severe 'health warning' because they seemed to contradict the fundamental beliefs of the institution.

However, there were notable exceptions to the predominant emphasis on the academic teaching of spirituality. One course, in particular, seemed to give space for some experimentation in prayer. One evangelical college begins the week with a morning dedicated to both the teaching and practice of spirituality, beginning with an hour's academic input on a spiritual tradition (for example, the Jesus Prayer, or Ignatian meditation), which is followed immediately by students going to their rooms to implement the ideas personally: 'We were then given a further hour to spend in praying this through or reflecting on it. First the teaching, which might be practical or theoretical, then time for reflection' (g). Another evangelical college separates the practical from the academic. All ordinands participate in what is called 'a practical devotional course' with this stated aim: 'to equip students to maintain and develop both their own spiritual health and that of those for whom they will care'. Instruction is followed by twenty minutes of prayer within the classroom – as the tutor says: 'There doesn't seem much point in just teaching it academically without the practice' (k). This course is supplemented by a more critical, scholarly spirituality course at degree level.

Interestingly, Catholic tutors tend to omit guided prayer-exercises, perhaps assuming that they were already known, while evangelical colleges take greater pains in providing more practical guidelines for the implementation of the theory.

A reciprocal relationship between prayer and theology

Interviewees used different expressions to convey a sense that there is a two-way relationship between theology and spirituality. We noted above this comment: 'The praying side is actually forcing me to do the reflecting bit' (e). Another puts it like this:

> A number of modules, if you study them from the perspective of a faith-life, of a journey, then they can't help but someway speak into how you pray, how you live your life, your attitudes, all sorts of things. This has to change who I am, because I can't compartmentalize my prayer-life from all the other bits of my life, because that's so much part of who I am that it reflects onto all sorts of things. (c)

A tutor puts it more precisely:

> What we learn from our study of theology . . . may feed our praying. But our prayer will also feed our theology. For instance, one test of different theological views (of atonement, let us say) may be how well they make

sense of what we are doing in prayer. What we do in prayer will help us do our theology better and more coherently. I think it is also sometimes in our praying that we may become aware of links between different theological topics that we may subsequently be able to tease out in study. (j)

Thus, in best practice, there will be a dialectic relationship enabling both a mutual feeding and a mutual questioning between prayer and theological study. The key theme is making connections:

a lot of it was [the college] trying to get you to make the connections between what you were doing and your life of prayer and actually making you bring these two together not as two separate things but as things that were intrinsically interwoven and interlinked all the way along. (a)

One tutor sums up the interrelationship succinctly: 'To me, the best theology is theology which comes from the heart, that's found its way to the heart, but not afraid with wrestling with the really tough questions given to the heart to ponder' (m). But there remains a danger of separating elements which should belong closely together in a creative relationship; as an evangelical interviewee put it: 'My biggest critique of the college is that there is a very strong emphasis on the academic ... My constant struggle was to redress the balance, with prayer and reflection and contemplation' (e).

The greatest challenge, perhaps, is to achieve a creative integration between intellectual formation and prayer. Several interviewees spoke of the integrating effect of prayer in terms of enabling a process of internalizing teaching input, a process of 'percolating down into the whole being' in which the individual appropriates and makes his or her own what is taught. As a staff member of a Catholic college put it, this is how wisdom is achieved:

Silence enables recollection and reflection. If we can foster within ourselves (and therefore if we can encourage students to foster within themselves) a spirit of recollection, this will help with integrating the spiritual, the academic, and the pastoral, and within the intentionality of formation will aid the interiorization of what has been learned. The real hope is that recollection will enable learning to produce an increase in wisdom. (j)

One minister was emphatic that this is a divine work:

I use the phrase 'trying to get theology into my bones' which means basically, making it a part of *me*, the whole me. It's very hard to describe ... It's really talking about that integration at the deepest level. The danger is having an academic understanding but one that actually doesn't fire you and enthuse you and impassion you for ministry, and I think prayer is absolutely vital in making that integration process . . . It's a case of allowing God to let study change you and make you more like Himself. It's recognizing that for that transformation at the deepest level to happen, that must be a work of God's Spirit. It's not just a human process. (e)

The contrast is between superficial study and learning, in which things stay on the surface of understanding, and a more profound process in which the learning makes a difference to the student and achieves its potential to affect both thinking and behaviour. One evangelical tutor put it more bluntly: 'The meditative form of prayer helps them to drive Scripture home, rather than just keeping it at the study level or even at the level of an understanding of a principle. It really drives it home from head to heart, and into life' (k). Thus there is evidence that silent reflective prayer can have a function in healing a divide and dichotomy between spirituality and learning.

Reflections

A great divide: the divergence between theology and spirituality

This vexed relationship of spirituality and the doing of theology stretches back a thousand years to the opening up of a rift between the two in the scholastic period, as we noted. The picture of two rivers flowing together provides a strong visual image for the confluence of streams of thinking and praying. It does not, however, necessarily suggest a peaceful flowing together of prayer and theology, or a comfortable synthesis, merging or fusion of spirituality and theology, for in a confluence there are strong cross-currents and the collision of materials borne by the rivers. There is the risk of a muddying of the waters. At the same time, there is a new energy and richer synergy from combined rivers, a renewed dynamism, a greater momentum, a new drama and creativity from the interpenetration of diverse streams: the possibility of 'deep speaking to deep' as the psalmist puts it.

There are various perspectives on the divide between theology and spirituality. McIntosh (1998: 63), who notes that 'a large-scale historical analysis of this period of divorce remains to be written', focuses on the increasing tendency towards individualism from the tenth century, and a movement towards the privatization of the mystical experience which had earlier been thought of as a corporate venture. He observes a growing medieval split between love and knowledge:

> By the later Middle Ages, the assumption has become in some cases nearly insurmountable that knowing is the task of theologians, while loving is a task for mystics; and instead of perceiving knowing and loving as one coinherent activity in God, they come to appear as strangers, rivals, even enemies struggling for dominance in the drama of the inner self.
>
> (1998: 71)

Sheldrake (1998b: 43) writes about the divorce: 'This division went deeper than method or content. It was, at heart, a division between the affective side of faith (or participation) and conceptual knowledge.' While scholars locate the divide as opening up with the development of the rational or scientific approach to theology advanced in Scholasticism, it is important not to lay the charge entirely at the feet of Aquinas, for he wrote out of the context of monastic spiritual disciplines. Others (such as McGrath, 1998: 115f) consider the split to grow with the nominalist teaching of Duns Scotus (1265–1308) and William of Ockham (1285–1347).

The nature of the knowledge and the knower, East and West

Insufficient attention has been given in considerations of ministerial formation to two major questions: What is the nature of the knowledge we seek? What is the nature of the human person as knower?

It is possible to identify the growing divergence of thought, East and West (Sherrard, 1959: 139ff). A western perspective emerges from Augustinian thinking. Augustine advocated a tripartite division of the human being, with the faculties of memory (akin to consciousness), understanding and will. In his thinking about the soul, he also posited the existence of a faculty superior to reason, calling it intelligence or intellect: *intelligentia*. This independent created faculty is capable of receiving illumination from God, but is not capable of participation in or intuition of the Divine being. Aquinas shares with Augustine a limited role for the intellect: the human person cannot enjoy, in this life, direct apprehension or intuition of God. Rather, 'there is no intellectual power in man distinct from his reason, and the mode of knowledge proper to man is reasoning or discursive knowledge' (Sherrard, 1959: 60). Sherrard detects in Aquinas the beginning of a movement from theology to philosophy; while prayer retains its place in the background, there opens up a chasm between *ascesis* and scholarship.

Thus theological anthropology is closely related to epistemology. It is significant that while the West maintains a polarity between nature and grace, no such distinction is found in eastern thought. As Meyendorff (1983: 13) puts it: 'Of course, in Greek patristic terminology. . . "nature" presupposes divine presence in man, that is, "grace". No opposition between "nature" and "grace " is therefore possible.' An eastern perspective seems more optimistic in its view both of the human person and the potentialities of prayer. The divinely formed faculty that apprehends God is called the *nous*, the spiritual mind or intuitive intellect. It is carefully distinguished from *dianoia*, the faculty of reason: 'The intellect does not function by formulating abstract concepts . . . it understands divine truth by means of immediate experience, intuition or "simple cognition" . . . It is the organ of contemplation' (Palmer, Sherrard and Ware, 1979: 362). As Ware (1985: 401) puts it: 'Here is no head–heart dichotomy, for the intellect is *within* the heart. The heart is the meeting point between body and soul, between the subconscious, conscious and supraconscious, between the human and the divine.' As Abbot Ephraim of Mount Athos (2006) reminds us: 'St John Damascene remarks that "as the eyes are to the body, so the intellect is to the soul" . . . this function of the intellect is an internal insight.' Simeon the New Theologian (1977: 158) writes of *moving* or relocating the mind to the heart:

The mind should be in the heart . . . Keep your mind there (in the heart), trying by every possible means to find the place where the heart is, in order that, having found it, your mind should constantly abide there. Wrestling thus, your mind will find the place of the heart.

If the Orthodox perspective emerges from a particular view of the human person, what kind of knowledge is to be sought? Maximos (1981: 69) in the seventh century put it thus:

When the intellect (*nous*) practises contemplation, it advances in spiritual knowledge . . . the intellect is granted the grace of theology when, carried on wings of love . . . it is taken up into God and with the help of the Holy Spirit discerns – as far as this is possible for the human intellect – the qualities of God.

Such knowledge is transforming: 'The intellect joined to God for long periods through prayer and love becomes wise, good, powerful, compassionate, merciful and long-suffering; in short, it includes with itself almost all the divine qualities' (1981: 74).

A key concept is participation in God. Fourteenth-century Gregory Palamas of Mount Athos, a main proponent of the prayer of *hesychia* (stillness), puts it: ' In prayer . . . man is called to *participation* in divine life: this participation is also the true knowledge of God' (Meyendorff, 1975: 77). In his controversy with the Calabrian philosopher Barlaam, Palamas is insistent: 'But hesychasts know that the purified and illuminated mind, when clearly participating in the grace of God, also beholds other mystical and supernatural visions . . .' (Meyendorff, 1983: 58). Palamas and Maximos represent developments from the seminal thinking of Evagrius of Pontus (346–99) who very succinctly expressed the intermingling waters of spirituality and theology: 'He who prays is a theologian; a theologian is one who prays' (Louth, 2000: 4).

Present perspectives: possibilities for confluence

Are these historic concepts only or do they live in the present? In fact, theological education in the Orthodox tradition is shaped by this approach. With such prayer 'the reading of a spiritual book is a revelation, a theophany . . . It is an encounter with Christ, a mystical union with Christ' (Aimilianos, 2005: 143).

Indeed, such an approach heals the divide and opens a path to wholeness. In an interview with the author, one monk of Mount Athos explains:

> True theology is coming to know God. It comes down to the difference between assimilating and accumulating. It is far more important to assimilate knowledge of God than accumulate ideas from books. The Church needs theologians equipped with a spiritual life. It is the mind *and* the heart working together: one integrated whole. The whole person needs to approach God using *all* the faculties of human being.

Here is another possibility for confluence: eastern theological perspectives, shaping an epistemology in which the role of prayer is taken seriously, flowing into western consciousness and into western educational practice.

In the West, there *are* significant voices calling for a reuniting of prayer and the doing of theology. First, there has been renewed interest in recent years in historic western sources of spirituality that celebrate 'mystical knowing'. Particular attention has been given to works which represent developments from the thought of

Pseudo-Dionysius' *Mystical Theology.* For example, John of the Cross writes: 'Extraneous to its common experience and natural knowledge, the soul will have a very abundant and delightful divine sense and knowledge of all divine and human things' (Kavanaugh and Rodriguez, 1991: 414). However, such knowledge becomes 'dark' and inexpressible. As Matthew (1995: 130–1) puts it:

> We are capable of knowing at one level and not knowing at another: there is the knowledge of words, of images, of concept, of feeling, of presence . . . A person can know God more and be able to talk about God less . . . The mystics are familiar with depths of spirit which have their own mode of knowing, untranslatable on to more customary levels.

Studies of *The Cloud of Unknowing* attend to its apophaticism represented in its allusive maxim: 'He [God] may well be loved, but not thought' (Wolters, 1961: 60; Cooper, 1991).

Secondly, an increasing number of theologians in the West are recognizing the crucial contribution of spirituality. McIntosh (1998: 10), who seeks to offer a hermeneutic as a tool for the theological use of spirituality sources, makes clear the dilemma: 'Put as bluntly as possible, theology without spirituality becomes ever more methodologically refined but unable to know or speak of the very mysteries at the heart of Christianity, and spirituality without theology becomes rootless, easily hijacked by individualistic consumerism.' Rowan Williams (1979: 181) appeals: 'we must look at this area of reflection and interrogation that we call "spirituality" at least as much as we look at the systematic theology which is properly inseparable from it'. Andrew Louth (1983: 93) echoes such a call to theologians: 'Receptiveness, and attentiveness: these are qualities deepened and realized in prayer . . . this is something we need to cultivate, we need to learn.' In his study *Spirituality and Theology,* Sheldrake argues for the reunion of theology and spirituality in terms of the need for mutual critique: 'Spirituality without theology runs the danger of becoming private or interior. Theology, however, needs the corrective of spirituality to remind us that true knowledge of God concerns the heart as much as the intellect [in its Western sense]' (1998a: 32). Elsewhere (1999: 61, 63) he goes further and asks whether prayer and its practice are 'optional extras for a theologian to be kept in a separate compartment of life lest they compromise "objectivity?" Or are they important components of the theological life?' His own answer is:

spirituality is another way of knowing and learning. In fact, the key to good theology is prayer, understood as a relationship with the divine rather than simply devotions and techniques of meditation. Perhaps we may go further and affirm that true prayer is true theology and vice versa.

Macquarrie (1972: 71) rightly claims it is a question of theological method: 'when it comes to the deepest and most significant problems of theology, the method is that of meditation, letting the mind become immersed in the concepts, symbols, teachings, dogmas, stories of the Christian faith'. For Louth (2000: 16, 19), 'Knowledge comes by prayer ... contemplation makes theology possible'. Earlier, Merton (1972: 197–8) had called for the flowing together of these two streams:

> Contemplation, far from being opposed to theology, is in fact the normal perfection of theology. We must not separate intellectual study of divinely revealed truth and contemplative experience of that truth ... Unless they are united, there is no fervour, no life and no spiritual value in theology, no substance, no meaning and no sure orientation in the contemplative life.

Gutiérrez, writing from the painful context of seeking liberation amidst oppression, argues strongly for the primacy of the encounter with God:

> Spiritual experience is the terrain in which theological reflection takes root. Intellectual comprehension makes it possible to carry the experience of faith to a deeper level, but the experience always comes first ... a theology that is not located in the context of an experience of faith is in danger of turning into a kind of religious metaphysics or a wheel that turns in the air without making the cart advance.
>
> (1984: 35–8)

Yet, despite these calls, the confluence remains largely unexplored territory. In particular, very little has been written about what could be called a 'spirituality of education', integrating the practice of prayer within the process of learning. A rare exception is *Living in Praise:Worshipping and Knowing God*:

> We see knowing and praising God to be intrinsic to each other ... Our conclusion about the rationality of knowing and praising God is that in this movement not only is God known ... but also God enhances our rational powers. By knowing the reality of God we are changed by it, not only morally but also rationally. We are freed from the fixations and obsessions of reason ... and are gently opened to being knit into a reality

that is delightful as well as true. Then we realize that our very capacity to know and enjoy God has only been kept alive by the respect of God.

(Ford and Hardy, 2005: 142)

Such realization needs to find practical expression in theological education today.

Questions for reflection

✦ How do these findings resonate with your educational practice or with your experience as a learner?

✦ What strikes you most about them?

✦ To what extent do you find yourself agreeing or disagreeing with the reflections?

10

Rivers in the desert: formation, prayer and postmodern mission

O God, you are my God, I seek you, my soul thirsts for you;
My flesh faints for you, as in a dry and weary land where there is no water.
So I have looked upon you in the sanctuary . . .

(Ps. 63: 1, 2a)

Let anyone who is thirsty come . . . and drink.

(Jn 7: 37, 38)

Let justice roll down like waters, and righteousness like an ever-flowing stream.

(Amos 5: 24)

Findings

This chapter examines empirical evidence that illustrates a final theme that was identified as pivotal to ministerial formation: *formation is oriented towards mission in the world.* The function of prayer in mission, and the requisite skills needed for innovative and responsive evangelism within today's culture, can be summed up under four headings.

Prayer and mission strategy

As the Church finds itself in 'an alien land' and facing the challenge of engaging creatively with a fast-changing culture, the role of prayer in discernment becomes imperative.

One interviewee contrasted two approaches to a mission situation in her parish, working with a colleague of another denomination:

> His approach to beginning work in the area was very much one of going to hit them over the head with a Bible really. Whereas I think my

approach is very much about being a presence in such a community, making connections, walking alongside, and taking it from there – it's something about not taking God *to* people but helping them to discover that He's already there and I think that links quite strongly in with prayer. It involves, yes, getting involved, but also being able to take a step back and actually trying to be aware of where God is at work and praying for those people there.

She spoke of the discerning function of prayer in this context:

> It's about discerning and trying to find out where we are called to be, rather than where we think we might be called to be, or even where we would necessarily like to be. And that does come back, in various differ- ent ways, to prayer . . . It reminds me for some reason of the road to Emmaus story – it was in the context of a conversation with Christ (prayer?) that the true perspective was revealed. (a)

Prayer opportunities for enquirers and seekers

A developing evangelistic strategy can involve providing accessible, non-threatening experiences of Christian spirituality that attract people by their beauty and simplicity and provide inspiration in their spiritual search. A key skill here for clergy is how to design and lead such prayer exercises open to visitors and those of the fringe. An NSM working priest said:

> In this post-modern society you've got to be able to meet individual people where they are – there's no one model that fits everyone, in a way it possibly did in more modernist society . . . One skill we need is to be very adaptable – to be aware of a whole range of different approaches to prayer. (b)

He gave an example of an experimental venture:

> At a mini-fair this summer, we set up prayer stations – things like prayer- trees, pebbles in water, candles on a map of the world – to try to offer the full range of different ways to pray, to the community. People respond to different things in different ways. We were trying to raise the profile of the church on the estate and to reach people with Christian spirituality, to break down the possible perceptions they have of the Church, that we are a very rigid organization. We haven't seen any results in terms of numbers – I don't think we can measure it in attendance figures – it's about helping them on their journey. (b)

Other examples include welcoming enquirers to contemplative prayer walks (not advertised as such) which include Christian reflec- tions in the midst of creation, and developing various prayer exercises using the body and silence. There is a particular sensitivity here to the different way adults and children learn, and the way personality differences shape praying preferences. This approach is not without controversy, however, as one wary evangelical tutor stated:

> Putting experience of Christian spirituality before the unchurched . . . that's putting the cart before the horse, I would have thought . . . I don't for a moment believe that 'anything goes' – 'it's prayer to you so it must be real' – so there needs to be some sort of analytical ability in the light of Scripture. (k)

But a Catholic tutor is emphatic:

> What is needed is the ability to be articulate about prayer and its significance, to understand a variety of types of prayer and to tell others about them. The ordained need to be able to meet an interest in spirituality and make of it a desire to pray. (j)

A role for holy people in society

There is evidence that people today still expect clergy to be people of holiness and ready to pray with and for parishioners.

> One has had increasing awareness that one is perhaps performing a useful role in society . . . I can say without any embarrassment, when someone might tell me that their sister's got cancer, 'I'll remember you in my prayers'. I wouldn't have found that so easy to do a few years ago. In a sense they expect this of you – and it's part of the job really. (f)

This priest has discovered the importance of being known as a person of prayer, and within his village setting is once again opening up a sacred space for enquirers:

> Also I think the fact that one is saying the Office in church regularly, it means something to the village: 'Oh, he's going down there to pray.' I open up the church at Morning Prayer and leave it open all day till Evening Prayer. This tells people that prayer is something that goes on in the church on a regular basis – it's not just for Sundays. The church is not an historic pile – it is a functioning house of prayer. (f)

As clergy have lost over the centuries additional roles in society which were accrued to them, they have the opportunity to become specialists once again, and rediscover their fundamental vocation: to be, and to be known as, 'a man of God', 'a woman of prayer'. There is evidence that theological colleges and courses are beginning to recognize this ancient but contemporary vocation in the priesthood: 'In formation, I would expect an increasing awareness of the "job" of prayer . . . I think there should be more intentional development of prayer for students and more attention to the task of leading others and teaching them to pray' (j). Certainly, a wide cross-section of the sample echoes this conviction: 'My work *is* prayer. And there is a deepening sense that . . . it's important that I am teaching others to pray – gifting others, enabling others to pray. Yes, prayer *is* mission' (d).

Prayer as empowering mission

There is evidence that clergy are finding prayer to be energizing and empowering, both prayer that sustains them throughout the day of ministry and also reflective or silent prayer where there is opportunity to find renewal. Times apart from people become essential for times engaging with people:

> It's only recently that I am beginning to find out more about the value of silence . . . I think initially I felt this was something I felt I needed – that sounds quite selfish – but actually, when I have honoured that desire I have been better able to serve . . . that stillness seems to breathe life into everything else that is going on. It's God's way of equipping me, to become his tool. (d)

A tutor links the search for courage with the need for discernment:

> I think we need tremendous courage at the moment . . . Sticking at a discipline of prayer is important, because mission is about having your head knocked against a brick wall, and refusing to budge at certain points, while being infinitely flexible in others . . . it is about the heart, having the disciplines of the heart and finding the courage to be daring, resolute, and to discern. (m)

Reflections

In the prophets, the hope of renewal and of new beginnings is often depicted by the image of water flowing amongst desert sands. Isaiah alludes in this image to humanity's deep thirst or longing for God (Is. 41: 17–18). Divine grace is envisioned as refreshing streams coursing through an arid landscape. The prophet Ezekiel visualizes renewal in terms of an ever-deepening river that issues from the sacred space of the temple. He is emphatic that it is a river of prayer and worship that makes a difference, evidenced in trees flourishing on the riverbank: 'they will bear fresh fruit every month, because the water for them flows from the sanctuary' (Ez. 47: 12). Such a river brings renewal not only to the desert but even to the waste places of the earth, symbolized in the Dead Sea's coming back to vitality. The river is hidden no longer: it emerges to make a difference to the very earth and give a glimpse of paradise restored.

This primordial image of thirst symbolizes contemporary culture very powerfully. Today's clergy face a *kairos* moment in mission: the empirical research discovered that clergy believe that the use of spirituality in outreach opens up profound new opportunities to lead enquirers forward in their spiritual search, through exposing them to spiritual experiences such as the Christian use of silence, stillness and meditation. This has become possible because of significant shifts taking place in British culture; equipping the clergy for these new opportunities becomes an urgent task of their ministerial formation.

The present context of mission: from secularization to 'a spiritual age'
Sociological perspectives on today's culture

Ever since Bryan Wilson's seminal *Religion in Secular Society* (1966), sociologists have used the concept of secularization to make sense of what is happening in British society. He defined this as 'the process whereby religious thinking, practice and institutions lose social significance' (1966: 14). Wilson's predictions about the decline of religious practice linked to institutions seem to have been fulfilled, but religious thinking and private religious practice are more ambiguous areas to interpret. Indeed, the very concept of secularization has been vigorously debated by sociologists over recent years, questioning whether this is an inevitable process. Berger himself, a key proponent of the idea, now talks (2000) of desecularization: in terms of describing or symbolizing the spiritual landscape, the 'sacred canopy' of overarching religious provision has been replaced by the spiritual marketplace characterized by religious pluralism. Brown and Davie represent different perspectives on this process of change. In his *Death of Christian Britain*, Callum Brown (2000: 272) concludes a pessimistic view of church life maintaining: 'the Britain of the new millennium is showing the world how religion as we have known it can die'. Grace Davie (2000) is more nuanced, attending not only to statistical decline but also to the unwritten story of less institutional indicators of religious practice, such as feelings, experience and numinous religious beliefs which, for her, 'represent considerable persistence in some aspects of religious life'. In *Religion in Britain since 1945*, she points out that religion has become a leisure pursuit competing alongside sport and shopping since the advent of Sunday trading. She claims (1994: 198): 'Religious life . . . is not so much disappearing as mutating, for the sacred undoubtedly persists and will continue to do so, but in forms that may be very different from those which have gone before.'

Partridge (2004) has sought to describe the emergence of alternative and 'new age' spiritualities in terms of 'the re-enchantment of the West'. Heelas and Woodhead (2005) ask whether in fact a sacralization is taking place in the West with the increasing popularity of subjective forms of spirituality. They advocate a 'subjectivization thesis' identifying a turn within the culture away from forms of religion marked by traditional dutiful sources of significance towards forms of spirituality which resource inner subjective life. Such a perspective has significance for contemporary missiology, as we shall see.

Philosophical perspectives on today's culture
'Postmodernism' is a slippery concept, but reflects something of what is happening philosophically in the shifts now taking place in Western culture, since an apparent fading away of the confidences of modernist and post-enlightenment society. It asks radical questions about the nature of language, truth, identity and values. Negatively, it implies a complete marginalization of institutions like the Church, and a cavalier attitude to history, celebrating discontinuities rather than continuities. Negatively, too, it encourages the privatization of religion, dismissing the idea that there can be any 'public truth': religious 'truth' is assigned to the private sphere of the individual. But postmodernist writers *can* assist an evaluation of the Church's role in society. First, postmodernism encourages creativity, innovation, experimentation and evolution of new forms, prompting exploration of new ways of being Church. Secondly, postmodernism exposes the moral and spiritual vacuum at the heart of British society. Tracy (1995: 227) puts it thus: 'postmodern thinkers often seem, at best, ethically underdeveloped . . . the postmoderns sometimes seem more determined by *ennui* than by ethics'. A sense of spiritual bankruptcy cries out for an authentic experience of God: fragmentation not only of society but also of the individual points to the need to make available a uniting and integrative kind of spirituality. Thirdly,

postmodernism's celebration of diversity and difference opens up for the Church an opportunity to recover a confidence in its capacity for evangelistic dialogue in the marketplace of ideas. Fourthly, in the face of materialistic, consumerist ways of living the Church is challenged afresh to pioneer lifestyles that are different, alternative, countercultural in this present age (Hauerwas and Willimon, 1989 and 1996; Budde and Brimlow, 2000). Fifthly, postmodernism's questioning of the all-sufficiency of the Enlightenment's rationalistic approach to knowledge affords the Church the opportunity to explore with searchers a mystical, non-rational, way of knowing, arising from the experience of prayer.[1]

Theological perspectives on today's culture
In *The Gospel in a Pluralist Society*, Newbigin (1989) rejects both the seductive power of the idea of pluralism and what he calls the disastrous dualism of culture/gospel: for him Christianity will always be culturally embodied and incarnate, requiring Christians to have a sharp discerning approach to the surrounding culture. But recent writers have wanted to go beyond the idea of religious pluralism as the most accurate categorization of British society and talk of 'a spiritual age'. Several recent independent pieces of research have uncovered not only a marked increase in people reporting frequency of spiritual experiences, but also their preparedness to sample expressions of Christian spirituality as a step on a journey of discovery: the BBC's Soul of Britain Survey 2000 and the diocese of Coventry's 'Beyond the Fringe' 2003 (Croft, Frost et al., 2005); see also Heelas and Woodhead (2005), reporting on Lancaster University's Kendal Project 2001. One survey in 2000 discovered that while many people in the sample had tried a range of spiritual experiences, it was prayer that was most valued (Barley, 2006: 7).

The report *Mission-shaped Church* (Archbishops' Council, 2004) calls on the clergy and Christian leaders not only to open up innovative entry points into the Christian community where enquirers can encounter authentic spirituality, but also to develop these in the community beyond the confines of the church. See also Croft, Dalpra and Lings (2006) and the website *www.freshexpressions.org.uk*.

---

[1] Cf. the links between postmodernism and apophaticism in D. Turner (1995). He is wary, however, of 'experientialism', focusing on the dialectical role of apophaticism in relation to theology.

A number of writers draw attention to the need to develop a new apologetics which includes what could be called 'a turn to personal experience'. Grenz, writing from the Evangelical tradition, puts it thus:

> Experience and interpretive concepts are reciprocally related. Our concepts facilitate our understanding of the experiences we have in life, and our experience shapes the interpretive concepts we employ to speak about our lives . . . Propositions can thus be said to have a second-order importance.
>
> (1996: 170–1)

He suggests that there is closer attention paid to the 'transformative religious experience'. In similar vein Vanhoozer calls for the embodiment of Christian claims in religious practices – which might include patterns of praying:

> We have learned from the postmoderns that knowledge is not disembodied. On this point, postmodernity and incarnational Christian faith are agreed. What is needed, therefore, is a translation of the Gospel that goes beyond conveying propositions – a translation that would *concretize* the Gospel in individual and communal shapes of living. Proclamations of the Gospel must be accompanied by performances that embody in new situations the wisdom and love of God embodied in the cross.
>
> (2003: 24)

Matthews (2000: 20–1) puts it succinctly: 'The integrity of the evangelistic work of the Church requires a retrieval of the mystical tradition . . . the secular world is still fascinated by a spirituality of mystery.'

The present challenge: from confrontation to engagement
In his magisterial study *Transforming Mission*, Bosch (1991: 519) concludes: 'The mission of the church needs constantly to be renewed and re-conceived.' Indeed, the world has moved on since he wrote in 1991; his book has no reference to the role of prayer or spirituality in mission. Harvey (1999: 93) cautions: 'Christendom is indeed a hard habit to break . . . The body of Christ, with precious few exceptions, continues to yearn nostalgically for the *modus vivendi* that characterized the sixteen centuries of Christendom.'

Drane (2005: 7) develops a missiology in reference to the new generation of spiritual searchers experimenting with expressions of spirituality beyond the confines of the Church. He observes: 'What is needed is not a Christendom model of confrontational denunciation, but a biblical model of cross-cultural mission, which values people as individuals made in God's image.' Clergy hoping to develop new patterns of engagement with seekers might look again to Paul's approach with the Athenians in Acts 17, a cultural situation with parallels with our own time in its diversity of religious and spiritual options available. It suggests a twofold challenge which can be explored through the river metaphor:

The first challenge is to understand the nature of the contemporary desert. Paul records: 'I went through the city and looked carefully at the objects of your worship' (Acts 17: 23). He was attentive to the spiritual landscape of the city. Clergy pioneering new patterns of mission through the use of spirituality need to understand the characteristics of the spiritual desert through which the river of prayer runs. Deserts vary greatly, from hot, parched subtropical wastes to cold winter deserts and icy polar wildernesses. There is an acute need to study and understand the terrain of today's context, to observe its topography and defining features. This involves discernment and close listening to people, as the empirical research revealed. In exploring the way forward in using spirituality in evangelism, clergy must understand the nature of people's spiritual thirst and the questions that they are asking.

The second challenge concerns opening up the river of prayer to seekers. In the midst of his dialogue with the Athenians, Paul uses accessible language. He speaks in concepts that make sense to his audience, with which they can easily identify. He can do this because first he has listened and has learnt the language, as it were, of the locals. An emerging theme in the present empirical data was that clergy need to learn again how to make connections with the culture. Some are opening up a diversity of entry points and pathways which enable searchers to make a journey towards faith via spiritual experiences. The approach is, initially at least, experiential: affording opportunities for enquirers to experience, first hand, aspects of prayer through silence, music, images and guided meditation, and thus to offer glimpses of the transcendent. Such an approach might explore themes which resonate with the contemporary thirst, including healing/wholeness, reconciliation, spiritual journey and care for the planet. See, for example, the evangelistic resource by Frost (2002) *Essence: an Exploration of Contemporary Spirituality which*

Looks towards a Lifestyle Integrating Body, Mind and Spirit. This calls for clergy to clear 'sacred spaces' along a crowded riverbank where people can come and find refreshment; to create drinking places along the river of prayer. Perhaps it is significant that the mission to Europe began at a riverbank of prayer which became a place of dialogue and conversion (Acts 16: 18). As Middleton and Walsh (1995) remind us, contemporary mission in a postmodern context must be characterized by deep humility. In the face of postmodern doubt about the possibilities of knowing the truth, which is seen as socially constructed, they commend what they call a 'sojourning epistemology': 'We must totally abandon any lingering aspirations of epistemological arrival, of having finally got it right . . . All knowing is provisional, open to correction, redirection and deepening.'

The present opportunity of mission: two complementary approaches

There are two major dimensions to an approach to mission engaging with the current thirst for spirituality, and clergy need to attend to both to ensure a healthy balance in evangelization.

The first approach emphasizes personal spirituality: attentiveness to the needs of the individual and to the key life issues that they face – identified by the recent research as concern for destiny/afterlife, purpose, the universe's origins, the spiritual realm, the existence and presence of God and the question of suffering, summarized in Hollinghurst, Richmond and Whitehead (2006). In their pastoral and evangelistic ministry, clergy will need to engage patiently one-to-one with searchers. As they seek to teach people to pray and lead them into encounter with God through the experience of prayer, they will need to respect the unique and personal needs and aspirations of each enquirer.

The second approach enables prophetic spirituality. Ministerial formation itself must be located within the corporate and communal setting so that spiritual formation is seen in ecclesial as well as individual terms in the context of the wider world. Similarly, clergy will seek both to lead enquirers from individualism to the experience of the community of the Church and to reveal in their lifestyle and actions the cutting edge of prophetic spirituality – to be able to speak a godly critique both to the world and to the enquirer. There is a need not only to understand the culture and be earthed incarnationally *within* it – inculturating evangelistic approaches – it is also necessary to uphold the integrity of the Christian witness by speaking *against* the culture, especially against its gods of consumerism and militarism. Wallis (1994: 38, 47) laments and affirms: 'Personal piety has become an end in itself instead of the energy for social justice ... Prophetic spirituality will always fundamentally challenge the system at its roots and offer genuine alternatives based on values from our truest religious, cultural and political traditions.'

Duraisingh (1992: 39) highlights the importance of locating ministerial formation within this kind of perspective, calling for:

> an *empowering-others-for-mission* model that arises out of an ideological option for, participation in and learning from the struggles and hopes of the poor and the marginalized. It is out of such a process of formation that comes the capacity, so badly needed today, to envision a new social order, the alternative, and even the impossible.

An indispensable dimension of ministerial formation must be to equip clergy with spiritual resources, not only to help them make sense of their own ministry, but also to enable them to engage seriously with the spiritual thirst increasingly evident in their communities (Egan, 2001).

Questions for reflection

✦ How do these findings resonate with your educational practice or with your experience as a learner?

✦ What strikes you most about them?

✦ To what extent do you find yourself agreeing or disagreeing with the reflections?

Part III
Possibilities for the Future

11

Conclusion: benefits of the formation paradigm and proposals for renewed practice

Introduction

This concluding chapter aims to identify recommendations for changed practice in respect to the role of spirituality and prayer in theological education. The Church of England, with its partner churches, is at a critical and decisive moment as it seeks, within the emerging regional training partnerships, to redesign the theological curriculum and reshape patterns of training. This is a *kairos* moment of great opportunity for the Church, and these recommendations are addressed primarily to those responsible for the renewal of ordination training.[1]

Benefits and dangers of formation paradigm

First, we must survey the benefits and limits of the formation paradigm and summarize the role of prayer in it. What difference does the formation paradigm make? What are the limitations of formation language, as mentioned in the interviews?

Formation understood as a lifelong process of inner transformation

A significant majority of the sample found the language of formation enriched their understanding of the process of preparing for ordination, seeing formation as a continuing lifelong process of inner change. An evangelical could say: 'I think formation is a good word.

---

[1] While the recommendations are framed in Anglican terminology, it is hoped that they will be of relevance to ecumenical partners and the wider Church.

It reminds us that we're not there yet – there's a constant formation in us. It reminds us that we constantly wear L-plates!' (e)

Those who appreciated the language of formation saw it in terms of as a dynamic process of inner transformation related to the *telos* of becoming more like Christ for the purpose of pastoral ministry. Several wished to emphasize formation as a divine work, two tutors speaking of the Orthodox concept of *theosis* in this regard, while others highlighted the role of the Holy Spirit. One put it succinctly: 'Something deep is happening' (d). Significantly, the formation paradigm can be appreciated by a diversity of traditions. It is not confined to the catholic tradition from which it sprung. An evangelical put it thus:

> the formation is going on at the deepest level . . . Theologically, you'd want to say that the Holy Spirit is the agent through which the change is happening. I think He uses prayer in that process. As we pray we're inviting the Holy Spirit to be doing that work of formation, change, within us, to be guiding that process. He's key to the whole thing! (e)

A Catholic concurred: 'During the process of formation, you actually make yourself more aware of the Holy Spirit and you make yourself more accessible to the Holy Spirit' (f).

Formation contrasted with training

Those who valued the formation language highlighted the limitations of training terminology, which was described several times as a 'mind-set' which did not seem to be so attentive to the process of inner change but rather viewed the minister as a functionary. Training language

> had the unfortunate implication of 'right, that's it, you're done – tick the box and you're off'. And it did feel very much like that initially. In a structure full of modules to be covered and lists of things to have studied, it felt very much task-orientated. (a)

Another put it thus: 'The language of formation is very helpful. Training to me is about tasks – "can you do this? Can you do that?" Formation recognizes that this is a journey and also that bad experiences can be formative too' (d). One person exemplified the attention to inner change:

> I find it helpful because it's more than just training – you are, with God's guidance, in fact going through a process of change – it may, in fact, be more of an inner change than an outward one. By inner change I mean

that one is more conscious of the presence of God in one's everyday life.
(f)

The limitations of formation language

Two interviewees, from the evangelical tradition, were very cautious about the formation paradigm. One thought it elitist:

> I find formation language aggravating, especially phrases like 'the spiritual formation of lay people' – it's arrogant of ordained people to imply that lay people are not adequately spiritually formed. If it's used of clergy formation it's fine, but I struggle with the idea that clergy need forming any more than other people – it sounds too distinctive, elitist even. In the Anglican Church we mistake leadership for spiritual superiority . . . (g)

Another critic of formation found the formation model alien and imposed:

> It's perceived as Min Div [Ministry Division] language – it's not conceived as traditional evangelical language. Formation is not a term I was brought up with. It goes, in my mind, with phrases like 'spiritual director' and 'rule of life' and all those other sort of phrases that are not from my particular background, that all need interpretation. It all seems slightly alien . . . the impression it conveys is that it's too human-centred a process, it's somehow what a college or a faculty or some other Christians can do for their fellows. (k)

A Catholic staff member recognized that standing alone it might convey individualism: 'the danger is that it could become self-centred, too exclusively about me and my gifts' (j). Certainly, several clergy were keen to emphasize the role of others in their formation, both within the college/course community and within the parish.

Formation model linked with attentiveness to prayer and growth

Where the formation paradigm is in use, there seems to be a greater appreciation of the creative functions of prayer and especially the role of silent reflective prayer. Three correlations were noted in the data.

First, where the formation language is welcomed, people are more articulate about the value of prayer within the learning process. As one put it: 'You can't separate prayer out from the process. It's the gateway to God's hand in shaping you, to open up the channel for this to take place' (b).

Secondly, those who were critical of formation also had less developed understanding of the diversity of prayer. Thus one of the critics of formation also said: 'Prayer is, by definition, talking to God, primarily . . . I don't see in Scripture the idea of prayer as a space for reflection. When I look at Scripture and prayer, that's not there. I wouldn't understand listening under the heading of "prayer"' (k). This is not just a question of semantics, but uncovers widely differing understandings of prayer. Staff from colleges which did not use the formation paradigm in their public documents revealed a lack of clarity about the wider functions and potentialities of prayer. A critic of formation could make this response in answer to the question 'How do you expect the practice of prayer to contribute to this process of personal change?'

> I'm not sure what the question's getting at . . . It's not the mechanism of prayer, as such, that does that, but keeping in touch with the Lord. It's a mixture of prayer, and reading His Word, and hearing His Word to us, – that's even more important than talking to Him. (k)

Thirdly, use of the formation paradigm in colleges and courses also correlated positively with more explicit, self-conscious attention to issues of personal growth; negatively, a minister from a college where the formation paradigm was not used at all implied an inattention to the relationship between personality and prayer, for in her experience 'Colleges often treat people as all the same – we must understand that we need opportunities to explore what is *your* best way of praying, for you personally' (g).

From the evidence in this sample, the use of the formation paradigm correlates with an unequivocal attention both to a key role for reflective prayer and to explicit mention of issues of personal development. One minister could see a vivid and unmistakable difference of approach when formation was introduced:

> I think they actually did quite a big U turn whilst I was at college. It was very 'training' orientated language when I arrived . . . A new Pastoral Studies tutor did a fantastic job of broadening the picture and actually saying 'this is about formation – it is not about training' . . . By the time I left college, it felt much more as if we were trying to engage with the process of formation rather than merely tick off a list of things we had to do before we left. (a)

These findings resonate with research recently undertaken by the Carnegie Foundation among a range of US seminaries; see Foster, Dahill et al. (2006: 289).

Types of prayer promoting formation

It was significant that all prayer-types identified in Urban Holmes's (1980) Circle of Sensibility were represented in this small sample of ministers. Holmes proposes two major axes or inclinations in prayer. The first axis is between a tendency in prayer towards the intellect, where prayer is characterized as thinking through concepts, and a tendency in prayer towards the affections, prayer having a higher emotional content. A second axis is between the *apophatic* and the *kataphatic*, the former representing the *via negativa* and moving towards the unknowability and hiddenness of God, the latter representing the *via affirmativa* celebrating the revelation of God.

These two axes create a framework for identifying prayer-types, four quadrants suggesting a fourfold typology of prayer:

1. speculative/kataphatic spirituality, where prayer is characterized by conceptual thinking and reasoning, often attending to the written word of scripture and of doctrinal writers; more head than heart and more revealed than hidden;
2. affective/kataphatic prayer which gives room for the expression of feelings and celebrates the immanence and closeness of God. Such prayer can include a focus on the quest of personal renewal and holiness;
3. affective/apophatic prayer having an emphasis on listening to God, rather than speaking to God, and enjoyed by people who are often introspective, contemplative and intuitive;
4. speculative/apophatic prayer is marked by an outward focus and a commitment to working for peace and justice and building the Kingdom. Such prophetic prayer encompasses both action and the ability to grapple with issues; it includes 'contemplatives in action'.

Holmes's typology is being widely used as a tool for gauging different types of prayer (Boa, 2001: 469; Sager, 1990: 3), though it incorporates only two sets of polarities. Others not considered in this model are solitude/community; action/stillness (being/doing); or engagement/withdrawal (the desert and the city). Nevertheless, Holmes provides a basic map where we can locate contrasting types of prayer (see figure 11.1). Thus a wide range of prayer-practices was found to advance formation.

MIND TO KNOW GOD	SPECULATIVE
Prayer linked with concern for the community Commitment to intercession Prayer fires engagement with ministry Examples in sample: Eucharist when seen in dynamic terms Daily Office related to demands of ministry 'Continuous prayer' in the heart of ministry (a) and (c)	Prayer linked with intellectual thought Focus on Scripture: the Word Prayer seeking insight Examples in sample: Prayer at computer amd desk Meditation as 'driving home scripture' Prayer linked with theological reflection (e) and (f)
APOPHATIC	**KATAPHATIC**
THE MYSTERY OF GOD	**THE REVEALED GOD**
Prayer seeking union with God Mystical prayer & contemplation Attention to the inner life Examples in sample: Search for stillness and silence Search for solitude Praying with the saints (b) (d)	Prayer & personal renewal A place for expressing feelings in prayer Prayer making sense of experience Examples in sample: Creativity and the arts in prayer Charismatic prayer Praying with a healing function (g)
HEART TO SENSE GOD	AFFECTIVE

Figure 11.1 Mapping of research findings within Holmes's typology

In summary, four major functions of prayer in formation were identified, which together make a dynamic which can rightly be called spiritual formation:

1. Creative function: prayer as the seedbed of theology; prayer energizing mission; prayer enabling the discernment of new mission strategies, including innovative and risky approaches in evangelism; spirituality as a doorway or entry point into the Church for enquirers and seekers.
2. Reflective function: enabling the doing of theology, enabling a space where issues of ministry can be wrestled with and thought through; as one noted: 'Prayer gives that stillness to reflect on what's happening. It's hard to find the words to describe it – the two have to be together, the formation is *in* the prayer, it's in the reflection' (c).
3. Restorative function: prayer enabling a space for refreshment and renewal amidst the pressures of ministry; bringing one's fragility

and woundedness before God, receiving a sense of healing into stressful and bruising days, and a sense of personal affirmation: 'the silence rejuvenates my spirit' (g).

4. Integrative function: enabling a dynamic relationship between intellectual thinking and reflective prayer; giving a space where a minister can unite person and role in the search for a ministerial identity; enabling an interplay between different aspects of forma-tion, which can be represented diagrammatically (see figure 11.2).

The research thus revealed a variety of factors that influence the practice of prayer both in the training institution and in the parish. These include the context of prayer, the personality of the pray-er and the degree of openness to different traditions. The very under-standing of prayer itself is influential, and narrower views of prayer correlated with limited opportunities to experiment. But the single most repeated factor that impeded spiritual formation was that of lack of time, both in the curriculum and in ministry.

Types of formation viewed separately

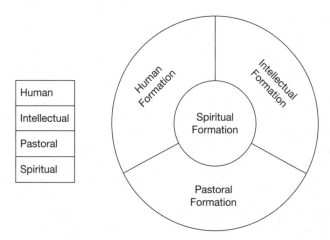

The types of formation seen in dynamic interrelationship, spiritual formation playing an integrative role.

Figure 11.2 Interplay between aspects of formation

Recommendations for theological educators involved in initial ministerial education (IME)

Articulate a vision for a 'spirituality of education'

As each emerging regional training partnership (RTP) seeks now to develop its curriculum for theological education, it should underpin this with an explicit statement of its educational philosophy, making as clear as possible how it envisages the role of spirituality and prayer in the formational process. This will require discussion and debate between educators which will be an invaluable opportunity to move on from current shallow views of spirituality in training (which often see prayer as either a pious preface to study or optional bolt-on/add-on) towards a more dynamic understanding of spiritual formation. The newly written learning outcomes on spirituality will be a useful starting point, even though they do not go far enough:

> At selection candidates should show evidence of a commitment to a spiritual discipline, involving individual and corporate prayer and worship. Their spiritual practice should be such as to sustain and energize them in their daily lives . . . At completion of IME candidates should . . . be rooted in a life of prayer shaped faithfully within the expectations of public ministry, corporate and personal worship and devotion.
>
> (Archbishops' Council, 2006: 69)

Such a condensed statement needs to be supplemented by an inspiring and energizing vision of the indispensable role of prayer in the very doing of theology. It would be a missed opportunity if RTPs fail to grasp this nettle and the chance to move beyond a vague acknowledgment of importance of prayer towards statements making more explicit the significant links between prayer and the doing of theology. This is an opportunity to rediscover how spiritual formation impacts both on how people teach and on how people learn: its crucial role in both epistemology and pedagogy.

One theme that demands special attention by educators has recurred throughout both the documentary and empirical research: the integrative function of spiritual formation and prayer. This has become an especially urgent issue because those currently rewriting the theological curriculum are facing again the danger of its fragmentation into separate areas of study. The evidence of this research points to how spiritual formation can heal and restore a number of potential dichotomies and divorces: the divide between the head and the heart, between affective and academic learning; the divide between the classroom and the chapel, between study and prayer, between *scientia* and *theoria*; between contemplation and action, withdrawal and engagement, between outward ministry and inner life or interiority.

In working out their educational philosophy, educators are challenged to discover how spirituality can infuse, unite and energize the whole process of ministerial formation, bringing into a creative organic relationship the domains of intellectual, human and pastoral formation. Policy documents now being prepared in the RTPs should address such questions as: What policy for spiritual formation is in place? What is our understanding of spiritual formation and what models do we find most helpful? By what means will spiritual formation be promoted? Will it be taught or caught? Thus, the present research invites educators to work out how spiritual formation strengthens the intentionality of the whole formation process, and how prayer becomes the very matrix, rather than appendix, of ministerial formation. Some US books and articles on the philosophy and spirituality of education may assist this process (see, for example, Astley, 1994; Jones, 2005). Also relevant to the task of developing a philosophy of education which takes account of spirituality is the debate in schools about the character of 'spiritual education' (Carr, 1995; Lewis, 2000).

One symbol that may evoke and stimulate theological reflection on the unity of thinking and praying is the biblical symbol of the heart. As *The Catechism of the Catholic Church* reminds us,

> according to Scripture, it is the *heart* that prays ... The heart is the dwelling-place where I am, where I live; according to the Semitic or biblical expression, the heart is the place 'to which I withdraw.' The heart is our hidden centre ... the place of encounter, because as image of God we live in relation.
>
> (Catholic Church, 1994: 545)

Moreover, according to the Hebraic tradition, the heart is the centre of the human, uniting the intellectual, emotional and volitional functions of the person (Wolff, 1974). It stands as a potent symbol of the inner life that is embodied and incarnate. Explorations in a spirituality of education will need to bring together Christian insights into epistemology and anthropology. The 'heart' image could well help to open up a much needed dialogue between eastern and western Christian perspectives on prayer and education (see above, chapter 9). As Ware (2000: 62) reminds us, in Orthodox theology the heart signifies the deep self; it is the seat of wisdom and understanding, the place where our moral decisions are made, the inner shrine in which we experience divine grace and the indwelling of the Holy Trinity. It indicates the human person as a 'spiritual subject,' created in God's image and likeness.

The image has resonances with contemporary attempts to develop a spirituality of education (see, for example, Apps, 1996; Glazer, 1999; Moore, 1998; cf. below on 'theology by heart').

Explore silence/reflective prayer as a discipline for deep learning

Many institutions prepare induction packs for new students which identify requisite study skills to be developed and disciplines of reading, writing and research. Those being prepared for theological students should make explicit the practices which will heal the divide between private study and prayer and include reflective prayer in the 'tool kit' of learning. IME learners should also be encouraged and taught to include times of reflective prayer in midst of study, by programmes of induction at the start of theological training which include attention to the role of reflective prayer in cognition, enabling a deeper kind of knowing identified above. This may include renewed attention to the role of *lectio* or prayerful reading of texts.

Particular guidance should be offered in developing the skills of contemplation. As several interviewees testified, familiarity with such a creative use of silence is either ignored or taken for granted in colleges and courses alike. This typical comment was noted:

> It was assumed you already knew all about praying, like the 6.45 am meditation – you weren't told this is the way to do it. You could say that by the time somebody gets to theological college they should know something about it anyway, but that is an assumption that shouldn't always necessarily be made, whether you're an older student or younger candidate . . . What we need is an introduction to prayer, not assuming people already know all about it. (f)

Contemplation itself may prove to be a useful concept with which to work, as it derives from the Latin *templum* as a temple or open space for observation. This resonates with the idea of the sanctuary within (Jamison, 2006). Working with the metaphor of looking, it invites the learner to seek insight and vision, to glimpse new possibilities, by attentiveness, looking deeper, going beneath the surface and widening perspectives. As Louth (2004) has recently stated, this is the very purpose of the university, but pressures to produce 'results' push the educational institution towards a consumerist model of education where 'the principle of leisure to contemplate is not only not conceded, it is no longer even understood'. It becomes all the more important, then, for theological institutions prophetically to model a different way where silence and recollection are acknowledged as key values in the learning process. The challenge is to nurture contemplative learners, exploring silence as a discipline for 'deep learning' (Hopkins-Powell, 2007).

Reunite prayer and theology through approaches to theological reflection explicitly incorporating the practice of reflective prayer

Theological reflection was identified in the research as a powerful means of reintegrating prayer and study. It can reclaim prayer as the seedbed of theology only if the practice of prayer is woven into the very process and not considered only as a pious supplement to serious study. Few western approaches to theological reflection in fact explicitly explore the role of prayer: it is not mentioned in the index, for example, of such standard textbooks as Bevans's *Models of Contextual Theology* (2002), nor is the practice of prayer mentioned in reference to models of education for ministry in van der Ven's *Education for Reflective Ministry* (1998b). Green (1990: 140) does give examples of how prayer can be incorporated in the reflective process, but writers such as Ballard and Pritchard (2006: 183) talk of spirituality in terms of forms of discipleship without attending greatly to the actual practice of prayer. They do acknowledge that what matters is 'that the individual has both a measure of self-awareness and also a knowledge of the riches of Christian spiritual traditions, which enable him or her to make the necessary connections'. Graham, Walton and Ward (2005) identify as one method of theological reflection what they call 'theology by heart', with 'the interior life' generating theological reflection through the practice of writing, but again there is no explicit exploration of the kinds of reflective prayer, identified in the present research, that actually facilitate this process. It might prove fruitful to learn again from base ecclesial communities where prayer is more explicitly integrated into the whole process of theological reflection (Marins, 1989). Renewed attention should be given to the *praxis* model where Christ's own ministry exemplifies a movement between time apart and the demands of ministry. One way prayer practices can be introduced into the classroom is precisely through corporate exercises in theological reflection.

Despite significant efforts to develop skills of theological reflection, especially in regional courses, its poor practice among the newly ordained has prompted the authors of one recent study to conclude 'methods and practices of theological reflection offered in theological education may need to be radically reconsidered' (Pattison, Thompson and Green, 2003: 119). Certainly, the present research reveals the urgent need for training ordinands in skills of discernment which integrate reflective prayer.

This resonates, of course, with the concept, in several disciplines and professions, of the reflective practitioner (Schön, 1988). It also resonates with researches by both cognitive psychologists and philosophers of education. Claxton (1994; 1997), for example, distinguishes between two modes of knowing: 'd-mode' mental activity, involved in rational, conscious and intellectual thinking, and slow ways of knowing: the more non-rational, less linear processes of what he calls the 'undermind'. He argues that western educational practice favours the 'd-mode' activity and that the use of the 'undermind' should be nurtured:

> D-mode must be developed and refined, but so must be the powers of intuition and imagination, of careful, non-verbal observation, of listening to the body, of detecting (without harvesting them too quickly) small seeds of insight . . . If they were more aware of both the possibility and the value of doing so, teachers would be able to find a host of opportunities to vary more widely the learning modes which their lessons encouraged or demanded.
>
> (Claxton, 1997: 12)

Moon (1999), following Entwistle (1996), distinguishes between deep approaches to learning and surface approaches. Deep approaches are characterized by the process of reflection and the relating of material studied to the learner's previous experience and knowledge; surface learning is marked by a failure to make connections between pieces of knowledge so they remain disjointed and unrelated. He appeals for practices that encourage the process of reflection in the classroom and study. Such writers build on the work on Mezirow (1981 and 1991) who developed the concept of transformative learning. For Mezirow the practice of reflection, facilitating the revising of perspectives and meaning, is the crucial catalyst that enables a transformation in consciousness and understanding (cf. Jarvis, 2004). Such writings call out for a dialogue between advocates of transformational education and the practice of ministerial formation, where the theme of transformation is a such key element (see above, chapter 7).

Open up spaces in the curriculum and in teaching for both experience and experimentation in prayer

A recurrent call among the interviewees in the present research was for an exploration of spirituality that is experiential as well as academic. The following is typical:

> In terms of actually looking at different ways of praying, there was very little input at all other than the spirituality course (a compulsory module) which looked at different spiritual traditions, from Ignatius to the Desert Fathers, but it was more of an academic course rather than filtering down into the actuality of prayer-life on a more experiential level. I think that theological colleges and courses often seem to shy away from the experiential aspect of prayer. They very much have their targets in mind, which are often academic or practical, and so prayer is addressed as a corporate rhythm, as an academic historical module to be studied, but very rarely as something experiential to be reflected upon and engaged with. They almost seem afraid to engage in a course which actually focuses on enabling different approaches to prayer. There was never any forum for someone to come in and talk about their experiences of different traditions of prayer. Such 'touchy-feely' things were left to individuals to discuss with their spiritual directors but, to my mind, prayer is too much of an important thing for those overseeing formation to simply trust that someone will be sorting it out somewhere else . . . I do actually think that they need people to start saying, for example, 'what *is* the Ignatian tradition?' Not just looking at it from a historical point of view and writing an essay on it, but actually engaging with what that approach is all about in an experiential way. (a)

Pressures on the curriculum entail filling the 'space of learning', even cramming students with information or data. An evangelical student commented, as we noted:

> My biggest critique of the college is that there is a very strong emphasis on the academic and I think the danger with that is that you spend your energies and attentions on the academic side of things. My constant struggle was to redress the balance, with prayer and reflection and contemplation. I think the danger is getting over-busy with the work, that the time of prayer – that side of your development – can be squeezed out. (e)

In the research, the single most repeated factor sidelining the role of prayer was that of time. Referring to parish ministry, interviewees spoke of the 'rush of the day', life as 'frenetic' and even of 'running around like a headless chicken'. Referring to college or course, similar expressions were used to describe the intensity of the workload and the danger of prayer becoming marginal or 'squeezed out'. One tutor referred to more time for prayer as 'what one might want in one's dreamworld' (k).

The challenge is for educators to take the risk of opening up a reflective space, where both dialogue about spiritual experience and prayer exercises themselves can take place. This does not have to stand in opposition to traditional teaching methods or to the scholarly study of spiritual or mystical texts. Rather, it represents an attempt to enable truths to be perceived at deeper levels. The opening up of a sacred space in teaching conveys the sense of both making time for shared reflection and also establishing a climate or educational ecology where sharing at a deeper level becomes possible. As Moon (1999: 166), writing from a secular standpoint, puts it:

> Not only is separate time needed for specific activities of reflection, but time is needed for more interaction within periods of teaching or lectures. An overfilled curriculum is one of the greatest disincentives for teachers to give time for reflection and for the learner to take time to reflect.

This could be considered with students through the image of the desert, a key symbol in Christian spirituality since the time of the Desert Fathers, resonating with the biblical images of the Exodus/ wilderness and Christ in the desert. For the Israelites, the desert was a place of pilgrimage, discovery and revelation. In Mark's gospel, it is not only a place of spiritual combat, solitude and struggle, a place of angels and wild beasts (Mk 1: 13) but also a discipline which becomes indispensable to Christ and his disciples throughout the course of his ministry, as the place of debriefing and communal reflection (Mk 6: 30–2). The Desert Fathers and Mothers sought not only an outer physical space, free from the noise and clutter of the city, but also an inner space where truth is to be discovered. In the Christian tradition, prayer itself has often been viewed as a desert experience (Louth, 2003). Like the idea of desert, opening up a prayerful space within teaching could be viewed fearfully as a wasteland or 'inefficient use of time' in the midst of 'productive' seminars and lectures. However, what seems at first negative can come to be experienced as the very place of transformation and conversion (Merton, 2004; Nouwen, 1990). The image of the desert suggests a terrain to be explored, the place of face-to-face encounter with God, and also, as the *Sayings of the Desert Fathers* (Ward, 1975) testify, the place of life-giving dialogue between spiritual searchers. The image of the desert stands as a prophetic symbol questioning the crowded timetables and information overload characteristic of recent theological training. However, the desert image if pursued too rigorously in spirituality leads to withdrawal and not engagement. The desert must be complemented by the city (Sheldrake, 2003).

The opening up of an exploratory space in lecture or seminar as 'holy ground' where people need to tread softly is a risky business for student and teacher alike. Palmer (1983: 69ff; 1998: 74) identifies the paradoxes involved in creating such space, including the tensions between its being both open and bounded, hospitable and focused, valuing alike the 'little' stories of the students and the 'big' stories of the tradition, welcoming both silence and speech.

While it demands a certain vulnerability and openness in participants, as they learn to speak of inward things, it can be maintained as a safe space by the acceptance by all of ground rules concerning respect, confidentiality, mutual listening and the absence of pressure to share personal matters beyond what one is comfortable with, honouring the freedom of all. Particular care needs to be taken in those university settings where, in modules open to the general public, ordinands may find themselves studying alongside those of no explicit faith or those of other faiths. Nevertheless, it is possible to incorporate reflective silence, rather than explicitly Christian prayer, creatively within such situations. Such elements can be made explicit in a learning covenant what is expected of students/teachers (see below).

In respect of spirituality modules, such space would fulfil three functions. First, it would enable the opportunity for students and teachers to share 'from the heart' their experience of spiritual life and prayer. Secondly, it would afford the opportunity for students actually to experience different forms of prayer, giving teachers the chance to be as attentive to fruitful patterns of prayer as to preferred learning styles (Honey and Mumford, 1986). Thirdly, it would afford the opportunity for students to experiment creatively, perhaps in practical workshops, with unfamiliar patterns of prayer and meditation, involving the use of art, music, poetry, bodily movement, symbols and visual aids. As Berntsen (1996: 229–43) notes: 'The point is that the good health of Christian education is dependent upon the operation of both lobes of the brain, so that Christian truth is learned both affectively and cognitively . . . Religion is a cognitive-affective activity.' These work on different levels for different people, encouraging affective learning, intuition and attentiveness to feelings to complement the more usual analytical methods of teaching (Sheldrake, 2001). The writing of reflective learning journals, now widely used, can give an opportunity to evaluate these.

However, it is important to note that the potential of opening up a prayerful reflective space extends to all subjects across the theological curriculum and can fruitfully be explored in such areas as doctrine and biblical studies, ethics and pastoral theology (Charry, 1997). Nouwen (1998: 232) reminds us of the experiential origins of doctrine: 'Doctrines are not alien formulations which we must adhere to but the documentation of the most profound human experiences.' It is to be hoped that the reconfiguring of initial ministerial education as a seven-year process will allow more time and opportunity for the creative incorporation of silence and prayer into theological method within all subjects. As Klimoski (2004: 47) puts it: 'Formation wedged in after everything else is done meets a requirement; formation that reminds a community of learners to create space, to reverence time, and to drink deeply at wisdom's well is transforming.' Perhaps UK educators can learn from the apparently greater readiness of North American seminary teachers to incorporate 'sacred spaces', as reported in the research by Foster et al.:

> Seminary educators draw on a variety of pedagogical methods and strategies to facilitate the presence of God, mystery, or transcendence. The most common involve some form of prayer or meditation. We discovered in the Auburn 2003 faculty survey [of half of all faculty members in accredited seminaries in the US and Canada] that 67 percent of the respondents agreed that it is 'important to open or close class sessions with some form of prayer or meditation.' For some, the daily liturgies of the whole seminary community establish the religious contact for the interplay of their teaching and student learning. For others, leading the class in prayer (or asking a student to do so), marking times of 'centering silence' . . . or using guided meditation flows seamlessly into the class session.
>
> (2006: 109)

Reassess the role of the theological teacher within the learning community

The role of the theological teacher has received very little attention in recent years. It is not addressed in such key documents as *Education for the Church's Ministry* (ACCM, 1987), *Mission and Ministry* (ABM, 1999), nor, indeed, in the *Hind Report*. How is the role of the teacher to be conceived in formational terms? The Roman Catholic Church speaks of theological educators as 'agents of formation' (John Paul II, 1992), or as 'formators' (Congregation for Institutes of Consecrated Life and Societies of Apostolic Life, 1990; Congregation for the Clergy, 1998). Even if the Church of England would not want to adopt such titles the question remains: what difference does the formation paradigm of learning make to patterns of teaching? In reflecting on the role of teacher in formation, two major possibilities might be explored.

First, fulfilling a role as exemplar and pilgrim, the theological educator has the opportunity to provide a vulnerable but inspiring example of integrating theology and prayer. To some extent, the spiritual formation of students will be dependent on the ways in which staff themselves resource and nurture their own spiritual life. In a Christian setting, it should be possible for teachers to show that their theological quest is rooted in their spiritual quest. They will model how spiritual formation integrates other dimensions of formation and especially heals the spiritual/academic divide. Teachers stand before students not as professionals having all the answers but as fellow pilgrims, explorers and companions asking similar questions. Indeed, courses of study can be seen in terms of spiritual pilgrimage and adventure as well as modules leading to academic award.

Secondly, the theological educator has a key role as co-creator of a learning community, called not only to impart knowledge, but also to facilitate a process of discovery, to be a catalyst sparking off new growth, a stimulus. Once again we are reminded of the recurrent need, highlighted by Freire (1970), for the banking model of education to give way to a participative model: the provider model to yield to the process of a liberating 'conscientization'. Barr and Tagg (1995) sum up the crucial differences between an instructional model of teaching and a learner-centred model. Palmer contrasts the pyramidical view of the classroom with a circular, interactive image (1998: 101, 103).

A learning community becomes an ecology of collaboration, in which teachers become learners and learners become teachers in a mutual sharing of spiritual experience. This demands the developing of more open relationships between learners and teachers and a lowering of self-protective barriers on all sides. As Nouwen (1998: 33) has said: 'people only become human when they are received and accepted. In this way, many students could be better students than they are if there was someone who could make them recognize their capacities and could accept these as a real gift.'

The issue of boundaries and limits is especially pertinent in the question of prayer and spirituality in the learning process. One student valued the chance 'to actually have a conversation with the lecturer and in that conversation, the conversation almost becomes the prayer – not a formal idea of prayer, but that coming together of people of like mind in the presence of God and having a conversation' (c). Her tutor commented, independently:

> I can see there's a role for conversations to supplement the formal teaching . . . to enable people to talk about how the spirituality session has affected them, especially if it has brought to the surface something painful, or I can see someone is really struggling with the topic. Some people would take the material one way and others would see it differently. Sometimes you can have really deep conversations with people, and that helps. But it's almost straying into spiritual direction, so you have to be careful. (h)

In reflecting on their role in facilitating conversations about prayer and learning, whether within or outside the seminar time, educators will need to be alert to avoiding such role confusions (Sheldrake, 1998b). Simmons (2006: 37) comments from the context of US university teaching:

> To the extent that the religious concepts . . . inherently inspire personal transformation, how can a boundary exist between the ideas students encounter and the power of those ideas to transform? Spiritual guidance emerges naturally in the academic study of religion, and those of us who teach in the field might as well get used to it.

Thus, educators will need to give careful thought to how their role might be clarified, perhaps within a learning covenant (see below). Certainly, those who serve as personal tutors will need to reflect on the adequacy of their availability and ability to give support, as one student in the present research pointed out:

With my tutor, we would meet once a term, and he would ask me how my prayer-life was going and how I was doing spiritually, as well as picking up the academic side . . . Through the tutor system, perhaps greater support could be given in terms of 'how's it going?' on a more frequent basis. 'How's your spiritual life?' Perhaps almost formalizing it can help to actually force people to think it through. Perhaps using some sort of questionnaire about how it's going in these different areas and giving that chance of reflecting with your tutor. (e)

In this way, the seminary or course will model something of the caring congregation into which the ordinand is to be sent, where there is an attentiveness to the mutual nurture of gifts and prayer between church members. Within the teaching situation, it will also require the grace of creating an environment where experiential sharing is possible without the student's fear that this will be taken up into the assessment process. As one tutor put it, 'Here's a challenge: how do you enable prayer to go on, notice its benefits, without putting it into a framework that is about monitoring and performance? How do you really enable prayer in the community to form people?' (m)

From the point of view of a tutor on a course, caring for the student's prayer-life did entail stepping across the boundary of the job into a private, personal realm:

The reality was: if you didn't do your essays all sorts of alarm bells went. If you didn't pray – that would be about you getting exhausted and feeling discouraged, and maybe an alarm signal would appear some way down the line – when you saw your student they would say 'I'm feeling far away from God' and then you'd have a prayer about it and you would encourage them to talk with their spiritual director. But the whole course culture is so much about assessment, and judgment – it's very hard to step out of that role to say 'How are *you*? How's your journey with God?' (m)

Educators might learn from ancient models of theological education in community such as that Augustine's (Cola, 1991). One practical way in which the mutual roles of teachers and students could be explored is through the designing of a learning covenant (Wickett, 2000). Taking a fresh look at the idea of learning contract, this invites participants to explore the mutual responsibility of teachers and students in contributing to developing the spiritual dimensions of learning and teaching. It might include specific commitments about confidentiality in order to help create a safe space for deep sharing. It might also serve to remind students of the need to take a high level of responsibility for their own formation.

This research raises the importance of critical reflection on practice by theological educators. As Hillier writes: 'We need . . . a commitment to the systematic questioning of our teaching as a basis for development' (2002: 13). One of the challenges to this may be a feature reported by James of US seminary staff: 'It is apparent that many faculty have not received formal training in educational theories or principles. As a result, they teach according to personal theories about good teaching that often are unexamined . . .' (*www.religiouseducation.net*).

Reconceive worship as a learning and formative event

In order to help heal the dichotomy between classroom and chapel, between learning and piety, educators should integrate worship creatively into the educational process and not see it as an extra-curricular activity. Exploring parallels between learning and worship in the Orthodox tradition, Ware observes: 'The word "education" comes from the Latin *educere*, "to evoke"; and so a school or university is precisely a place in which with rigour and discipline we evoke and cultivate a sense of wonder' (2000: 71). Worship with its words and spaces can provide a contemplative arena in which the thinking of the classroom can be lifted up to God and transformed through the gaining of new insights. As we noted, Ford and Hardy (2005: 142) write of worship 'in this movement . . . God enhances our rational powers' (see also Neville and Westerhoff, 1978). Educators should ensure that study flows seamlessly into worship, either in classroom or chapel, so that the one energizes the other.

The empirical evidence revealed how, for some, the Eucharist is experienced as a place of profound affirmation of diaconal and priestly identity, remoulding the celebrant towards a greater Christlikeness as a servant leader. The liturgical texts themselves have become more explicit in revealing a formational intentionality in worship, with a recent Eucharistic Prayer making the petition: 'Form us into the likeness of Christ' (Archbishops' Council, 2000). Explicit concepts of liturgical formation have a longer history in the Roman Catholic Church. The Ordination Rite for Presbyters includes the words at the presentation of the chalice: 'Realise what you are doing; imitate what you handle' (Hurley, 1978; see also Congregation for Catholic Education, 1979). Seeing worship as a transformational process, Irvine observes: 'to elucidate the formational meaning of worship we need to work with a more developed pneumatology . . . and accordingly give a greater logical priority to the presence and active working of God [in worship]' (2005: 85). Educators should view worship not as a separate activity but as the very crucible of learning and formation.

Support ordinands with spirituality resources that will equip them for the actual challenges of ministry

An oft-repeated criticism from both college and course students in the empirical research was that pathways of prayer considered in spirituality modules were often irrelevant to and remote from the actual practice of ministry. They were predominantly historical or theoretical in content, very rarely experiential or practical. There is a limited relation between what is taught in spirituality modules or modelled in chapel and what would actually be useful in the parish: some subjects were taught that had no obvious relation to pastoral ministry. Conversely, ways of praying that were discovered to be absolutely essential to their survival as ministers, such as the way in which forms of intercession or meditation can alleviate stress, were never considered in this way in college or course or mentioned as being considered there by interviewees. There was a notable lack of correlation in responses to two questions asked in the interviews: 'What opportunities for experiencing different types of prayer did your *college provide*?' and 'Please describe the forms of praying which are helping you in *ministry now*'.

Educators should consider providing a workable 'toolbox' of prayer resources related to ministry's demands and issues, rather than providing a purely historical introduction to sources of spirituality. Where historical sources are commended, there needs of course to be a two-way conversation utilizing the hermeneutic of generosity and the hermeneutic of suspicion (Miles, 1989). While it is recognized that spirituality must always be contextual, springing up in actual situations of ministry and life, it is possible to explore wellsprings and sources that are likely to provide inspiration and challenge. Useful general works on spirituality of ministry include: Holmes, 2002; Wicks, 1995; Boa, 2001; Schwartz, 1989; Philibert, 2004; O'Leary, 1997; Runcorn, 2006.

In the light of the empirical research's discovery of significant needs among the newly ordained, certain types of spirituality suggest themselves as examples which may contribute to the building of a spirituality of priesthood and ministry, not forgetting the need both to respect personality differences and to coax people out of their comfort zones.

Anticipating the experience of fatigue and stress in ministry, and the danger of burnout, Benedictine spirituality might be explored, with its concern to seek a creative balance between prayer, study and work, an interplay between the seeking solitude and building community, pursuing both engagement and withdrawal (see de Waal, 1997; Taylor, 1989).

Anticipating the need for a hopeful, embodied, sacramental and incarnate spirituality, finding God in creation and amongst the poor, and supporting a countercultural lifestyle characterized by simplicity, Franciscan spirituality might be explored (see Short, 1999; Boff, 1990; Puls, 1985).

Supporting evolution of a ministerial identity, making sense of its paschal transitions and making generous allowance for all-too-human failings, a spirituality might look to George Herbert's poem-prayers as a stimulus to encourage honest questioning and struggle in spirituality (Herbert, 1995; Sheldrake, 2000). A latter-day example of compassionate ministerial spirituality would be the writings of Henri Nouwen, including *The Wounded Healer: Ministry in Contemporary Society* (1972).

An energizing spirituality would look to sources that celebrate the empowering of the Holy Spirit in ministry, for example the writings of Simeon the New Theologian (Symeon, 1996).

The need to hone skills of discernment by recognizing and celebrating the presence and action of God amidst the world's struggles and injustices would find rich inspiration in the various spiritualities of liberation. This would also enable a greater practice of spirituality in community and the avoidance of the dangers of individualism and what Brown (1988) calls the 'Great Fallacy' of dividing spirituality from life; it also alerts the participant to a more global perspective (see Gutiérrez, 1984; Casaldaliga and Vigil, 1994; Kleissler, Lebert and McGuinness, 1991).

The challenge to develop spirituality as a seedbed of theology would be inspired by those practices which facilitate a prayerful rediscovery of the biblical tradition, for example, through the practice of *lectio divina* or such meditative approaches as commended by the Ignatian tradition (Hughes, 1985 and 2003).

The challenge for educators and spiritual directors is to identify sources of spirituality which both resource and challenge contemporary ministerial practice. Another approach to identifying key sources in spirituality which meet the demands of ministry today would be to recognize that the historic models of training suggest complementary patterns of prayer. As has been seen, each tradition throws up its own pertinent questions and challenges to contemporary practice. Thus they invite us to consider the place of a range of patterns of prayer, namely: *praxis*: prayer and theological reflection; *paideia*: personality and prayer; *ascesis*: the role of spiritual disciplines in prayer; *scientia*: the need to unite prayer and study; *seminarium*: practices of community prayer; *Wissenschaft*: spirituality resources which underpin leadership skills.

Students should be asked to pay closer attention in their pastoral placements to recognizing which types of spirituality most sustain ministry today. Usually such projects, which make up a significant aspect of pre-ordination training, have focused on the pastoral skills required and less on spirituality resources needed. What is really needed is training for ordinands to become 'contemplatives in action', not only using spirituality resources in detached 'prayer-times' but cultivating a way of living in the world that is contemplative and discerning because it involves an attentive way of looking. Traditional resources which encourage this perhaps can be reworked for ministry today (see Muggeridge, 1996; Blaiklock, 1981; Ashwin, 1991; compare Ashley, 2001).

Recommendations for theological educators involved in continuing ministerial education (CME) – the ongoing development of the Church's ministers

For me, formation isn't instant, it's a life-long process. There is a dynamic to formation, in which God is continually working in you. (h)

In the context of ministerial formation I would want to say that something deep is happening. It's about development, taking time – it doesn't happen overnight. (d)

A recurring theme in the empirical research was the importance of understanding formation as a continuing process sustaining and stimulating the whole course of ordained ministry.

Reframe CME in terms of ongoing formation
There are four models currently in use, each with different emphases. *In-service training* tends to work with a functionalist model of ministry and stresses the acquisition of skills needed to

accomplish the tasks of ministry (General Synod, 1980). *Continuing professional development* likewise has an emphasis on sustaining effective practitioners in an ever-changing environment and the need to adapt to new challenges; one can compare the model of 'equipping' in Archbishops' Council, 2001. *Continuing ministerial education* itself often communicates a propensity towards refreshing academic qualifications and intellectual study. *Lifelong learning* most often includes updating skills (see Ward, 2005).

In contrast to these, the model of ministerial formation, with its attentiveness to ongoing spiritual formation, emerges as an inspiring and refreshing alternative, encouraging the dynamic integration of human, spiritual, intellectual and pastoral growth. The theology of formation is considerably richer than that of training, because it explores more fully the role of the Holy Spirit in the divine/human synergy of formation. To appreciate the value of formational theology it is instructive to set side-by-side John Paul II (1992) *Pastores Dabo Vobis* and the Anglican report *Mind the Gap* (Archbishops' Council, 2001). There are two areas in particular which would benefit from a renewed alertness to the role of spirituality in ongoing ministerial support:

Resource the spiritual dimensions of ministry through CME
A review of CME programmes from a number of southern dioceses reveals that much current CME training in dioceses focuses on resourcing clergy and readers for change management, team building and the development of ministerial skills in a changing culture. The present research reveals the need to develop a strategy to cultivate spiritually reflective pastors. It invites those planning CME to look again at the provision of spirituality resources and training better to support those ministry roles which involve prayer. These include teaching others to pray and nurturing the spiritual life of Christians to sustain their ministry and witness in the workplace. CME providers will also need to be more alert to what inspires and sustains a priestly ministry and lifestyle which will often be countercultural in character.

Utilizing the formation paradigm in CME can also overcome the dichotomy between doing and being in ministry, as it is recognized, for example, that skilled preaching, delivered with authority and depth, emerges from the life of prayer while skilled listening in pastoral encounters is honed in the art of meditative prayer. CME should be playing a role in the nurture of what Peterson (1993) calls 'the contemplative pastor'. Within this, there is an urgent need, independently attested, to resource and train clergy and lay leaders in skills of theological reflection which enable them prayerfully to recognize the action of God in the world, equipping them for a prophetic ministry discerning 'what the Spirit is saying to the Churches'.

The question of what role CME should take in helping to develop ministerial spirituality needs to be openly discussed. Is it to be left to spiritual directors, spiritual writers and retreat conductors? If it underpins the very practice of ministry, as the present research shows, it should be a central not marginalized element in any CME provision in a diocese, both providing resources and reminding clergy and lay leaders of the need to take responsibility for their essential ongoing spiritual formation. The increasing challenges facing public ministry in today's world make supporting the spiritual formation of the clergy and lay leaders all the more imperative: it is not a luxury or optional extra but an essential and urgent priority.

Develop CME's pastoral role in the ongoing formation of ministerial identity

The present findings confirmed other research that clergy, even in their early years, face high levels of stress, fatigue and frustration and the danger of burn-out (Society of Mary and Martha, 2002; Warren, 2002). This is often linked with priests' problem of identity confusion in a church with a plethora of ministries. The research has shown how prayer can often take on a paschal or turbulent character in the light of this. CME should provide a safe space where struggles about priestly identity can be explored within confidential dialogue – not in an inward-looking, narcissistic way but in a manner that gives inspiration and energy for ministry. The research discovered that ministerial identity is a key aspect of ministerial formation demanding ongoing attention throughout ministry. Moreover, it revealed that, where a formational model is being used, there is more explicit attention to issues of personal growth. Thus, use of such a model in CME would further its ability to renew confidence and to strengthen self-understanding in the Church's ministers.

In addition, penetrating questions about spiritual practice should be included in ministerial reviews currently being redesigned as a tool for clergy development in the light of such documents as

Archbishops' Council (2005). This will affirm the importance of recognizing spirituality as a key dimension contributing to clergy effectiveness. Ministerial review itself should help create a space where clergy can reflect and take stock of the impact of spiritual formation on their ministry and on their evolving sense of vocation.

Equip clergy and lay leaders through CME for ministry at the cutting edge of evangelism

The challenge of 'opening rivers in the desert' considered above identified the ways in which exploring Christian spirituality is becoming a significant pathway into the Christian community for postmodern seekers. The issues which concern them are such precisely formational concerns as discovering identity and vocation. The research in Croft and Frost (2005) uncovered as seekers' frequently recurring questions: What is the purpose of life? Whose life and values will inspire me? What is the relevance of the spiritual realm to my life? CME should not only resource the spiritual formation of clergy but also equip them to grasp the present opportunities for innovative forms of outreach utilizing spirituality (Hope, 2006).

Recommendations for theological educators involved in adult education

Explore the benefits of a formational model in adult education

Initial Christian formation

The formational model has been utilized fruitfully for some time in the Roman Catholic Church through the use of the *Rite of Christian Initiation of Adults* (Congregation for Divine Worship, 1974). It has been powerfully restated in the Papal Exhortation (John Paul II, 1988), *Christifideles Laici*, a rich exposition of an integrated Christian formation, making explicit its links to Christians' role in mission: 'The fundamental objective of the formation of the lay faithful is an ever-clearer discovery of one's vocation and the ever-greater willingness to live it so as to fulfil one's mission.' The growth of Small Christian Communities in the Roman Catholic Church and beyond provides a significant expression of a formation reintegrating theology and spirituality within Christian discipleship (O'Halloran, 1996).

Thus far there has been limited application in the Anglican Church of the formational model in the training of new Christians (for examples, see Ball, 1984, and Mayes and Warner, 1990). The *Emmaus* course works with a model of personal growth but has no explicit references to Christian formation (Cottrell and Croft, 2004). The *Alpha* course, with its highly didactic and instructional approach, leaves little room for prayerful theological exploration (Gumbel, 2005). Its 'Holy Spirit weekend', though experiential in character, entails a very restricted understanding of prayer, with no space for reflection. Those preparing courses for enquirers or confirmation materials should study how a formational model can enrich and deepen pedagogical approaches for enquirers.

Continuing Christian formation

In developing Christians towards discovering the ministry of all the baptized, there has been a failure to learn ecumenically from sources where the formational model has been used to good effect. This is evidenced, for example, in its absence from such basic Church documents as *Christian Education and Training for the 21st Century* (General Synod, 1996). Indeed, *Learning for Life*, a widely used handbook for adult Christian education has no references to Christian formation (Craig, 1994). Utilizing a formational model would enable lay participants to develop a spirituality that feeds their vocation and the doing of theology.

Recent proposals for *Education for Discipleship*, emerging in the wake of the *Hind Report*'s concern for lay development, have failed to take forward creatively the clues in the report about the benefits of a formational model. In the report from the Implementation Task Group (Archbishops' Council, 2006), there is but one reference to prayer and an aim in the methodology to 'provide education and training in a way which resources the mind, emotions and spirit'. The proposals for developing a well-equipped laity give more attention to academic accreditation. A formational model would enable explicit attention not only to progression in spiritual maturity but also to the discernment of vocation that springs from growth in Christian identity.

A useful starting point might be Gangel and Wilhoit (1997). In the UK, there is a dearth of Christian writing both on Christian formation and the role of the Christian lay educator. The bibliography 'Books for Adult Educators' issued by the Education Division of the Church of England contains fourteen titles of which only three are by Christian authors, Hull (1985) and Craig (1994), Green

(1990). This suggests there is a need for some new creative work in this area.

Reframe the training of lay leaders and readers in formational terms

A recent review of reader/preaching training gives closer attention to the role of spirituality in training. *A Vision for Good Practice* presents an 'educational and training framework' in terms of three overlapping circles of knowledge/understanding; competence/skills; conviction/spirituality. It states: 'While each area is important in itself, formation occurs in their dynamic interaction . . . Together, in balance, they shape the life and ministry of a Preacher/Reader' (Archbishops' Council, 2006: 38). It goes on to make an important formational statement:

> In order to nurture their Christian life, it is essential that Readers/ Preachers are meeting with God as they continue to test their calling throughout their training and ministry. Who they are, as people, their spirituality, attitudes, qualities and maturity, in their home church community and in the wider world, are as important as their knowledge and competence.
>
> (Archbishops' Council, 2006: 40)

This is a welcome statement and it is to be hoped that the theory will bear fruit in practice and also influence clergy training as lay and clergy training become more closely intertwined. The report *Readers Upbeat: Quickening the Tempo of Reader Ministry in the Church Today* (General Synod, 2008), however, reveals how difficult it is to hold on to this vision: the report is dominated by the need to balance skills-based training with greater higher-education accreditation in conjunction with universities. Attention to spiritual development is separated out as a kind of holy activity from the learning process, with desired support from spiritual directors or companions: 'Specific attention needs to be given in Reader training to spiritual formation and maturity' (General Synod, 2008: 63). The challenge is to integrate and imbed such spiritual formation into the learning process itself.

Much remains to be done in terms of articulating a spirituality of leadership which could be applicable to clergy and lay leaders alike. While books on Christian leadership abound, there is a paucity of writing on spirituality resources or spiritual disciplines which might underpin such leadership, revealing a real need to develop spiritual formation in relation to Christian leadership. Ten widely used text-books on Christian leadership contain no reference to prayer or spirituality: Adair and Nelson (2004); Adair (2001); Finney (1989); Greenslade (1984); Lawrence (2004); Marshall (1991); Nelson (1999); Rendle (1998); Sofield and Kuhn (1995); Wright (2000). For spirituality and Christian leadership, see Johnson and Dreitcer (2001).

Many of the elements of ministerial formation identified in the research are of direct relevance to this wider field of training about leadership, such as issues of ministerial identity, handling stress and doing theology. A spirituality of leadership could be explored by working with the functions of prayer which the research identified.

Conclusion: questions for the wider Church

What should be the role of spirituality in ministerial formation? The research has clarified the character of formation as an intentional, transformational process with significant implications for the prac-tice of theology. It has identified the creative, reflective, restorative and integrative functions of prayer in such formation. It has revealed the significance of prayer in ministerial formation from many angles: attentiveness to spirituality is demanded by mission in today's cul-ture, by the need to make sense of stress and identity confusion, by the very nature of theology itself.

The research reveals the different dimensions of the mystery of prayer in formation as expressed by two interviewees:

> We need to see prayer as the thing that undergirds everything, the hidden stream from which everything comes from and goes back to, a way of being . . . Prayer is a stream running through formation, and it is that stream which gives it life. (a)

> prayer is like that hidden stream: how do we make courses so that there is that hidden stream running through Jerusalem, through the heart of the city? (m)

As a river plays a unique role in the formation of the physical land-scape, sometimes building up, and sometimes eroding stubborn rock, so the river of prayer fulfils inalienable functions within the process of the shaping of ministers, priests and lay leaders. It is truly dynamic, not only energizing ministry but opening up ancient yet ever new possibilities in the quest of 'doing theology'. As a river may flow underground or be unseen, so the role of prayer in the learning process itself has often been unacknowledged in the past, yet its hidden or mysterious role can be decisive in the making of ministers capable of the theological reflection demanded by today's changing culture.

Yet the issue of the role of prayer in ministerial formation also raises two huge questions for the wider Church.

What kind of priest is needed today?

If formation is a transformational process of learning and growth towards a 'form' of ministry, oriented to the *telos* developing the clergy needed today, what 'shape' of priesthood is most engendered by a process where spiritual formation finds its rightful place? The research suggests three main dimensions of ministry:

Priests as holy people, people of prayer

The research has shown that church members look to their clergy to be teachers of prayer and guides for the spiritual journey. Moreover, there is evidence that in a postmodern society there persists a role for holy men and women who can act as 'soul friends' to the wider community beyond the Church, who are known as authoritative and authentic exemplars and representatives of a spiritual tradition. One young priest put it thus:

> my approach is very much about being a presence in such a community, making connections, walking alongside, and taking it from there – not taking God *to* people but helping them to discover that He's already *there* and I think that links quite strongly in with prayer. (a)

Such a priestly presence and availability in the local community, radiating a quality of spiritual depth and accessible, unselfconscious holiness, represents a type of spiritual leadership which is self-authenticating and which springs from an empowering of the Spirit.

Priests as 'stewards of the mysteries of God'

The phrase, from 1 Corinthians 4: 1–2, suggests that priests will not only be guardians of the spiritual traditions of the Church but also the ones who open these resources to others. Priests' role as teachers of divine mysteries will spring from their relationship with God, their glimpse of eternity and their encounter with the Transcendent and the Incarnate, nurtured by prayer and silence. As Barron puts it:

If the priest is to be a mediator between heaven and earth, if he is to speak symbolically of the all-embracing and ever elusive mystery of Being itself, he must be in habitual contact with the Mystery, he must stand stubbornly in the presence of God. He must take with utmost seriousness the command of St Paul to pray continually, to orient the whole of his being to the love of God. In short, the priest must be a mystic, a contemplative, a person of prayer . . . who must be, in every fibre of his being, formed by prayer.

(1999: 96)

This needs to be affirmed in all ordination training, as one tutor interviewed put it:

The training mindset tends to take over, especially in a culture where you've got competencies, learning outcomes, and it all has to be accredited, bite-sized and modularized, standardized . . . If we are to have a potency in our post-enlightenment, post-modern world, we have to recover confidence in what is less measurable, less quantifiable, much more fruitful and more relational . . . in a sense, this is the big *metanoia* for the Church: it's returning to its roots in the mystery of Christ. (m)

Priests as prophets and theologians

The evidence suggests that clergy accept their vocation to be seers of a different vision, singers of a different song; in the words of the *Ordinal*: 'They are to proclaim the word of the Lord and to watch for the signs of God's new creation. They are to be messengers, watchmen . . .' While seeking to engage with the culture, in many ways they model a way of life which is profoundly countercultural and which throws up many questions to modern consumerist society. From the river of prayer they draw resources to enable them to 'do theology' in today's context, seeing theological reflection, as one put it, in terms of

a way of approaching things and a way of looking at things and interpreting things, which is actually, almost a way of prayer. It's trying to look for where God is in this and be open to where God is . . . Prayer and theological reflection are in many ways one and the same – the eyes through which you look at things. (a)

Priests accept their calling to try to articulate, both for congregation and community, a theology which discerns the action of God in the world.

What kind of Church is needed today?

The research raises the perennial issue of the relation of the ordained ministry to the ministry of all the baptized. Recent understandings of this relationship help elucidate the wider significance of the spiritual formation of the clergy. The ordained ministry is seen as a focus encapsulating the ministry of all (General Synod, 1997; compare Anglican–Roman Catholic International Commission, 1973: 14). Writers describe the ordained ministry as a sacramental sign, giving a clear image of the priorities of Christian ministry (Hannaford, 1991). Others describe the ordained ministry in terms of an icon or mirror of all God's people, revealing in a focused and symbolic way, in their being and doing, the vocation of all Christians.

Thus, priests reveal to all the baptized *their* calling to be holy people, people of prayer, bearers of God's mystery, prophets and theologians. Indeed, it is possible to go further and affirm very radically that an ordained priesthood provides a visible sign to the world of the very vocation of humanity: the divine calling inviting every man and every woman to be in a real sense priests who encounter and reveal God to each other (Countryman, 1999).

Thus the spiritual formation of priests, far from being a marginal or secondary matter in theological training, speaks symbolically of humanity's very vocation and destiny. The river of prayer is truly a universal symbol of the transformational possibilities present in Christian spirituality. As the writer to the Ephesians puts it:

> I pray that, according to the riches of his glory, he may grant that you may be strengthened in your inner being with power through his Spirit, and that Christ may dwell in your hearts through faith, as you are being rooted and grounded in love. I pray that you may have the power to comprehend, with all the saints what is the breadth and length and height and depth, and to know the love of Christ that surpasses knowledge, so that you may be filled with all the fullness of God.

> (Eph. 3: 16–19)

Photocopiable sheets for personal or group use

QUESTIONS FOR REFLECTION BY THEOLOGICAL EDUCATORS IN INITIAL MINISTERIAL EDUCATION

What is our vision for ministerial formation?

How far does it reflect the elements of ministerial formation identified in *Spirituality in Ministerial Formation*: transformation through prayer; integrating prayer and theology; nurturing identity and virtue; resourcing mission?

What do we understand by spiritual formation within this process?

What policy for spiritual formation is in place in our institution?

What would we put into a 'learning covenant', in terms of mutual (teacher–student) responsibility about developing the spiritual dimensions of learning and teaching?

How can we link spiritual formation more organically into the very learning process?

How can we nurture 'deep knowing'?

Is there any place for silence or communal or individual reflection in our teaching/seminars?

How will we describe spiritual formation in the student induction pack? Dare we include reflective prayer as a study skill?

What would we want to say about the relationship between prayer and theological reflection in our induction or welcome for new students?

How might reflective prayer/silent contemplation be promoted, especially for those whose background or personality is unfamiliar with the practice?

How can we model and actually practise in our setting the integration of prayer and 'doing theology'?

What 'sacred spaces' do we open up in our teaching?

How are we equipping people to be 'contemporary mystics' (Croft, Frost et al., 2005: 118)?

How can we explore spirituality and different spiritual traditions experientially as well as academically?

To what extent are we prepared to have 'spiritual conversations' with our students?

What does this require of teachers?

How does all this relate, if at all, to the question of assessment?

How can we see prayer as 'the matrix, not the appendix' of learning?

How can we see worship as 'the very crucible of learning and formation'?

'The future of the Church at the present moment depends most of all on the spiritual formation of future priests' (Catholic Church, 1980, quoted in chapter 3). How far do you agree with this?

How wide is the scope of spirituality resources we make available to students?

QUESTIONS FOR REFLECTION BY THOSE INVOLVED IN CME, ADULT EDUCATION AND LAY LEADERSHIP TRAINING

What would our programmes look like if we recast them in terms of formation?

What would need to change?

How can we incorporate the practice of prayer into the learning process?

How can we develop worship times more creatively as learning events?

How can we nurture 'contemplative pastors'?

What can we do to support and resource a spirituality of leadership?

What spirituality resources do we offer to sustain ministry in the long term?

What formational resources can we provide to help avoid 'burn-out'?

How are we equipping ministers to engage creatively with the spiritual search in today's culture?

What opportunities do we provide for exploring and resourcing innovative forms of evangelism which attend to the current spiritual search evident in some places in society?

What forms of spirituality are most appropriate in our context?

QUESTIONS FOR REFLECTION BY THEOLOGICAL STUDENTS

How do I understand ministerial formation? What kind of transformations do I expect to experience within this process – how might I change?

How can I incorporate the practice of prayer into my learning process?

How can I reunite the activities of prayer and theological reflection in my practice? Do I want to revise the way I do theological reflection in the light of the book *Spirituality in Ministerial Formation*?

How do I understand the dynamic of spiritual formation?

What fragmentation or disconnectedness, if any, do I experience in the process of theological studies? How do I think the practice of prayer might be healing and integrative in my studies?

How can I achieve 'deep knowing' rather than 'superficial knowing'? How can I spot the difference?

What would I like to see in a 'learning covenant' in terms of my responsibility to develop the spirituality of learning?

How do I see and experience the role of prayer in nurturing ministerial identity and healing stresses?

In what ways might I experience prayer as a process of perception or cognition?

How can I develop as a 'contemporary mystic'?

In what ways can I develop forms of prayer that will be of encouragement for enquirers?

What role do I see for 'wrestling with God' and 'wrestling with difficult issues' in prayer?

How do I see the role of the Holy Spirit in my formation?

Bibliography

Adair, J. (2001). *The Leadership of Jesus and its Legacy Today*, Norwich: Canterbury Press.

Adair, J. and Nelson, J. (eds) (2004). *Creative Church Leadership*, Norwich: Canterbury Press.

Advisory Board of Ministry (ABM) (1992). *Integration and Assessment: the Report of an ABM Working Party on Educational Practice*, London: Church House Publishing.

Advisory Board of Ministry (1993). *The Report of a Working Party on the Criteria for Selection for Ministry in the Church of England*, London: ABM.

Advisory Board of Ministry (1994). *Ministerial Review: Its Purpose and Practice*, London: Church House Publishing.

Advisory Board of Ministry (1998). *Beginning Public Ministry: Guidelines for Ministerial Formation and Personal Development for the First Four Years after Ordination*, London: Church House Publishing.

Advisory Board of Ministry (1999). *Mission and Ministry: the Churches' Validation Framework for Theological Education*, London: Ministry Division, Archbishops' Council.

Advisory Council for the Church's Ministry (ACCM) (1981). *Spirituality in Ordination Training*, London: Occasional Paper 9, ACCM.

Advisory Council for the Church's Ministry (1987). *Education for the Church's Ministry*, London: Church House Publishing.

Advisory Council for the Church's Ministry (1988). *Theology in Practice*, London: ACCM, Church House Publishing.

Advisory Council for the Church's Ministry (1990). *Residence – an Education*, London: Church House Publishing.

Aimilianos, Archimandrite of Simonopetra (2005). *The Church at Prayer*, Athens: Indiktos.

Alfeyev, H. (1988). 'The problems facing Orthodox theological education in Russia', *Sourozh: A Journal of Orthodox Life and Thought*, 73, 5–22.

Allen, J. J. (1986). *The Ministry of the Church*, New York: St Vladimir's Seminary Press.

Alson, W. P. (1991). *Perceiving God: the Epistemology of Religious Experience*, Ithaca and London: Cornell University Press.

Amirtham, S. and Pryor R. (eds) (1989). *The Invitation to the Feast of Life: Resources for Spiritual Formation in Theological Education*, Geneva: World Council for Churches (WCC): Programme on Theological Education.

Anglican–Roman Catholic International Commission (1973). *Ministry and Ordination*, London: Catholic Truth Society.

Apps, J. W. (1996). *Teaching from the Heart*, Florida: Krieger.

Archbishops' Council (2000). *Holy Communion*, London: Church House Publishing.

Archbishops' Council (2001). *Mind the Gap: Integrated Continuing Ministerial Education for the Church's Ministers*, London: Church House Publishing.

Archbishops' Council (2002). *The Structure and Funding of Ordination Training: the Interim Report*, London: Ministry Division of Archbishops' Council.

Archbishops' Council (2003). *Formation for Ministry within a Learning Church (Hind Report)*, London: Church House Publishing.

Archbishops' Council (2004). *Mission-shaped Church: Church Planting and Fresh Expressions of Church in a Changing World*, London: Church House Publishing.

Archbishops' Council (2005). *Review of Clergy Terms of Service*, London: Church House Publishing.

Archbishops' Council (2006). *Shaping the Future: New Patterns of Training for Lay and Ordained*, London: Church House Publishing.

Arseniev, N. (1979). *Mysticism and the Eastern Church*, London: Mowbrays.

Ashley, J. M. (2001). 'The mysticism of everyday life', *The Way*, supp. 102, 61–70.

Ashwin, A. (1991). *Heaven in Ordinary: Contemplative Prayer in Ordinary Life*, Great Wakering: McCrimmon.

Astley, J. (1994). *The Philosophy of Christian Religious Education*, Birmingham, AL: Religious Education Press.

Astley, J., Francis, L. J. and Crowder C. (1996). *Theological Perspectives on Christian Formation*, Leominster: Gracewing.

Avis, P. (1999). *God and the Creative Imagination: Metaphor, Symbol and Myth in Religion and Theology*, London: Routledge.

Backhouse, H. C. (ed.) (1988). *A Plain Man's Guide to Holiness*, London: Hodder and Stoughton.

Ball, P. (1984). *Journey into Faith*, London: Society for Promoting Christian Knowledge (SPCK).

Ballard, P. and Pritchard, J. (2nd edn, 2006). *Practical Theology in Action*, London: SPCK.

Banks, R. (1999). *Reenvisioning Theological Education*, Grand Rapids: Eerdmans.

Barley, L. (2006). *Christian Roots, Contemporary Spirituality*, London: Church House Publishing.

Barr, R. B. and Tagg, J. (1995). 'From teaching to learning: a new paradigm for undergraduate education', in *Change*, Helen Dwight Reid Educational Foundation, *http://critical.tamucc.edu*.

Barrett, C. K. (1968). *A Commentary on the First Epistle to the Corinthians*, London: A & C Black.

Barron, R. E. (1999). 'Priest as bearer of the mystery', in K. S. Smith (ed.), *Priesthood in the Modern World*, Wisconsin: Sheed & Ward, pp. 93–100.

Barry, P. (1995). *Saint Benedict and Christianity in England*, Ampleforth: Abbey Press.

Basil of Caesarea (1986). 'Letter 2', in G. A. Barrois, *The Fathers Speak*, New York: St Vladimir's Seminary Press, pp. 47–52.

Basil of Caesarea (1997). *On The Holy Spirit* 1:1, in A. Roberts and J. Donaldson (eds), *The Ante-Nicene Fathers*, Albany: Ages Digital Library.

Battle, M. (2002). 'Teaching and learning as ceaseless prayer', in L. G. Jones and S. Paulsell (eds), *The Scope of our Art: The Vocation of the Theological Teacher*, Grand Rapids: Eerdmans, pp. 155–72.

Beit-Hallahmi, B. and Argyle, M. (1997). *Religious Behaviour, Belief and Experience*, London: Routledge.

Berg, B. L. (1989). *Qualitative Research Methods for the Social Sciences*, Boston: Allyn & Bacon.

Berger, P. (1967). *The Sacred Canopy: Elements of a Sociological Theory of Religion*, New York: Anchor Books.

Berger, P. (2000). *The Desecularization of the World: Resurgent Religion and World Politics*, Grand Rapids: Eerdmans.

Berntsen, J. A. (1996). 'Christian affections and the catechumenate', in J. Astley, L. J. Francis and C. Crowder (eds), *Theological Perspectives on Christian Formation*, Leominster: Gracewing, pp 229–43.

Best, E. (1981). *Following Jesus: Discipleship in the Gospel of Mark*, Sheffield: Press of Journal for Study of New Testament.

Bevans, S. B. (2002). *Models of Contextual Theology*, Maryknoll, NY: Orbis.

Binns, J. (2005). 'Theological education in the Ethiopian Orthodox Church', *Journal of Adult Theological Education*, 2 (2), 103–13.

Blaiklock, E. M. (tr.) (1981). *Brother Lawrence: the Practice of the Presence of God*, London: Hodder & Stoughton.

Boa, K. (2001). *Conformed to His Image: Biblical and Practical Approaches to Spiritual Formation*, Grand Rapids: Zondervan.

Board of Education (1996). *Taking the Credit: NVQ's and the Churches*, London: Church House Publishing.

Boff, L. (1988). *Trinity and Society*, London: Burns & Oates.

Boff, L. (1990). *Saint Francis: A Model for Human Liberation*, New York: Crossroad.

Borg, M. J. (1993). *Jesus: A New Vision*, London: SPCK.

Bosch, D. J. (1991). *Transforming Mission: Paradigm Shifts in Theology of Mission*, Maryknoll, New York: Orbis.

Bourne, Cardinal (1926). *Ecclesiastical Training*, London: Burns Oates & Washbourne.

Bridger, F. (2003). 'A theological reflection', in Convocations of Canterbury and York, *Guidelines for the Professional Conduct of the Clergy*, London: Church House Publishing, pp. 13–20.

Briggs Myers, I. and Myers, P. B. (1995). *Gifts Differing: Understanding Personality Type*, Mountain View, CA: Davies-Black Publishing.

Bright, P. (tr.) (1986). *Early Christian Spirituality*, Philadelphia: Fortress Press.

Brodie, T. L. (1997). *The Gospel According to John: A Literary and Theological Commentary*, Oxford: Oxford University Press.

Brooks, T. M. (1998). 'Spirituality and its impact on theological education,' *Ministerial Formation*, 80, 39–41.

Brown, C. (2000). *The Death of Christian Britain*, London: Routledge.

Brown, L. B. (1994). *The Human Side of Prayer: The Psychology of Praying*, Birmingham, AL: Religious Education Press.

Brown, R. M. (1988). *Spirituality and Liberation*, London: Spire.

Broyles, C. (1989). *The Conflict of Faith and Experience in the Psalms: A Form-Critical & Theological Study*, Sheffield: Journal for the Study of the Old Testament Press.

Brueggemann, W. (1982). *Genesis: A Bible Commentary for Teaching and Preaching*, Atlanta: John Knox Press.

Brueggemann, W. (1991). *Interpretation and Obedience*, Minneapolis: Fortress Press.

Brueggemann, W. (2001). *The Prophetic Imagination*, Minneapolis: Fortress Press.

Bryant, C. (1978). *The River Within: The Search for God in Depth*, London: Darton, Longman & Todd.

Bryman, A. (2001). *Quantity and Quality in Social Research*, London: Routledge.

Bryman, A. (2004). *Social Research Methods*, Oxford: Oxford University Press.

Budde, L. and Brimlow, R. W. (eds) (2000). *The Church as Counterculture*, New York: State University.

Bullock, F. W. B. (1955). *A History of Training for the Ministry of the Church of England in England and Wales from 1800 to 1874*, St Leonards on Sea: Budd & Gillatt.

Bullock, F. W. B. (1969). *A History of Training for the Ministry of the Church of England in England and Wales From 598 to 1799*, St Leonards on Sea: Budd & Gillatt.

Bunker, D. E. (1991). 'Spirituality and the four Jungian personality functions,' *Journal of Psychology and Theology*, 19 (1), 26–34.

Callahan, V. W. (tr.) (1967). *The Fathers of the Church: St Gregory of Nyssa: Ascetical Works*, Washington: Catholic University of America Press.

Canon Law Society Trust (1983). *The Code of Canon Law*, London: Collins Liturgical Publications.

Carr, D. (1995). 'Towards a distinctive conception of spiritual education', *Oxford Review of Education*, 21 (1), 83–98.

Cartledge, M. J. (2003). *Practical Theology*, Carlisle: Paternoster Press.

Casaldaliga, P. and Vigil, J. M. (1994). *The Spirituality of Liberation*, Tunbridge Wells: Burns & Oates.

Catholic Church (1994). *The Catechism of the Catholic Church*, London: Chapman.

Central Board of Finance of the Church of England (1998). *Common Worship Initiation Services*, London: Church House Publishing.

Cetuk, V. S. (1998). *What to Expect in Seminary: Theological Education as Spiritual Formation*, Nashville: Abingdon Press.

Charry, E. (1997). *By the Renewing of Your Minds*, Oxford: Oxford University Press.

Chilton, B. (2002). *Rabbi Jesus*, London: Image/Doubleday.

Claxton, G. (1994). *Noises from the Dark Room: The Science and Mystery of the Mind*, London: Aquarian.

Claxton, G. (1997). *Hare Brain, Tortoise Mind: Why Intelligence Increases When you Think Less*, London: Fourth Estate.

Clement of Alexandria (1986). 'Exhortation to the Greeks' (*Protreptikos*), in P. Bright (tr.), *Early Christian Spirituality*, Philadelphia: Fortress Press, pp. 51–5.

Clement of Alexandria (1997a). *Paedagogus* in A. Roberts and J. Donaldson (eds), *The Ante-Nicene Fathers*, Albany: Ages Digital Library.

Clement of Alexandria (1997b). *Stromateis* in A. Roberts and J. Donaldson (eds), *The Ante-Nicene Fathers*, Albany: Ages Digital Library.

Cocksworth, C. (2003). *Wisdom: the Spirit's Gift*, Cambridge: Grove.

Coggan, D. (1970). *The Prayers of the New Testament*, London: Hodder & Stoughton.

Cola, S. (1991). 'The relevance of a communitarian spirituality in the process of formation', in M. Mulvey (ed.), *Formation and Communion: Priests of the Future*, New York: New City Press, pp. 38–45.

Commission for Priestly Formation (1979). *Cherwell Report: A Report by the Commission's Working Party on Priestly Training*, Roman Catholic Episcopal Conference of England and Wales.

Congar, C. Y. (1983). *I Believe in the Holy Spirit*, vol. I: *The Experience of the Spirit*, London: Geoffrey Chapman.

Congregation for Catholic Education (1970). *The Basic Plan for Priestly*

Formation (Ratio Fundamentalis Institutionis Sacerdotalis), Washington, DC: National Conference of Catholic Bishops.

Congregation for Catholic Education (1979). *Instruction on Liturgical Formation in Seminaries.*

Congregation for Catholic Education (1980). *Spiritual Formation in Seminaries (www.catholicculture.org).*

Congregation for Catholic Education (1985). *Ratio Fundamentalis Institutionis Sacerdotalis: Basic Norms for Priestly Formation.* These documents are in National Conference of Catholic Bishops (1993). *Norms of Priestly Formation*, vols I & II, Washington DC: US Catholic Conference.

Congregation for the Clergy (1994). *Directory on the Ministry and Life of Priests*, London: CTS.

Congregation for the Clergy (1998). *Basic Norms for the Formation of Permanent Deacons*, Rome: Libreria Editrice Vaticana.

Congregation for the Clergy (1999). *The Priest and the Third Christian Millennium: Teacher of the Word, Minister of the Sacraments and Leader of the Community*, Vatican City: Congregation for the Clergy.

Congregation for Divine Worship (1974). *Rite of Christian Initiation of Adults*, London: Catholic Truth Society.

Congregation for Institutes of Consecrated Life and Societies of Apostolic Life (1990). *Directives on Formation in Religious Institutes*, London: Catholic Truth Society.

Connelly, C. (1850a). 'Constitutions(or Rule) of the Society of the Holy Child Jesus', unpublished, from archives of the society, Oxford.

Connelly, C. (1850b). 'Customal of the Society of the Holy Child Jesus', unpublished, from archives of the society, Oxford.

Cooper, A. (1991). *The Cloud of Unknowing: Reflections on Selected Texts*, Tunbridge Wells: Burns & Oates.

Coptic Orthodox Church Network (2008). *An Introduction to the School of Alexandria (www.copticchurch.net).*

Costello, T. (2002). *Forming a Priestly Identity: Anthropology of Priestly Formation in the Documents of the VIII Synod of Bishops and the Apostolic Exhortation Pastores Dabo Vobis*, Rome: Editrice Pontificia Universita Gregoriana.

Cottrell, S. and Croft, S. (2004). *Emmaus: The Way of Faith: Growing as a Christian*, London: Church House Publishing.

Countryman, L. W. (1999a). *The Poetic Imagination: An Anglican Spiritual Tradition*, London: Darton, Longman & Todd.

Countryman, L. W. (1999b). *Living on the Border of the Holy: Renewing the Priesthood of All*, Harrisburg, PA: Morehouse.

Cousins, E. (tr.) (1978). *Bonaventure: the Soul's Journey into God*, London: SPCK.

Craig, Y. (1994). *Learning for Life: A Handbook of Adult Religious Education*, London: Mowbray.

Cram, R. H. and Saunders, S. P. (1992). 'Feet partly of iron and partly of clay: pedagogy and the curriculum of theological education', *Theological Education*, 28, 21–50.

Creswell, J. W. (1997). *Qualitative Inquiry and Research Design*, London: Sage.

Croft, S., Dalpra, C. and Lings G. (2006). *Starting a Fresh Expression*, London: Church House Publishing.

Croft, S. and Frost, R. (2005). *Evangelism in a Spiritual Age*, London: Church House Publishing.

Croft, S. and Walton, R. (2005). *Learning for Ministry: Making the Most of Study and Training*, London: Church House Publishing.

Cullmann, O. (1995). *Prayer in the New Testament*, London: SCM.

Danielou, J. (1973). *Gospel Message and Hellenistic Culture*, London: Darton, Longman & Todd.

Davie, G. (1994). *Religion in Britain since 1945*, Oxford: Blackwell.

Davie, G. (2000). *Religion in Modern Europe*, Oxford: Oxford University Press.

Davis, C.F. (1989). *The Evidential Force of Religious Experience*, Oxford: Clarendon Press.

de Waal, E. (1997). *Living with Contradiction*, Norwich: Canterbury Press.

Deane-Drummond, C. E. (2000). *Creation Through Wisdom: Theology and the New Biology*, Edinburgh: T & T Clark.

Dey, I. (1993). *Qualitative Data Analysis*, London: Routledge.

Downey, M. (ed.) (1993). *The New Dictionary of Catholic Spirituality*, Collegeville, Minnesota: Liturgical Press.

Drane, J. (2005). 'New spirituality and Christian mission', in Bible Society, *The Bible in Transmission: A Forum for Change in Church and Culture*, Swindon: Bible Society, pp. 6–8.

Driver, J. (1989). 'Spirituality and theological education', *Ministerial Formation*, 46, 12–25

Duffy, E. (1992). 'Common things raised up to angelhood: priestly formation then and now', in J. H. Murphy (ed.), *New Beginnings in Ministry*, Mount Merrion, Co. Dublin: Columba Press, pp. 160–78.

Dulles, A. (1976). *Models of the Church*, Dublin: Gill & Macmillan.

Duncan, B. (1993). *Pray Your Way: Your Personality and God*, London: Darton, Longman & Todd.

Dunn, J. D. G. (1998). *The Theology of Paul the Apostle*, Edinburgh: T & T Clark.

Dunn, J. D. G. (2003). *Jesus Remembered*, Michigan/Cambridge: Eerdmans.

Duraisingh, C. (1992). 'Formation for mission', *International Review of Mission*, LXXXI (321), 33–45.

Edwards, T. H. (1980). 'Spiritual formation in theological schools: ferment and challenge', *Theological Education*, 17, 7–52.

Egan, R. J. (2001). 'The mystical and the prophetic: dimensions of Christian experience', *The Way*, supp. 102, 92–106.

Eliot, T. S. (1974). *Collected Poems 1909–1962*, London: Faber & Faber.

Entwistle, N. (1996). 'Recent research on student learning and the learning environment', in J. Tait and P. Knight (eds), *The Management of Independent Learning*, London: SEDA/Kogan Page.

Ephraim, Archimandrite of Vatopedi Monastery (2006). 'The soul and repentance', *Friends of Mount Athos Annual Report 2006*, Oxford: Friends of Mount Athos.

Erickson, J. H. (2002). 'Orthodox theology in a changing world', *St Vladimir's Theological Quarterly*, 46 (4), 307–14.

Ethiopian Orthodox Church (1997). *The Church of Ethiopia: A Panorama of History and Spiritual Life*, Addis Ababa: Ethiopian Orthodox Church.

Faber, J. (1991). 'Content and human development', *The Way*, supp. 71: *Formation in Religious Life*, 54–63

Farley, E. (1983). *Theologia: the Fragmentation and Unity of Theological Education*, Philadelphia: Augsburg Fortress.

Farley, E. (1988). *The Fragility of Knowledge*, Philadelphia: Fortress Press.

Farley, E. (2003). *Practicing Gospel*, London: Westminster John Knox Press.

Finney, J. (1989). *Understanding Leadership*, London: Darton, Longman & Todd.

Finney, J. R. and Maloney, H. N. (1985). 'Empirical studies of Christian prayer: a review of the literature', *Journal of Psychology and Theology*, 13 (2), 104–15.

Fiorenza, F. S. (1988). 'Thinking theologically about theological education', *Theological Education*, 24, supp. 2, reprinted in J. Astley, L. J. Francis and C. Crowder, *Theological Perspectives on Christian Formation*, Leominster: Gracewing, pp. 318–41.

Flannery, A. (ed.) (1975). *Vatican Council II: the Conciliar and Post Conciliar Documents*, Dublin: Dominican Publications.

Flew, R. N. (1934). *The Idea of Perfection in Christian Theology*, Oxford: Clarendon.

Fokkelman, J. P. (1991). *Narrative Art in Genesis: Specimens of Stylistic and Structural Analysis*, Sheffield: Journal for the Study of the Old Testament Press.

Follent, J. (1994). 'Negative experience and Christian growth', in P. Slattery (ed.), *St John of the Cross*, New York: Alba House.

Ford, D. F. (1997). *The Shape of Living*, London: Fount.

Ford, D. F. and Hardy, D. W. (2005). *Living in Praise: Worshipping and Knowing God*, London: Darton, Longman & Todd.

Foster, C. R., Dahill, L. E., Golemon, L. A. and Tolentino, B. W. (2006). *Educating Clergy: Teaching Practices and Pastoral Imagination*, San Francisco: Jossey-Bass.

Foster, R. (1980). *Celebration of Discipline*, London: Hodder & Stoughton.

Foster, R. (1992). *Prayer: Finding the Heart's True Home*, London: Hodder & Stoughton.

Fowke, R. (1997). *Personality and Prayer: Finding and Extending the Prayer Style that Suits your Personality*, Guildford: Eagle.

Fox, M. (2001). *Prayer: A Radical Response to Life*, New York: Tarcher/Putnam.

Francis, L. J. and Astley, J. (2001). *Psychological Perspectives on Prayer*, Leominster: Gracewing.

Francis, L. J. and Evans, T. E. (2001). 'The psychology of Christian prayer: a review of empirical research', in L. J. Francis and J. Astley, *Psychological Perspectives on Prayer*, Leominster: Gracewing, pp. 2–22.

Freire, P. (1970). *Pedagogy of the Oppressed*, New York: Herder & Herder.

Frost, R. (2002). *Essence: an Exploration of Contemporary Spirituality which Looks Towards a Lifestyle integrating Body, Mind and Spirit*, Eastbourne: Kingsway.

Fry, T. (ed.) (1982). *The Rule of St Benedict in English*, Collegeville, MN: Liturgical Press.

Fuller, E. (ed.) (1957). *The Christian Idea of Education*, New Haven: Yale University Press.

Gangel, K. O. and Wilhoit, J. C. (1997). *The Christian Educator's Handbook on Spiritual Formation*, Michigan: Baker Books.

Garrigou-Lagrange, R. (1954). *The Priesthood and Perfection*, Dublin: Dominican Publications.

Garrigou-Lagrange, R. (1961). *The Priest in Union with Christ*, Cork: Mercier Press.

General Synod (1980). *The Continuing Education of the Church's Ministers*, London: General Synod, (GS Misc. 122).

General Synod (1996). *Christian Education and Training for the 21st Century*, London: Church House (GS Misc. 389).

General Synod (1997). *Eucharistic Presidency*, London: House of Bishops, Church House Publishing.

General Synod (2003). *The Revised Catechism*, London: SPCK.

General Synod (2005). *Common Worship Ordinal*, London: Church House Publishing.

General Synod (2008). *Readers Upbeat: Quickening the Tempo of Reader Ministry in the Church Today*, London, General Synod (GS 1689).

Gibbard, M. (1970). *Why Pray?*, London: SCM.

Gill, R. (2002). *Changing Worlds: Can the Church Respond?*, London: T & T Clark.

Gilliat-Ray, S. (2001). 'The fate of the Anglican clergy and the class of 97: some implications of the changing sociological profile of Anglican ordinands', *Journal of Contemporary Religion*, 16 (2), 209–25.

Glazer, S. (ed.) (1999). *The Heart of Learning: Spirituality in Education*, New York: Tarcher/Penguin.

Godin, A. (ed.) (1968). *From Cry to Word: Contributions towards a Psychology of Prayer*, Brussels: Lumen Vitae Press.

Graebner, T. (2003). *Sacred Waters: Modern Pilgrimages to the Fountains, Seas and Rivers of the Bible*, Whitefish, MT: Kessinger.

Graham, E., Walton, H. and Ward, F. (2005). *Theological Reflection: Methods*, London: SCM.

Green, L. (1990). *Let's Do Theology*, London: Continuum.

Greenslade, P. (1984). *Leadership: Reflections on Biblical Leadership*, London: Marshall Morgan & Scott.

Greenwood, R. (1999). *Transforming Priesthood*, London: SPCK.

Greer, R. A. (1992). 'Who seeks for a spring in the mud? Reflections on the ordained ministry in the fourth century', in R. J. Neuhaus (ed.), *Theological Education and Moral Formation*, Grand Rapids: Eerdmans, pp. 22–55.

Gregory of Nyssa (1962). 'On Perfection', in H. Musurillo (tr.), *From Glory to Glory: Texts from Gregory of Nyssa's Mystical Writings*, London: John Murray, pp. 83–4.

Gregory the Great (1978). 'Regula Pastoralis II:7:68', in J. Quasten and J. C. Plumpe (eds), *Ancient Christian Writers: The Works of the Fathers in Translation*, New York: Newman Press.

Grenz, S. J. (1996). *A Primer on Postmodernism*, Grand Rapids: Eerdmans.

Gula, R. M. (1996). *Ethics in Pastoral Ministry*, New York: Paulist Press.

Gumbel, N. (2005). *Alpha Course Manual*, London: Alpha International.

Gunton, C. E. (1988). *The Actuality of Atonement*, Edinburgh: T & T Clark.

Gutiérrez, G. (1984). *We Drink from Our Own Wells*, London: SCM.

Gutiérrez, G. (1988). *A Theology of Liberation*, London: SCM.

Habgood, J. (1998). *Being a Person: Where Faith and Science Meet*, London: Hodder & Stoughton.

Hall, D. J. (1988). 'Theological education as character formation?', *Theological Education*, 24, supp. 1, 153–79.

Hannaford, R. (1991). 'Towards a theology of the diaconate', in C. Hall (ed.), *The Deacon's Ministry*, Leominster: Gracewing, pp. 25–44.

Hardy, D. W. (1996). *God's Ways with the World*, Edinburgh: T & T Clark.

Hart, D. G. and Mohler, R. A. (eds.) (1996). *Theological Education in the Evangelical Tradition*, Grand Rapids: Baker Books.

Harvey, B. (1999). *Another City*, Pennsylvania: Trinity Press.

Hassel, D. J. (1984). *Radical Prayer*, New York: Paulist Press.

Hauerwas, S. (1981). *Vision and Virtue*, Notre Dame, IN: University of Notre Dame Press.

Hauerwas, S. and Willimon, W. H. (1989). *Resident Aliens*, Nashville: Abingdon Press.

Hauerwas, S. and Willimon, W. H. (1996). *Where Resident Aliens Live*, Nashville: Abingdon Press.

Heelas, P. and Woodhead, L. (2005). *The Spiritual Revolution*, London: Routledge.

Heiler, F. (1937). *Prayer: A Study in the History and Psychology of Religion*, London: Oxford University Press.

Herbert, G. (1995). *The Complete English Works*, London: Everyman's Library, David Campbell Publishers.

Hiller, D. (2000), 'Faith, experience and the concept of prayer', *Neue Zeitschrift fur Systematische Theologie und Religionsphilosophie*, 42 (3), 316–29.

Hillier, Y. (2002). *Reflective Teaching in Further and Adult Education*, London: Continuum.

Hinton, M. (1994). *The Anglican Parochial Clergy*, London: SCM.

Hodge, M. (1986). *Patterns of Ministerial Training*, London: ACCM.

Hoge, R. (2002). *The First Five Years of the Priesthood*, Collegeville, MN: Liturgical Press.

Hoge, R. and Wenger, J. E. (2003). *Evolving Visions of the Priesthood*, Collegeville, MN: Liturgical Press.

Hollinghurst, S., Richmond, Y. and Whitehead, R. (2006). *Equipping Your Church in a Spiritual Age: A Resource Workbook for Local Churches*, London: Group for Evangelism.

Holmes, A. (2000). *A Life Pleasing to God: The Spirituality of the Rules of St Basil*, London: Darton, Longman & Todd.

Holmes, A. F. (2001). *Building the Christian Academy*, Grand Rapids: Eerdmans.

Holmes III, U. T. (1980). *A History of Christian Spirituality*, New York: Harper & Row.

Holmes III, U. T. (2002). *Spirituality for Ministry*, Harrisburg, PA: Morehouse.

Honey, P. and Mumford, A. (1986). *Using Our Learning Styles*, London: Honey Publications.

Hope, S. (2006). *Mission-shaped Spirituality*, London: Church House Publishing.

Hopkins-Powell, S. (2007). 'Creating silence on the campus', *Journal of College and Character*, 2 (*www.college.values.org*).

Horsley, R. A. (1998). *1 Corinthians*, Nashville: Abingdon Press.

Howells, E. (2001). 'Mysticism and the mystical: the current debate', *The Way*, supp. 102, 15–27.

Hughes, G. W. (1985). *God of Surprises*, London: Darton, Longman & Todd.

Hughes, G. W. (2003). *God in All Things*, London: Hodder & Stoughton.

Hughes, P. (1961). *The Church in Crisis: The Twenty Great Councils*, London: Burns & Oates.

Hull, J. (1985). *What Prevents Adults from Learning?*, London: SCM Press.

Humphreys, C. (1992). *From Ash to Fire: A Contemporary Journey through the Interior Castle of Teresa of Avila*, New York: New City Press.

Hurley, D. E. (ed.) (1978). *Roman Pontifical: Ordination*, Rome: International Commission on English in the Liturgy.

Hurley, D. E. and Cunnane, J. (1967). *Vatican II on Priests and Seminaries*, Dublin: Scepter Books.

Hylson-Smith, K. (1999). *Christianity in England from Roman Times to the Reformation: I From Roman Times to 1066*, London: SCM.

Irvine, C. (2005). *The Art of God: the Making of Christians and the Meaning of Worship*, London: SPCK.

Jacob, W. (1990). 'The development of the concept of residence in theological education in the Church of England', in Advisory Council for the Churches' Ministry, *Residence – an Education*, London: Church House Publishing, pp. 68–91.

Jaeger, W. (1945). *Paideia: The Ideals of Greek Culture*, vol. 1, Oxford: Oxford University Press.

Jaeger, W. (1961). *Early Christianity and Greek Paideia*, Cambridge, MA: Harvard University Press.

James, D. L. (2002). 'Theological faculty as religious educators: how personal beliefs about teaching, learning, and spiritual growth inform teaching practices', *www.religiouseducation.net*.

James, W. (1971). *The Varieties of Religious Experience*, London: Fontana Library Theology and Philosophy.

Jamison, C. (2006). *Finding Sanctuary: Monastic Steps for Everyday Life*, London: Weidenfeld & Nicolson.

Janssen, J., de Hart, J. and den Draak, C. (1989). 'Praying practices', *Journal of Empirical Theology*, 2 (2), 28–39.

Jarvis, P. (2004). *Adult Education and Lifelong Learning: Theory and Practice*, 3rd edn, London: Routledge Falmer.

Jeremias, J. (1974). *The Prayers of Jesus*, London: SCM.

John XXIII (1959). *Princeps Pastorum*, *www.vatican.va*.

John Paul II (1988). *Christifideles Laici*, *www.vatican.va*.

John Paul II (1992). *Pastores Dabo Vobis*, London: Catholic Truth Society.

Johnson, B. C. and Dreitcer, A. (2001). *Beyond the Ordinary: Spirituality for Church Leaders*, Grand Rapids: Eerdmans.

Johnson, W. (2002). 'We need a revolution', *The Tablet*, 1 June.

Jones, Alan (1987). 'Are we lovers anymore? (Spiritual formation in seminaries)', *Theological Education*, 24 (1), 9–29.

Jones, Anthea (2000). *A Thousand Years of the English Parish*, Moreton-in Marsh: Windrush Press.

Jones, L. (2005). 'What does spirituality in education mean? Stumbling toward wholeness', *Journal of College and Character*, VI (7), *www.collegevalues.org*.

Kavanaugh, K. and Rodriguez, O. (trs) (1979). *Teresa of Avila: The Interior Castle*, New York: Paulist Press.

Kavanaugh, K. and Rodriguez, O. (trs) (1991). *The Collected Works of St John of the Cross*, Washington DC: Institute of Carmelite Studies.

Kelsey, D. H. (1988). 'Reflections on a discussion of theological education as character formation', *Theological Education*, 25 (1), 62–75.

Kelsey, D. H. (1992). *To Understand God Truly: What's Theological About a Theological School*, Louisville: Westminster/John Knox Press.

Kelsey, D. H. (1993). *Between Athens and Berlin: The Theological Education Debate*, Grand Rapids: Eerdmans.

Kelsey, M. T. (1974). *Encounter with God: A Theology of Christian Experience*, London: Hodder & Stoughton.

Kelsey, M. T. (1977). *The Other Side of Silence: A Guide to Christian Meditation*, London: SPCK.

King, A. and Clifford S. (eds) (2000). *The Rivers' Voice: An Anthology of Poetry*, Totnes: Green Books.

Kinn, J. W. (2004). *The Spirit of Jesus in Scripture and Prayer*, Maryland: Sheed & Ward.

Kittel, G. (ed.) (1967). *Theological Dictionary of the New Testament*, Grand Rapids: Eerdmans.

Kleissler, T. A., Lebert, M. A. and McGuinness M. C. (1991). *Small Christian Communities: A Vision of Hope*, New York: Paulist Press.

Klimoski, V. (2004). 'Evolving dynamics of formation', in M. L. Warford (ed.), *Practical Wisdom: On Theological Teaching and Learning*, New York: Peter Lang, pp. 29–48.

Kudian, M. (tr.) (1986). *Nerses Shnorhali: Jesus the Son*, London: Mashtots Press.

Kuhrt, G. W. (2000). *An Introduction to Christian Ministry: Following Your Vocation in the Church of England*, London: Church House Publishing.

Kuhrt, G. W. (2001). *Ministry Issues: Mapping the Trends for the Church of England*, London: Church House Publishing.

Ladd, K. L. and Spilka, B. (2002). 'Inward, outward, and upward: cognitive aspects of prayer', *Journal for the Scientific Study of Religion*, 41 (3), 475–84.

Lane, W. L. (1974). *The Gospel According to Mark*, Grand Rapids: Eerdmans.

Lawrence, J. (2004). *Growing Leaders: Reflections on Leadership, Life and Jesus*, Oxford: Bible Reading Fellowship.

Leech, K. (1980). *True Prayer*, London: Sheldon Press.

Leech, K. (1985). *Experiencing God: Theology as Spirituality*, New York: Harper & Row.

Leech, K. (2005). 'Beware the bureaucrats', *Church Times*, 5 August.

Leo XIII (1902). *Fin Dal Principio* (Encyclical on the Education of the Clergy), *www.vatican.va*.

Lewis, J. (2000). 'Spiritual education as the cultivation of qualities of the heart and mind: a reply to Blake and Carr', *Oxford Review of Education*, 26 (2), 263–83.

Lincoln, A. T. (1990). *Ephesians: Word Biblical Commentary*, Dallas: Word Books.

Lincoln, A. T. (2005). *The Gospel According to St John*, London: Black's New Testament Commentaries, Continuum.

Lindbeck, G. (1988). 'Spiritual formation and theological education', *Theological Education*, 24, supp. 1, 10–32.

Lonsdale, D. and Sheldrake, P. (eds) (1986). *The Way*, supp. 56: *Formation for Ministry*.

Lossky, V. (1957). *The Mystical Theology of the Eastern Church*, Cambridge: James Clarke.

Louden, S. H. and Francis, L. J. (2003). *The Naked Parish Priest: What Priests Really Think They're Doing*, London: Continuum.

Louth, A. (1983). *Discerning the Mystery: An Essay on the Nature of Theology*, Oxford: Clarendon Press.

Louth, A. (2000). *Theology and Spirituality*, 5th edn, Fairacres: Oxford SLG Press.

Louth, A. (2003). *The Wilderness of God*, London: Darton, Longman & Todd.

Louth, A. (2004). 'Theology, contemplation and the university', *Studies in Christian Ethics*, 17, 169–79.

Luscombe, P. and Shreeve, E. (eds) (2002). *What is a Minister?*, Peterborough: Epworth Press.

McCloskey, G. N. (2004). *Augustine: Struggling to Learn*, accessed from *http://kahuna.merrimack.edu*.

McFadyen, A. I. (1990). *The Call to Personhood: A Christian Theory of the Individual in Social Relationships*, Cambridge: Cambridge University Press.

McFague, S. (1982). *Metaphorical Theology: Models of God in Religious Language*, Philadelphia: Fortress Press.

McGinn, B. (1991). *The Foundation of Mysticism*: vol. I: *Origins to the 5th Century*, London: SCM.

McGrath, A. E. (1998). *Historical Theology*, Oxford: Blackwell.

McIntosh, M. A. (1998). *Mystical Theology: the Integrity of Spirituality and Theology*, Oxford: Blackwell.

MacIntyre, A. (1985). *After Virtue: A Study in Moral Theory*, London: Duckworth.

McPartlan, P. (1993). *The Eucharist Makes the Church*, Edinburgh: T & T Clark.

Macquarrie, J. (1972). *Paths in Spirituality*, London: SCM.

Malherbe, A. J. & Ferguson, E. (trs) (1978). *Gregory of Nyssa: The Life of Moses*, New York: Paulist Press.

Marins, J. (1989). *The Church From the Roots: Basic Ecclesial Communities*, London: CAFOD.

Marmion, Abbot (1952). *Christ the Ideal of the Priest*, St Louis: B. Herder Book Co.

Marschisano, F. (1989). 'Spiritual formation in theological education: a Roman Catholic response', *Ministerial Formation*, 47, Geneva, WCC, 26–9.

Marshall, T. (1991). *Understanding Leadership*, Tonbridge: Sovereign World.

Martin, T. F. (1999). '*Clericatus sarcina*: Augustine and the care of the clergy', in *Devotion and Dissent: The Practice of Christianity in Roman Africa. Church Leadership: Roles and Requirements, http://divinity.library. vanderbilt.edu/burns/chroma/.*

Mary, A. and Bonner, G. (trs) (2004). *Saint Augustine: the Monastic Rules*, New York: New City Press.

Matthew, I. (1995). *The Impact of God: Soundings from St John of the Cross*, London: Hodder & Stoughton.

Matthews, M. (1996). *Rediscovering Holiness*, London: SPCK.

Matthews, M. (2000). *Both Alike to Thee: the Retrieval of the Mystical Way*, London: SPCK

Matthew the Poor (2003). *Orthodox Prayer Life: the Interior Way*, New York: St Vladimir's Seminary Press.

Maximos the Confessor, (1981). 'Four hundred texts on love', in G. E. H. Palmer, P. Sherrard and K. Ware (trs), *The Philokalia*, vol. 2, London: Faber & Faber, pp. 52–113.

Mayes, A. D. (2002). *Spirituality of Struggle: Pathways to Growth*, London: SPCK.

Mayes, A. D. and Warner, M. (1990). *Follow Me: Adult Confirmation Workbook*, Birmingham: Additional Curates' Society.

Meredith, A. (1985). *The Cappadocians*, London: Chapman.

Meredith, A. (1986). 'Clement of Alexandria', C. Jones, G. Wainwright and E. Yarnold (eds), *The Study of Spirituality*, London: SPCK, pp. 112–14.

Merick, R. (1988). 'An Orthodox pastor in a new world', in *A Legacy of Excellence: St Vladimir's Orthodox Theological Seminary 1938–1988*, New York: St Vladimir's Seminary Press, pp. 69–71.

Merton, T. (1972). *Seeds of Contemplation*, Wheathampstead: Anthony Clarke.

Merton, T. (2004). *The Wisdom of the Desert*, Boston and London: Shambhala.

Methodist Church (1996). *The Making of Ministry*, Ministerial Training Policy Working Group, Peterborough: Methodist Publishing House.

Methodist Church (2003a). *Church and Ministry: A Theological Framework – Formation in Ministry, Discussion Paper 1*, London: Methodist Formation in Ministry Office.

Methodist Church (2003b). *Vocational Discernment and Formation: Formation in Ministry, Discussion Paper 4*, London: Methodist Formation in Ministry Office.

Methodist Conference (2002). *What is a Presbyter?*, Peterborough: Methodist Publishing House.

Meyendorff, J. (1975). *Byzantine Theology: Historical Trends and Doctrinal Themes*, Oxford: Mowbray.

Meyendorff, J. (1983). *Gregory Palamas: the Triads*, New York: Paulist Press.

Mezirow, J. (1981). 'A critical theory of adult learning and education', *Adult Education*, 32, 3–23.

Mezirow, J. (1991). *Transformative Dimensions of Adult Learning*, San Francisco: Jossey-Bass.

Michael, C. P. and Norrisey, M. C. (1991). *Prayer and Temperament: Different Prayer Forms For Different Personality Types*, Charlottesville, VA: Open Door.

Michael, P. (ed.) (2000). *The Gift of Rivers: True Stories of Life on the Water*, San Francisco: Travellers' Tales.

Middleton, J. R. and Walsh, B. J. (1995). *Truth Is Stranger Than It Used to Be*, Downers Grove, IL: InterVarsity Press.

Midgley, M. (1989). *Wisdom, Information and Wonder: What is Knowledge For?*, London: Routledge.

Miles, M. R. (1989). *The Image and Practice of Holiness*, London: SCM.

Miller-McLemore, B. J. (2002). 'Contemplation in the midst of chaos', in L. G. Jones and S. Paulsell (eds), *The Scope of our Art: The Vocation of the Theological Teacher*, Grand Rapids: Eerdmans, pp. 48–74.

Moberly, R. C. (1969). *Ministerial Priesthood*, London: SPCK.

Moltmann, J. (2001). *The Spirit of Life: A Universal Affirmation*, Minneapolis: Fortress Press.

Monbourquette, J. (2001). *How to Befriend Your Shadow*, London: Darton, Longman & Todd.

Moon, J. (1999). *Reflection in Learning and Professional Development: Theory and Practice*, London: Kogan Page.

Moore, A. (2002). 'One song, two different tunes', *Church Times*, 24 May.

Moore, M. E. M. (1998). *Teaching from the Heart: Theology and Educational Method*, Harrisburg, PA: Trinity Press International.

Moorman, J. R. H. (1958). *A History of the Church in England*, London: A&C Black.

Mottola, A. (tr.) (1964). *The Spiritual Exercises of St Ignatius*, New York: Image/Doubleday.

Muddiman, J. (2001). *A Commentary on the Epistle to the Ephesians*, London: Continuum.

Muggeridge, K. (tr.) (1996). *The Sacrament of the Present Moment: Jean-Pierre de Caussade*, London: Fount.

Mulholland, M. R. (1993). *Invitation to a Journey: A Road Map for Spiritual Formation*, Downes Grove, IL: InterVarsity Press.

Muller, R. A. (1996). 'The era of Protestant orthodoxy', in D. G. Hart and R. A. Mohler, *Theological Education in the Evangelical Tradition*, Grand Rapids: Baker Books, pp. 103–28.

Murray, J. C. (1957). 'The Christian idea of education', in E. Fuller (ed.), *The Christian Idea of Education*, Yale: Yale University Press, pp. 152–63.

Musurillo, H. (tr.) (1962). *From Glory to Glory: Texts from Gregory of Nyssa's Mystical Writings*, London: John Murray.

Nelson, J. (ed.) (1999). *Leading, Managing, Ministering*, Norwich: Canterbury Press.

Neuhaus, R. J. (1992). *Theological Education and Moral Formation*, Grand Rapids: Eerdmans.

Neville, G. K. and Westerhoff III, J. H. (1978). *Learning Through Liturgy*, New York: Seabury.

Newbigin, L. (1989). *The Gospel in a Pluralist Society*, London: SPCK.

Nickerson, K. S. (1987). 'Spiritual formation in the United Methodist seminaries in the USA: a report', *Ministerial Formation*, 39, 28–31.

Norman, E. (2002). *Secularisation*, London: Continuum.

Northcott, H. (1962). *The Venture of Prayer*, London: SPCK.

Nouwen, H. J. M. (1972). *The Wounded Healer: Ministry in Contemporary Society*, New York: Continuum.

Nouwen, H. J. M. (1986). *Lifesigns: Intimacy, Fecundity and Ecstasy in Christian Perspective*, London: Image.

Nouwen, H. J. M. (2nd edn, 1990). *The Way of the Heart*, London: Darton, Longman & Todd.

Nouwen, H. J. M. (1998). *Ministry and Spirituality*, New York: Continuum.

O'Halloran, J. (1996). *Small Christian Communities: A Pastoral Companion*, Blackrock, Co. Dublin: Columba.

O'Leary, D. J. (1997). *New Hearts for New Models: A Spirituality for Priests Today*, Blackrock, Co. Dublin: Columba.

Pagura, F. J. (1988). 'Contextual spirituality and spiritual training', *Ministerial Formation*, 43, 15–22.

Palmer, G. E. H., Sherrard, P. and Ware, K. (trs) (1979). *The Philokalia*: vol. 1, London: Faber & Faber.

Palmer, G. E. H., Sherrard, P. and Ware, K. (trs) (1981) *The Philokalia*: vol. 2, London: Faber & Faber.

Palmer, P. J. (1983). *To Know As We Are Known: Education as a Spiritual Journey*, San Francisco: Harper & Row.

Palmer, P. J. (1998). *The Courage to Teach*, San Francisco: Jossey-Bass.

Partridge, C. (2004). *The Re-Enchantment of the West*, London: T & T Clark.

Patsavos, L. (1976). 'The image of the priest according to the three Hierarchs', *Greek Orthodox Theological Review*, XXI, 55–70.

Pattison, S., Thompson, J. and Green J. (2003). 'Theological reflection for the real world: time to think again', *British Journal of Theological Education*, 13 (2), 119–31.

Paul VI (1965). *Presbyterorum Ordinis*, in A. Flannery (ed.) (1975), *Vatican Council II: The Conciliar and Post Conciliar Documents*, Dublin: Dominican Publications, pp. 863–902.

Paul VI (1965). *Optatam Totius*, in A. Flannery (ed.) (1975), *Vatican Council II: The Conciliar and Post Conciliar Documents*, Dublin: Dominican Publications, pp. 707–24.

Pepe, E. (1991). 'Priestly formation in the history of the Church', in M. Mulvey (ed.), *Formation and Communion: Priests of the Future*, New York: New City Press, pp. 8–21.

Perri, W. D. (1996). *A Radical Challenge for Priesthood Today*, Mystic, CT: Twenty-Third Publications.

Peterson, E. H. (1993). *The Contemplative Pastor: Returning to the Art of Spiritual Direction*, Grand Rapids: Eerdmans.

Philibert, P. J. (2004). *Stewards of God's Mysteries: Priestly Spirituality in a Changing Church*, Collegeville, MN: Liturgical Press.

Phillips, D. Z. (1965). *The Concept of Prayer*, London: Routledge & Kegan Paul.

Pius X (1908). *Haerent Animo* (To the Catholic Clergy on Priestly Sanctity), from *www.catholiclinks.org.*

Pius XII (1950). *Menti Nostrae*, accessed from *www.ewtn.com/library.*

Pobee, J. (ed.) (1997). *Towards Viable Theological Education: Ecumenical, Imperative, Catalyst of Renewal*, Geneva: WCC.

Poloma, M. M. and Pendleton, B. F. (1991). *Exploring Neglected Dimensions of Religion in Quality of Life Research*, Lampeter: Edwin Mellen Press.

Porter, J. (1994). *The Recovery of Virtue*, London: SPCK.

Powell, M. A. (1998). *The Jesus Debate: Modern Historians Investigate the Life of Christ*, Oxford: Lion.

Prestige, G. L. (1940). *Fathers and Heretics*, London: SPCK.

Pryor, R. J. (1994). 'Nurturing spiritual development in the Uniting Church: spiritual development and theological education', *Ministerial Formation*, 66, 14–21.

Pryor, R. J. (1998) 'Spirituality and theological education', *Ministerial Formation*, 80, 35–41.

Puls, J. (1985). *Every Bush is Burning: A Spirituality for our Times*, Geneva: WCC.

Purkiser, W. T. (1983). *Exploring Christian Holiness*, vol. 1: *The Biblical Foundations*, Kansas: Beacon Hill Press.

Purves, A. (2001). *Pastoral Theology in the Classical Tradition*, Louisville: Westminster John Knox Press.

Quasten, J. and Plumpe, J. C. (eds) (1978). *Ancient Christian Writers: The Works of the Fathers in Translation*, New York: Newman Press.

Rahner, K. (1968). *Servants of the Lord,* Tunbridge Wells: Burns & Oates.

Ramsey, M. (1977). *Holy Spirit: A Biblical Study,* London: SPCK.

Rendle, G. R. (1998). *Leading Change in the Congregation,* Herndon, VA: Alban Institute.

Rice, H. L. (1991). *Reformed Spirituality,* Louisville, KY: Westminster/ John Knox Press.

Riem, R. (2003). 'Why calling matters more: weighing vocational and competency approaches to ministerial development', *British Journal of Theological Education,* 14 (1), 78–92.

Riley, J. (1990). *Getting the Most from Your Data: A Handbook of Practical Ideas on How to Analyse Data,* Bristol: Technical and Educational Services Ltd.

Robbins, V. K. (1984). *Jesus the Teacher: A Socio-Rhetorical Interpretation of Mark,* Philadelphia: Fortress Press.

Roberts, A. and Donaldson, J. (eds) (1997). *The Ante-Nicene Fathers,* Albany: Ages Digital Library.

Robson, J. and Lonsdale, D. (1987). *Can Spirituality be Taught?,* London: Association of Centres of Adult Theological Education/BCC.

Rolheiser, R. (1988). *Seeking Spirituality: Guidelines for a Christian Spirituality for the Twenty-First Century,* London: Hodder & Stoughton.

Rooy, S. (1988). 'Historical models of theological education', in C. R. Padilla (ed.), *New Alternatives in Theological Education,* Oxford: Regnum Books, pp. 51–72.

Rose, J. (2005). 'Educating the whole person an Orthodox perspective', in P. Schreiner, E. Banev and S. Oxley (eds), *Holistic Education Resource Book: Learning and Teaching in an Ecumenical Context,* Munster/New York: Waxman, pp. 69–76.

Rousseau, P. (1994). *Basil of Caesarea,* Berkeley: University of California Press.

Runcorn, D. (2006). *Spirituality Workbook,* London: SPCK.

Russell, A. (1984). *The Clerical Profession,* London: SPCK.

Sager, A. H. (1990). *Gospel-Centred Spirituality: an Introduction to our Spiritual Journey,* Minneapolis: Augsburg.

Samuelian, T. J. (tr.) (2002). *St Grigor Narekatsi: Speaking with God from the Depths of the Heart,* Yerevan, Armenia: Vem Press.

Sanders, J. N. (1975). *The Gospel According to St John,* London: A&C Black.

Sanford, J. A. (1982). *Ministry Burnout,* London: Arthur James Ltd.

Schaff P. (ed.) (1997). *Nicene and Post-Nicene Fathers,* Albany: Ages Digital Library.

Schmemann, A. (1966a). *Introduction to Liturgical Theology,* London: Faith Press.

Schmemann, A. (1966b). *The World as Sacrament,* London: Darton, Longman & Todd.

Schmemann, A. (1974). *Of Water and The Spirit,* London: SPCK.

Schner, G. (1993). *Education for Ministry: Reform and Renewal in Theological Education*, Kansas City: Sheed & Ward.

Schön, D. A. (1988). *Educating the Reflective Practitioner*, London: Jossey-Bass.

Schuth, K. (1989). *Reason for the Hope: The Futures of Roman Catholic Theologates*, Wilmington, DE: Michael Glazier, Inc.

Schwartz, R. M. (1989). *Servant Leaders of the People of God: An Ecclesial Spirituality for American Priests*, New York: Paulist Press.

Schwoebel, C. and Gunton, C. (eds) (1991). *Persons, Divine and Human*, Edinburgh: T & T Clark.

Shahovskoy, J. (1966). *The Orthodox Pastor: Outline of Pastoral Theology*, New York: St Vladimir's Seminary Press.

Sheldrake, P. (1991a). *Spirituality and History*, London: SPCK.

Sheldrake, P. (ed.) (1991b). *The Way of Ignatius Loyola: Contemporary Approaches to the Spiritual Exercises*, London: SPCK.

Sheldrake, P. (1994). *Befriending our Desires*, London: Darton, Longman & Todd.

Sheldrake, P. (1998a). *Spirituality and Theology*, London: Darton, Longman & Todd.

Sheldrake, P. (1998b). 'The role of spiritual direction in the context of theological education', *Anglican Theological Review*, 80 (3), 366–81.

Sheldrake, P. (1999). 'Spirituality as an academic discipline', in A. Thatcher (ed.), *Spirituality and the Curriculum*, London: Cassell, pp. 55–78.

Sheldrake, P. (2000). *Love Took My Hand: the Spirituality of George Herbert*, London: Darton, Longman & Todd.

Sheldrake, P. (2001). 'Teaching spirituality', *British Journal of Theological Education*, 12 (1), 53–64.

Sheldrake, P. (2003). 'Christian spirituality as a way of living publicly: a dialectic of the mystical and prophetic', *Spiritus: Journal of the Society for the Study of Christian Spirituality*, 3 (1), 19–37.

Sheridan, W. P. (1999). 'Functionalism undermining priesthood', *Human Development*, 20 (3), 12–16.

Sherrard, P. (1959). *The Greek East and the Latin West: A Study in the Christian Tradition*, London: Oxford University Press; reprinted Denise Harvey, Limni, Greece, 2002.

Shields, R. (1996). 'The dialogical challenge to Verstehen', *British Journal of Sociology*, 47, from *http://http-server.carleton.ca/~rshields/versdial.html*.

Short, J. (1999). *Poverty and Joy: the Franciscan Tradition*, London: Darton, Longman & Todd.

Simeon (Symeon) the New Theologian (1977). 'Three methods of attention and prayer', in E. Kadloubovsky and G. E. H Palmer, *Writings From the Philokalia*, London: Faber & Faber, pp. 152–61.

Simeon (Symeon) the New Theologian (1996). *On the Mystical Life: The Ethical Discourses*, vol. 2, New York: St Vladimir's Seminary Press.

Simmons, J. (2006). 'Vanishing boundaries: when teaching *about* religion becomes *spiritual guidance* in the classroom', *Teaching Theology and Religion*, 9 (1), 37–43.

Slattery, P. (ed.) (1994). *St John of the Cross*, New York: Alba House.

Smith, D. M. (1999). *John*, Nashville: Abingdon Press.

Smith, J. B. (1992). *A Spiritual Formation Workbook*, London: Hodder & Stoughton.

Society of Mary and Martha (2002). *Affirmation and Accountability*, Dunsford: Society of Mary and Martha.

Sofield, L. and Kuhn, D. H. (1995). *The Collaborative Leader*, Notre Dame, IN: Ave Maria Press.

Stronstad, R. (1984). *The Charismatic Theology of St Luke*, Peabody, MA: Hendrickson.

Stuart, E. (1997). *Religion is a Queer Thing: A Guide to the Christian Faith for Lesbian, Gay, Bisexual and Transgendered People*, London: Cassell.

Sumney, J. L. (2004). 'Do not be conformed to this age; biblical understandings of ministerial leadership', in M. L. Warford (ed.), *Practical Wisdom: On Theological Teaching and Learning*, New York: Peter Lang, pp. 127–42.

Sykes, S. (1994). 'Ministerial formation: liberating continuities from the past', *Ministerial Formation*, 64, 14–16.

Tartre, R. A. (1966). *The Postconciliar Priest: Comments on Some Aspects of the Decree on the Ministry and Life of Priests*, New York: Kenedy & Sons.

Taylor, B. C. (1989). *Spirituality for Everyday Living: An Adaptation of the Rule of St Benedict*, Collegeville, MN: Liturgical Press.

Taylor, J. V. (1972). *The Go-Between God*, London: SCM.

Temple, W. (1970). *Readings in St John's Gospel*, London: Macmillan.

Thatcher, A. (1993). *Liberating Sex: A Christian Sexual Theology*, London: SPCK.

Thomas, G. (1982). *Welcome: An Adult Education Program Based on RCIA*, New York: Paulist Press.

Thomson, J. G. S. S. (1959). *The Praying Christ: A Study of Jesus' Doctrine and Practice of Prayer*, London: Tyndale Press.

Thouless, R. H. (1971). *An Introduction to the Psychology of Religion*, Cambridge: Cambridge University Press.

Timiados, E. (1985). 'Theological education and spirituality', *Ministerial Formation*, 30, 18–23.

Timms, N. (2001). *You Aren't One of the Boys: Authority in the Catholic Priesthood*, Chelmsford: Matthew James Publishing.

Tolhurst, J. (1982). 'Training under stress', *The Clergy Review*, LXVII (10), 366–74.

Tracy, D. (1988). 'Can virtue be taught? Education, character, and the soul', *Theological Education*, 24, supp. 1, 33–52

Tracy, D. (1995). 'Theology and the many faces of postmodernity', in R. Gill (ed.), *Readings in Modern Theology*, London: SPCK, pp. 225–35.

Trull, J. E. and Carter J. E. (1993). *Ministerial Ethics*, Nashville, TN: Broadman & Holman.

Tucker, T. (2003). *Reformed Ministry: Traditions of Ministry and Ordination in the United Reformed Church*, London: United Reformed Church.

Turner, D. (1995). *The Darkness of God*, Cambridge: Cambridge University Press.

Turner, V. (1995). *The Ritual Process: Structure and Antistructure*, Nashville, TN: Aldine Transaction.

Tweedie, W. K. (1867). *Rivers and Lakes of Scripture*, London: T. Nelson & Sons.

Ulanov, A. and Ulanov, B. (1982). *Primary Speech: A Psychology of Prayer*, Atlanta: John Knox Press.

Underhill, E. (1991). *Practical Mysticism*, Guildford: Eagle.

United Reformed Church (1984). *Preparing Today for Tomorrow's Ministry*, London: United Reformed Church.

United Reformed Church (1994). *Patterns of Ministry: Interim Report 1994*, London: United Reformed Church.

United Reformed Church (2003). 'A considered response to Hind', The Training Committee of the United Reformed Church (unpublished paper for ecumenical consultation).

United Reformed Church (2004). *General Assembly 2004 Training Committee Report*, London: United Reformed Church.

Vanhooozer, K. J. (ed.) (2003). *The Cambridge Companion to Postmodern Theology*, Cambridge: Cambridge University Press.

Valuy, B. (1871). *Du Gouvernement des communautés religieuses*, Lyon and Paris: H. Pélagaud Fils et Roblot.

Vassiliadis, P. (2000). 'Theological education and Orthodox issues for the 3rd millennium', *Ministerial Formation*, 90, 15–21.

van den Blink, A. J. (1999). 'Reflections on spirituality in Anglican theological education', *Anglican Theological Review*, 81 (3), 429–50.

van der Ven, J. A. (1998a). *Practical Theology: An Empirical Approach*, Louvain: Peeters Press.

van der Ven, J. A. (1998b). *Education for Reflective Ministry*, Louvain: Peeters Press.

van Engen, J. (2004). *Educating People of Faith*, Michigan: Erdmans.

van Knippenberg, T. (2000). 'The structure and variety of prayer', *Journal of Empirical Theology*, 13 (2), 55–67.

von Balthasar, H. U. (1986). *Prayer*, San Francisco: Ignatius Press.

von Rad, G. (3rd revised edn, 1972). *Genesis*, London: SCM Press.

Vorgrimler, H. (ed.) (1968). *Commentary on the Documents of Vatican II*, vol. II, London: Burns & Oates.

Waaijman, K. (2002). *Spirituality: Forms, Foundations, Methods*, Louvain: Peeters,

Wainwright, G. (2002). *Eucharist and Eschatology*, Peterborough: Epworth Press.

Wakefield, G. (3rd edn, 1983). *A Dictionary of Christian Spirituality*, London: SCM.

Wakelin, M. (2005). *On Becoming Living and Knowing: the Fernley Hartley Lecture 2005 to the Methodist Conference*, London: Guy Chester Centre.

Wallis, J. (1994). *The Soul of Politics*, London: Fount.

Ward, B. (tr.) (1975). *The Sayings of the Desert Fathers*, Kalamazoo: Cistercian Publications.

Ward, F. (2005). *Lifelong Learning: Theological Education and Supervision*, London: SCM.

Ward, H. (1990). *The Gift of Self*, London: Darton, Longman & Todd.

Ward, J. N. (1967). *The Use of Praying*, Epworth: Epworth Press.

Ware, K. (1985). 'Ways of prayer and contemplation I: Eastern', in B. McGinn, J. Meyendorf and J. Leclerq (eds), *Christian Spirituality: Origins to the 12th Century*, London: SCM, pp. 395–414.

Ware, K. (2000). *The Inner Kingdom*, New York: St Vladimir's Seminary Press.

Warford, M. L. (ed.) (2004). *Practical Wisdom: On Theological Teaching and Learning*, New York: Peter Lang.

Warren, R. (1995). *Building Missionary Congregations: Towards a Post-Modern Way of Being Church*, London: Church House Publishing.

Warren, Y. (2002). *The Cracked Pot: the State of Today's Anglican Parish Clergy*, Stowmarket: Kevin Mayhew.

Watts, F. and Williams, M. (1988). *The Psychology of Religious Knowing*, London: Chapman.

Westcott, B. F. (1902). *The Gospel According to St John*, London: John Murray.

Westerhoff III, J. H. (1975). 'Learning and prayer', *Religious Education*, 70, 605–18.

Westerhoff III, J. H. (1982). 'Theological education and models for ministry', *Saint Luke's Journal of Theology* 25:2, 153–69.

White, J. M. (1989). 'How the seminary developed', in K. Schuth (ed.), *Reason for the Hope: The Futures of Roman Catholic Theologates*, Delaware: M. Glazier, pp. 11–28.

Whitney, D. S. (1991). *Spiritual Disciplines for the Christian Life*, Amersham: Scripture Press.

Wickett, R. E. Y. (2000). 'The learning covenant', in L. M. English (ed.), *Addressing the Spiritual Dimensions of Adult Learning: What Educators Can Do*, San Francisco: New Directions for Adult and Continuing Education, no. 85, Jossey-Bass, pp. 39–48.

Wicks, R. J. (ed.) (1995). *Handbook of Spirituality for Ministers*, vol. 1, New York: Paulist Press.

Wiles, M. (1977). *The Christian Fathers*, London: SCM.

Wilkin, R. L. (1984). 'Alexandria: a school for training in virtue', in P. Henry (ed.), *Schools of Thought in the Christian Tradition*, Philadelphia: Fortress Press, pp. 15–30.

Wilkin, R. L. (2004). 'Christian formation in the early Church', in J. van Engen, *Educating People of Faith*, Michigan: Eerdmans, pp. 48–62.

Williams, R. (1979). *The Wound of Knowledge*, London: Darton, Longman & Todd.

Williams, R. (1991). *Teresa of Avila*, London: Continuum.

Willimon, W. H. (2000). *Calling and Character: Virtues of the Ordained Life*, Nashville: Abingdon Press.

Willimon, W. H. (2002). *Pastor: The Theology and Practice of Ordained Ministry*, Nashville: Abingdon Press.

Wilson, B. (1966). *Religion in Secular Society*, London: C.A. Watts.

Wilson, D. (1999). *The Paideia of God*, Moscow, ID: Canon Press.

Winkelmes, M.-A. (2004). 'The classroom as a place of formation: purposively creating a transformative environment for today's diverse seminary population', *Teaching Theology and Religion*, 7 (4), 213–22.

Wolff, H. W. (1974). *Anthropology of the Old Testament*, London: SCM.

Wolters, C. (tr.) (1961). *The Cloud of Unknowing*, Harmondsworth: Penguin.

Wood, C. M. (1985). *Vision and Discernment: an Orientation in Theological Study*, Atlanta, Georgia: Scholars Press.

Wood, C. M. (1991). '"Spiritual formation" and "theological education"', *Religious Education*, 86 (4), 550–61.

World Council of Churches (1987). *Spiritual Formation in Theological Education*, Geneva: WCC.

Wright, T. (2004). *Luke for Everyone*, London: SPCK.

Wright, W. C. (2000). *Relational Leadership: A Biblical Model for Leadership Service*, Carlisle: Paternoster.

Wynkoop, M. B. (1972). *A Theology of Love: The Dynamic of Wesleyanism*, Kansas City: Beacon Hill Press.

Ziesler, J. (1989). *Paul's Letter to the Romans*, London: SCM.

Ziesler, J. (1990). *Pauline Christianity*, Oxford: Oxford University Press.

Zizioulas, J. D. (1985). *Being as Communion: Studies in Personhood and the Church*, New York: St Vladimir's Press.

Zizioulas, J. D. (1988). 'The mystery of the Church in Orthodox tradition', *One in Christ*, 24, 294–303.

Index